WAR
THE OVER
FAMILY

DAVID POPENOE

WAR OVER THE FAMILY

TRANSACTION PUBLISHERS
NEW BRUNSWICK (U.S.A.) AND LONDON (U.K.)

First paperback printing 2008
Copyright © 2005 by Transaction Publishers, New Brunswick, New Jersey.

All rights reserved under International and Pan-American Copyright Conventions. No part of this book may be reproduced or transmitted in any form or by any means, electronic or mechanical, including photocopy, record-ing, or any information storage and retrieval system, without prior permission in writing from the publisher. All inquiries should be addressed to Transaction Publishers, Rutgers—The State University, 35 Berrue Circle, Piscataway, New Jersey 08854-8042.

This book is printed on acid-free paper that meets the American National Standard for Permanence of Paper for Printed Library Materials.

Library of Congress Catalog Number: 2004046055
ISBN: 978-0-7658-0259-0 (cloth); 978-1-4128-0810-1 (paper)
Printed in the United States of America

Library of Congress Cataloging-in-Publication Data

Popenoe, David, 1932-
    War over the family / David Popenoe.
        p. cm.
    Includes bibliographical references and index.
    ISBN 0-7658-0259-7 (cloth : alk. paper)
        1. Family—United States. 2. Marriage—United States. 3. United
    States—Social conditions—1960-1980. 4. United States—Social
    conditions—1980- I. Title.

HQ536.P65   2005
306.85'0973—dc22   2004046055

Contents

Part 4: Looking Back

Acknowledgments

Chapter 1, "Family Decline in America," originally appeared in David Blankenhorn, Steven Bayme, and Jean Bethke Elshtain (editors), *Rebuilding the Nest* (Family Service America, 1990). Reprinted with permission of the Institute for American Values.

Chapter 2, "American Family Decline, 1960-1990: A Review and Appraisal," originally appeared in the *Journal of Marriage and the Family* 55-3 (August 1993). Reprinted with permission of National Council on Family Relations.

Chapter 3, "The Family Condition of America: Cultural Change and Public Policy," originally appeared in H. J. Aaron, T. E. Mann, and T. Taylor (editors), *Values and Public Policy* (Brookings Institution, 1994). Reprinted with permission of the Brookings Institution.

Chapter 4, "Family Values: A Communitarian Position," originally appeared in David Sciulli (editor), *Macro Socio-Economics: From Theory to Activism* (M. E. Sharpe, 1995). Reprinted with permission of M. E. Sharpe, Inc.

Chapter 5, "The Evolution of Marriage and the Problem of Stepfamilies: A Biosocial Perspective," originally appeared in A. Booth and J. Dunn (editors), *Stepfamilies: Who Benefits? Who Does Not?* (Lawrence Erlbaum, 1994). Reprinted with permission of Lawrence Erlbaum Associates.

Chapter 6, "A World Without Fathers," originally appeared in *The Wilson Quarterly*, Spring, 1996. It is adapted from my book *Life Without Father* (Free Press, 1996).

Chapter 7, "Fostering the New Familism: A Goal for America," originally appeared in *The Responsive Community* 2-4 (Fall, 1992).

Chapter 8, "The Roots of Declining Social Virtue: Family, Community, and the Need for a 'Natural Communities Policy,'" originally appeared in M. A. Glendon and D. Blankenhorn (editors), *Seedbeds of Virtue: Sources of Competence, Character and Citizenship in American Society* (Madison Books, 1996). Reprinted with permission of Rowman and Littlefield Publishing Group.

Chapter 9, "Modern Marriage: Revising the Cultural Script," originally appeared in D. Popenoe, J. B. Elshtain, and D. Blankenhorn (editors), *Promises to Keep: Decline and Renewal of Marriage in America* (Rowman and Littlefield, 1996). Reprinted with permission of Rowman and Littlefield Publishing Group.

Chapter 10, "Challenging the Culture of Fatherlessness," originally appeared in W. F. Horn, D. Blankenhorn, and M. B. Pearlstein (editors), *The Fatherhood Movement: A Call to Action* (Lexington Books, 1999). Reprinted with permission of Rowman and Littlefield Publishing Group.

Chapter 11, "The Marriage Movement," originally appeared as "Marriage" in Don Eberly (editor), *Building a Healthy Culture: Strategies for An American Renaissance* (William B. Eerdmans, 2001). Reprinted with permission of William B. Eerdmans Publishing Co.

Chapter 12, "Can the Nuclear Family Be Revived?" originally appeared in *Society* 36-5 (July/August, 1999).

Chapter 13, "A Marriage Research Agenda for the Twenty-First Century: Ten Critical Questions," originally appeared in A. J. Hawkins, L. D. Wardle, and D. O. Coolidge (editors), *Revitalizing the Institution of Marriage in the 21st Century* (Praeger Publishers, 2002). Reprinted with permission of the Greenwood Publishing Group.

Chapter 14, "Remembering My Father: An Intellectual Portrait of 'The Man Who Saved Marriages,'" was presented in an earlier version at the Symposium on Fatherhood in America, Institute for America Values, New York City, December 1991. It is published here for the first time.

Chapter 15, "The War Over the Family," was presented at the Tenth Annual International Meeting in Political Studies, Universidada Catolica Portuguesa, Lisbon, Portugal, November 2002. It is published here for the first time.

Introduction

The articles in this book come from a career in which I have been a major warrior in what has been called "the war over the family," that is, a heated national debate over the meaning and importance of marriage and the family in contemporary American life. The debate, essentially, is between those who believe that the weakening of the married-parent nuclear family should be a major focus of societal concern, especially in its effects on children, and those who do not.

The cultural war over the family is said to have begun in the 1960s when Daniel Patrick Moynihan, then a minor cabinet official in the administration of President Lyndon Johnson, wrote a report claiming the Negro family to be "in the deepest trouble" and involved in "a tangle of pathology." At that time 25 percent of black births were out of wedlock and close to 30 percent of black children lived with a single parent. President Johnson drew on Moynihan's views in his 1965 "war on poverty" speech, and the reaction from the cultural left was outrage. Moynihan was called, very simply, a racist, and was sent into intellectual exile—along with any official discussion of family weakening—for years.

It was not just the black issue that triggered the family war, however. Radical feminists saw the nuclear family as patriarchal and oppressive, gays and lesbians saw it as discriminatory, and the growing number of divorced people and unwed mothers feared stigma and isolation. The ideology that nothing was going wrong with families, they were only "diversifying," made its way strongly into the dominant culture of the intellectual elite in America. This was despite the fact that the rates of out-of-wedlock births and single parent households for whites soon climbed to the levels seen among blacks in the 1960s, and the national divorce rate skyrocketed to around 50 percent.

By the end of this book the reader will know in great detail where I stand in this debate. What she or he will not know from reading the articles in the book, however, is how I came to have the ideas and opinions that I now hold. That is the purpose of this introduction, a brief intellectual autobiography of how I came to be involved in one of the most contentious chapters in recent American social and cultural history. I will present two versions of how I started researching and writing about family issues and went on to become a national pro-marriage and family advocate. The first is the more objective and resume-based; the second is the more personal—the story behind the story.

I didn't start out as a family scholar. In the late 1950s and early 1960s I pursued graduate work in city planning and the then-new interdisciplinary field of urban studies at the University of Pennsylvania, receiving a Ph.D. there in 1963. Sociology was my minor field. This was a stimulating intellectual experience led by some well-known professors, including the distinguished sociologist Herbert Gans, with whom I disagreed often but learned much; social historian and critic Lewis Mumford, at one time America's leading humanist but now all but forgotten; ecologist Ian McCarg, the most influential environmental planner of his era and also one of the most colorful people I have ever known; and political scientist Martin Meyerson, who later became president of the University. The field of planning at this time was in a halcyon stage, joyful and carefree with the idea strongly entrenched that through government action massive and beneficial social change could be achieved.

My first jobs were in city planning and urban development in Philadelphia and Newark, New Jersey, but I soon shifted into academia, taking a job as research specialist in the new Ford Foundation-sponsored Urban Studies Center at Rutgers University. This was a period of growing urban strife and the idea there was to develop an "urban extension specialist," an equivalent of the highly successful agricultural extension specialist that had played a major role in making American agriculture one of the world's leading industries. Could we achieve the same success for cities?

My colleagues at the Urban Studies Center were mostly sociologists. We never were able to figure out how to create university-based urban extension specialists, much less save the city, but we had a lot of fun trying and, mostly through osmosis, I gradually drifted into sociology and took a Rutgers teaching position in that field in 1969. In 1972, with the help of a senior Fulbright research scholarship, I traveled to Sweden with my family to live for a year and study the planners' (and also the social workers') best extant version of utopia. Sweden at that time, and still, has the most perfectly planned cities in the world. My special interest was suburbs, and my Swedish research led to my first major book—*The Suburban Environment: Sweden and the United States* (1977)—which compared the lives of residents in a prominent Stockholm suburb with Levittown, Pennsylvania, both built in the 1950s. I was particularly interested in family life as it was lived in these two communities, and the Swedish suburb in many respects won top honors.

I made many return trips to Sweden (and the rest of Europe) over the years, writing mostly about housing and urban development issues. At the same time, I moved up the ranks at Rutgers, eventually becoming chair and graduate director of the sociology department and later social and behavioral sciences dean. I was considered highly pro-Swedish, so much so that one of my colleagues labeled me a "Swedish Zionist." But beginning in the late 1970s I became increasingly aware of what I came to think of as a "dark side of the welfare state." While most of the welfare-state measures, along with the urban planning, seemed highly desirable, something undesirable was happening to the Swedish family. According to all available data it was seriously weakening. Although seldom discussed in Sweden, Swedish divorce, nonmarital cohabitation, and single-parent family rates were among the highest in Europe and, with the lowest marriage rate in recorded history, the institution of marriage in that nation was rapidly in decline. This meant that, although the welfare measures were of great benefit in coming to the aid of children from broken homes (as well as intact families), a rapidly increasing number of Swedish children were missing out on what arguably they most wanted in their young lives: to grow up living with their own father and mother. Could the welfare state itself be sewing the seeds of its own destruction?

In the mid-1970s I started teaching sociology of the family courses, and it became ever more clear to me that family problems in the United States were as serious, if not more so, as those in Sweden. Still, why would two very different nations, one the quintessential individualistic market economy and the other the world's greatest welfare state, exhibit family trends of such striking similarity? Obviously, a broad cultural shift endemic to modern nations must be at work. The questions raised by this line of thinking led to my book *Disturbing the Nest: Family Change and Decline in Modern Societies* (1988), which was a broad comparative look at family trends in the United States and Sweden and, for additional comparison, Switzerland and New Zealand. Because it was in an economically advanced and socially engineered welfare state that family breakdown presented the greatest enigma, the book focused on the situation in Sweden. I became somewhat critical of the Swedish welfare state's response to family issues, and found out that Swedes do not take kindly to too much criticism of their society by an outsider. While I had been a long-time favorite of Swedes for my praise of their planning and urban development, suddenly my Swedish lecture invitations began to dry up. By that time, however, I had decided to concentrate much more on the American scene, the main focus of the articles in the present book.

The Swedish family revelations were clearly of great importance in my career shift from urban planner/sociologist to scholar of the family. But the story is incomplete without a consideration of certain personal circumstances in my life, and thus the need for a more subjective account of my intellectual career. I was born the youngest of four boys in a strong, intact family in southern California in which "family values" played a major role. My family was not religious, but my father Paul was a nationally known "family relations" expert in his own right for almost fifty years. (My brief biography of Paul Popenoe is published in this book for the first time.) Considered to be one of the founders of marriage counseling in America, he established in 1930 the nation's first family counseling and research center in Los Angeles and went on to become well known as the author of numerous popular books on marriage and a nationally syndicated family advice newspaper column, host of a national television program called *Divorce Hearing*, a frequent guest on Art Linkletter's *House Party* show first on radio and then television, and the professional founder of the marital advice feature in the *Ladies Home Journal* entitled "Can This Marriage Be Saved?" This monthly column still runs in the *Journal* where it is billed as the "most popular, most enduring women's magazine feature in the world," and for the first twenty-five years after its founding in 1952 it carried my father's picture as well as his introduction. All of the cases written up in the column came from his institute in Los Angeles.

My father thought of himself as a pioneer in the marriage and family field, which he clearly was, and he dearly hoped that one of his sons would follow in his footsteps. But the first three went into electrical engineering, government administration, and horticulture, respectively, leaving me as the last hope. Even though the close association I had with my father and his institute (where I occasionally worked in the summer during my high school years) caused me to absorb as a child a lot of the lore of family relations, it is not a field that I had ever considered going into. My father was a very strong personality and therefore a hard act to follow, and anyway I was too young, psychologically primitive, inexperienced with the opposite sex, and more interested in "the outdoors" (my original undergraduate field was geography). I married at age twenty-seven while still in graduate school, soon had two young daughters, and found family life to be quite a challenge, certainly not something on which I felt comfortable pronouncing as an expert. Yet I married a highly intelligent and educated woman who provided me a whole new realm of psychological insights and by the 1970s, having drifted into sociology and with my family well established, the family field grew in my interest. My father, then in his eighties, wanted me to move to California and take over his institute. I made a number of trips to the Coast, and considered it seriously, but in the end I just didn't think I had the maturity or wisdom for the job; moreover, the life of a tenured professor is not an easy thing to give up. I'm sure that my father and also my mother were quite disappointed.

My mother died suddenly in 1978 and my father died a year later, at age ninety. He never was able to get a stable and long-term replacement for himself at his institute, and shortly after his death it quickly faded from the national scene. Strangely, or perhaps not so strangely, his death seemed to free me to make yet another career shift. The year 1979, when he died, is just about the time when I was beginning to take an interest in the Swedish family. If I couldn't run his institute, at least I could pursue his interest in family relations. Which is what I started to do, and have been doing ever since.

It was difficult to find a publisher for my 1988 book on the family. Its topic was "family decline," and this had become an unpopular idea in the minds of many people in academia, publishing, and the intellectual left in general. The politically correct view was that the family was just changing, not declining, and there were many new family forms that were every bit as good as "the traditional nuclear family." The dominant motif in the family field was not family decline but "family diversity." This same ideology prevailed in Sweden, where my contention that the Swedish family was "declining" was met with disbelief and even antagonism.

To me, the reason for being concerned about family decline was, and still is, the well being of children. All the social scientific data that I could unearth, in Sweden, the United States, and other modern nations, pointed strongly to the fact that child outcomes were worse in all family forms apart from married couple families, whether the measure was crime, school completion, teen pregnancies, depression, and almost every other undesirable dimension one could think of. What a tragedy, I thought, that with all the blessings of modernity, children were being left behind.

My concern for children surely was influenced by own family experiences. I grew up in a strong family, and eventually came to live in a solid, intact family as an adult. I was blessed to marry a woman who was a devoted mother and deeply oriented to family life, as well as being a professional in her own right. We were (and are) very close to our two daughters, who have gone on to have strong families themselves in addition to professional careers. When our daughters were growing up one could plainly see, through their friends and associates, how family environments affected child outcomes. The statistical findings that stable, loving, attentive families produced the most successful and well-adjusted children were clearly in evidence, in real life, through personal observation. My experience of being a father was also of enormous value, of course, when it came to writing my book *Life Without Father.*

By the late 1980s the academic world, the media, and most of the so-called cultural elite seemed to be in deep denial about the effects of the changing family structure on child well being. After my book *Disturbing the Nest* was published, I felt alone and isolated in the academic world and sought to link up nationally with people who believed as I did, and such people also sought to link up with me. Much of the early linkage revolved around the Institute for American Values in New York City, founded in 1987 by community organizer David Blankenhorn. It was here that I met many of the colleagues with whom I would later work to develop a "marriage movement," notably Barbara Dafoe Whitehead, who helped me to found the National Marriage Project at Rutgers University in 1997. These early years were filled with excitement, intellectual stimulation, and hope.

The history of our pro-family efforts is described in final chapter of this book, suitably titled "The War Over the Family." Although we have not come close to achieving our stated goal of "rebuilding a marriage culture," there is now widespread acceptance among intellectuals as well as the general public that family change in recent decades has hurt children and that we, as a nation, should be striving to make amends. Also, by the early 2000s some of the most discouraging family trends had leveled off and even reversed direction. But the war over the family is far from over. Some of the trends, such as the declining marriage rate and the growth of nonmarital cohabitation, seem ironclad elements of modernity. And if the European nations are any guide for us, a weaker family is in our future—probably without most of the European family support systems such as child allowances and paid "family leaves" following the birth of a child. If sociology has taught us anything, however, it is that the direction and rapidity of social change can take us by surprise. Perhaps the younger generation will be able to undo what their parents have wrought.

Part 1

Family Decline

1

Family Decline in America

As a social institution, the family has been "in decline" since the beginning of world history, gradually becoming weaker through losing social functions and power to other institutions such as church, government, and school. Yet during the past twenty-five years, family decline in the United States, as in other industrialized societies, has been both steeper and more alarming than during any other quarter century in our history. Although they may not use the term "decline," most family scholars now agree, with a growing tinge of pessimism, that the family during this period has undergone a social transformation. Some see "dramatic and unparalleled changes" while others call it "a veritable revolution."[1]

Agreement about the dramatic nature of family change over the past few decades, together with a pessimistic assessment of it, represent a recent shift of viewpoint on the part of many scholars. In the 1970s, in sharp contrast to the prevailing mood of the general public, the outlook of many family experts was one of complacency. For example, in their 1981 book *What's Happening to the American Family?* economists Sar Levitan and Richard Belous noted that "currently fashionable gloom and doom scenarios miss the essential process of adjustment and change" and that "a critical analysis of the evidence does not paint such a dire picture, and thus a heartfelt 'hurrah' is in order."[2]

Yet after reviewing the events of the 1980s, their optimistic mood shifted strikingly. The second edition of this book, published in 1988, contains much apprehensive talk of "radical changes in family structure." The authors conclude, with some apologies for the "more sanguine scenario" of the earlier edition, that "American families are besieged from all sides" and "widespread family breakdown is bound to have a pervasive and debilitating impact not only on the quality of life but on the vitality of the body politic as well."[3]

The recent social transformation of the family has been so momentous that, in my opinion, we are witnessing the end of an epoch. Today's societal trends are bringing to a close the cultural dominance of what historians call the modern (I will use the term "traditional") nuclear family, a family situated apart from both the larger kin group and the workplace; focused on the procreation of children; and consisting of a legal, lifelong, sexually exclusive, heterosexual, monoga-

3

mous marriage, based on affection and companionship, in which there is a sharp division of labor, with the female as full-time housewife and the male as primary provider and ultimate authority. Lasting for only a little more than a century, this family form emphasized the male as "good provider," the female as "good wife and mother," and the paramount importance of the family for childrearing. (Of course, not all families were able to live up to these cultural ideals.) During its cultural heyday, the terms "family," "home," and "mother" ranked extraordinarily high in the hierarchy of cultural values.[4]

In certain respects, this family form reached its apogee in the middle of the twentieth century. By the 1950s—fueled in part by falling maternal and child mortality rates, greater longevity, and a high marriage rate—it is probably the case that a higher percentage of children than ever before were growing up in stable, two-parent families.[5] Similarly, this period witnessed the highest ever proportion of women who married, bore children, and lived jointly with their husbands until at least age fifty.[6]

Flight from the Nuclear Family

In the 1960s, however, four major social trends emerged to signal a widespread "flight" from both the ideal and the reality of the traditional nuclear family: rapid fertility decline, the sexual revolution, the movement of mothers into the labor force, and the divorce revolution. None of these changes was new to the 1960s; each represented a tendency that was already evident in earlier years. However, a striking acceleration of these trends occurred in the 1960s, which was made more dramatic by the fact that during the 1950s these trends had leveled off and in some cases even reversed their direction.[7]

The Decline in Fertility

First (taking up these four trends without reference to their relative importance or causal priority), fertility declined in the United States by almost 50 percent between 1960 and 1989, from an average of 3.7 children per woman to only 1.9. Although fertility has been gradually diminishing for several centuries (the main exception being the two decades following World War II), the level of fertility during the past decade was the lowest in U.S. history and below that necessary for the replacement of the population. As a percentage of the total population, children over the past twenty-five years have dropped from more than a third to about one-fourth.[8]

Growing dissatisfaction with parenthood is now evident among adults in our culture, along with a dramatic decrease in the stigma associated with childlessness.[9] Some demographers now predict that between 20 percent and 25 percent of today's young women will remain completely childless, and nearly 50 percent will be either childless or have only one child.[10]

The Sexual Revolution

Second, what is often called the sexual revolution has shattered the association of sex and reproduction.[11] The erotic has become a necessary ingredient of personal well being and fulfillment, both in and outside marriage, as well as a highly marketable commodity. The greatest change has been in the area of premarital sex: from 1971 to 1982, the proportion of unmarried girls in the United States aged fifteen to nineteen who engaged in premarital sexual intercourse jumped from 28 percent to 44 percent.[12] This behavior reflects a widespread change in values: in 1967, 85 percent of Americans "condemned premarital sex as morally wrong," compared with only 37 percent in 1979.[13]

The sexual revolution has been a major contributor to the striking increase in unwed parenthood. Nonmarital births jumped from 5 percent of all births in 1960 (22 percent of births among blacks) to 22 percent in 1985 (60 percent of births among blacks). This is the highest rate of nonmarital births ever recorded in the United States.

Working Married Mothers

Third, although unmarried women have long been in the labor force, the past quarter century has witnessed a striking movement into the paid work force of married women with children.[14] In 1960, only 19 percent of married women with children younger than six were in the labor force (39 percent with children between six and seventeen); by 1986, this figure had climbed to 54 percent (68 percent of those with older children).[15]

Increased Divorce Rate

Fourth, the divorce rate in the United States over the past twenty-five years (as measured by the number of divorced persons per 1,000 married persons) has nearly quadrupled, increasing from thirty-five to 130. This increase has led many to refer to a divorce revolution.[16] A landmark of sorts was passed in 1974, when for the first time in American history more marriages ended in divorce than in death.[17] The probability that a marriage contracted today will end in divorce ranges from 44 percent to 66 percent, depending upon the method of calculation.[18]

Reshaped Family Experience

These four trends signal a widespread retreat from the traditional nuclear family in terms of a lifelong, sexually exclusive unit, focused on children, with a separate-sphere division of labor between husband and wife. Unlike most previous family change, which reduced family functions and diminished the importance of the kin group, the family change of the past twenty-five years has tended to break up the "nucleus" of the family unit—the bond between husband and wife. Nuclear units, therefore, are losing ground to single-parent families, serial and stepfamilies, and unmarried and homosexual couples.[19]

The number of single-parent families, for example, has risen sharply as a result not only of marital breakup, but also of marriage decline (fewer persons who bear children are getting married) and widespread abandonment by males. In 1960, only 9 percent of children in the United States younger than eighteen were living with one parent; by 1986, this figure had climbed to nearly one-fourth of all children. (The comparable figures for blacks are 22 percent and 53 percent, respectively.) Of children born between 1950 and 1954, only 19 percent of whites (48 percent of blacks) had lived in a single-parent family by the time they reached age seventeen. But for children born in 1980, the figure is projected to be 70 percent (94 percent for blacks).[20]

During the past quarter century there has also been a retreat from family living in general. For instance, the percentage of "nonfamily" households (households other than those containing two or more persons living together and related by blood, marriage, or adoption) has nearly doubled, from 15 percent to 28 percent of all households. Approximately 85 percent of these new households consist of a person living alone.[21]

To summarize the state of the family today compared with that of twenty-five years ago:

- fewer persons are marrying and they are marrying later in life
- those marrying are having fewer children
- more marriages end in divorce

Trends such as these have dramatically reshaped people's lifetime family experiences, that is, their connectedness to the institution of the family: The proportion of an average person's adult life spent with spouse and children was 62 percent in 1960, the highest in our history. Today it has dropped to 43 percent, the lowest point in our history.[22]

In the United States, the changing family structure has helped to continue, and in some ways exacerbate, the tragedy of child poverty. Since 1974, the poverty rate among children has exceeded that among the elderly, and 40 percent of all poor people in this nation today are children.[23] According to a recent estimate, one out of every four American preschoolers in 1987 was living below the poverty line.[24]

In addition to family structural change, the psychological character of the marital relationship has also changed substantially over the years.[25] Traditionally, marriage has been understood as a social obligation—an institution designed mainly for economic security and procreation. Today, marriage is understood mainly as a path toward self-fulfillment: self-development is seen to require a significant other, and marital partners are picked primarily to be personal companions. Put another way, marriage is becoming deinstitutionalized. No longer comprising a set of norms and social obligations that are widely enforced, marriage today is a voluntary relationship that individuals can make and break at will. As one indicator of this shift, laws regulating marriage and divorce have become increasingly more lax.[26]

As psychological expectations for marriage grow ever higher, dashed expectations for personal fulfillment fuel our society's high divorce rate. Divorce also feeds upon itself. The higher the divorce rate, the more "normal" it becomes, with fewer negative sanctions to oppose it, and the more potential partners become available. In general, psychological need, in and of itself, has proved to be a weak basis for stable marriage.

These family trends are all interrelated. They are also evident, in varying degrees, in every industrialized Western country, which suggests that their source lies not in particular political or economic systems but in the broad cultural shift that has accompanied industrialization and urbanization. Although scholars do not agree on all aspects of this shift, clearly an ethos of radical individualism has emerged in these societies, in which personal autonomy, individual rights, and social equality have gained supremacy as cultural ideals. In keeping with these ideals, the main goals of personal behavior have shifted from commitment to social units of all kinds (families, communities, religions, nations) to personal choices, lifestyle options, self-fulfillment, and personal pleasure.[27]

Family Change as Family Decline

Despite the dramatic nature of the recent social transformation of the family, many family experts are still reluctant to refer to the transformation as "family decline." This is unfortunate, because the concept of the family as a declining or weakening institution provides a "best fit" for many of the changes that have taken place. The concept also alerts us to examine the consequences of a rapidly changing institution.

During the past twenty-five years, the institution of the family has weakened substantially in a number of ways. Individual family members have become more autonomous and less bound by the family group, and the group has become less cohesive. Fewer of its traditional social functions are now carried out by the family; these have shifted to other institutions. The family has lost more power and authority to other institutions, especially to the state and its agencies. The family has grown smaller, less stable, and has a shorter life span; people are therefore family members for a smaller percentage of their life. The outcome of these trends is that people have become less willing to invest time, money, and energy in family life. It is the individual him or herself, not the family unit, in whom the main investments are increasingly made.[28]

Why, then, are so many family scholars reluctant to speak of family decline? The short answer is that to speak of family decline within the intellectual community in recent years has been to be accused of opposing equality for women.

The dominance of the traditional nuclear family in the 1950s helped to fuel the modern women's movement. Reacting strongly to the lingering patriarchy of this family form, as well as to its separate-sphere removal of women from the labor market, the women's movement came to view the traditional nuclear family in very negative terms.[29] Today, those who believe in greater equality for women—and that includes most academics and other intellectuals—favor an egalitarian family form, with substantial economic independence for wives. With respect to these characteristics, the flight from the traditional nuclear family is regarded as progress, not decline.

To speak of decline under these circumstances, therefore, is perceived as being implicitly in favor of a discredited family form, one that oppressed women. Indeed, the term "decline" has been used most forcefully by those conservatives who tend to view every recent family change as negative and who have issued a clarion call for a return to the traditional nuclear family.

But properly used, the term "decline" should not carry such ideological baggage. To empirically conclude that the family is declining should not automatically link one to a particular ideology of family or gender. Moreover, not all decline is negative in its effects; decline is not necessarily the opposite of progress. All sorts of institutional forms that were once fully accepted have declined: theocracies, hereditary monarchies, imperialism. The results of their decline have been by no means merely regressive. It is important to distinguish an empirical trend, such as the weakening of an institution, from both its positive and negative consequences.

The Social Consequences of Family Decline

How are we to evaluate the social consequences of recent family decline? At the outset, it must be stressed that the issue is extremely complex. Society has been ill served by the simplistic, either/or terms used by both the political right and left in the national debate.

Certainly, one should not jump immediately to the conclusion that family decline is necessarily bad for our society. A great many positive aspects of the recent family changes stand out as noteworthy. During this same quarter century of family decline, women (and many minorities) have clearly improved their status and probably the overall quality of their lives. Much of women's gain in status has come through their release from family duties and increased participation in the labor force. In addition, given the great emphasis on psychological criteria for choosing and keeping marriage partners, it can be argued persuasively that those marriages today that endure are more likely than ever before to be emotionally rewarding companionships.[30]

This period has also seen improved health care and longevity as well as widespread economic affluence, all of which have produced, for most people, a material standard of living that is historically unprecedented. Some of this improvement is due to the fact that people are no longer so dependent on their families for health care and economic support; they no longer are so imprisoned by social class and family obligation. When in need, they can now rely more on public care and support, as well as self-initiative and self-development.

Despite these positive aspects, the negative consequences of family decline are real and profound. The greatest negative effect, in the opinion of nearly everyone, is on children. Because children represent the future of a society, any negative consequences for them are especially significant. Substantial, if not conclusive, evidence indicates that, partly due to family changes, the quality of life for children in the past twenty-five years has worsened.[31] Much of the problem is of a psychological nature and thus is difficult to measure quantitatively.

Perhaps the most serious problem is a weakening in many families of the fundamental assumption that children are to be loved and valued at the highest level of priority. The general disinvestment in family life that has occurred has commonly meant a disinvestment in children's welfare. Some refer to this as a national "parent deficit." Yet the deficit goes well beyond parents to encompass an increasingly less child-friendly society. The parent deficit is all too easily blamed on newly working women. But it is men who have left the parenting scene in large numbers, a phenomenon one scholar has called "A disappearing act by fathers."[32] More than ever before, fathers are denying paternity, avoiding their parental obligations, and absent from home (at the same time there has been a slow but not offsetting growth of the "housefather" role).[33] Indeed, a persuasive case can be made that men began to abandon the "good provider" role at about the same time that many women started to relinquish the role of the full-time homemaker.[34] Thus, men and women may have been equally involved in triggering the recent flight from the traditional nuclear family.

The breakup of the nuclear unit has been the focus of much concern. Virtually every child desires two biological parents for life, and substantial evidence exists that childrearing is most successful when it involves two parents, both of whom are strongly motivated for the task.[35] This is not to say that other family forms can not be successful, only that as a group they are not as likely to be successful. This is also not to say that the two strongly motivated parents must be organized in the patriarchal and separate-sphere terms of the traditional nuclear family.

Regardless of family form, a significant change has occurred over the past quarter century in what can be called the social ecology of childhood.[36] Advanced societies are moving ever farther from what many hold to be a highly desirable childrearing environment consisting of the following characteristics: a relatively large family that does a lot of things together, has many routines and traditions, and provides a great deal of quality contact time between adults and children; regular contact with relatives, active friendships in a supportive neighborhood; contact with the adult world of work; little concern on the part of children that their parents will break up; and the coming together of all these ingredients in the development of a rich family subculture that has lasting meaning and strongly promulgates family values such as cooperation and sharing.

As this brief sketch of the changing ecology of childhood suggests, not only the family has been transformed, but also the community environment in which families exist. Children are especially sensitive to their local environments; yet adults, too, have a big stake in the quality of their surroundings.

The family has always been a fundamental and probably essential unit of what some call "civil society"—the local society made up of kin and friendship networks, neighborhoods, religious institutions, and voluntary associations. Civil society provides meaning and attachment for people's lives and helps to protect them from the impersonal forces of market and state.[37] As the market and state "megastructures" grow ever more powerful, the need for the mediating structures of civil society becomes that much more compelling, both for psychic survival and political freedom.[38] Although reasonable doubt can be expressed about the empirical accuracy of the common phrase "as the family goes, so goes the nation," I am not so doubtful about the phrase "as the family goes, so goes civil society."

Family Decline and Today's Policy Debate

What should be done to counteract or remedy the negative effects of family decline? This is the most controversial question of all, and the most difficult to answer.

The problems of purposive social action are enormous. In remedying the negative effects, it is never easy to avoid canceling out the positive benefits. Also, if family decline in fact stems from a broad cultural shift, it will not be easy to modify. The underlying trend may simply have to play itself out. It could be, of course, that the problems we are seeing result not from the intrinsic character of the cultural shift, but rather from its extreme rapidity. From this perspective, as the changes become complete and society settles down, we may be able to adjust without great difficulty to the new conditions.

Let us assume, however, that purposive social action is both called for and can have a useful outcome. Among the broad proposals for change that have been put forth, two extremes stand out prominently in the national debate: (1) a return to the structure of the traditional nuclear family characteristic of the 1950s and (2) the development of extensive governmental family policies.

Aside from the fact that it is probably impossible to return to a situation of an earlier time, the first alternative has major drawbacks. Such a shift would require many women to leave the work force and to some extent become "deliberated," an unlikely occurrence indeed. Economic conditions necessitate that even more women take jobs, and cultural conditions stress ever greater equality between the sexes.

In addition to such considerations, the traditional nuclear family form, in today's world, may be fundamentally flawed. As an indication of this, one should realize that the young people who led the transformation of the family during the 1960s and 1970s were brought up in 1950s families. If the 1950s families were so wonderful, why didn't their children seek to emulate them? In hindsight, the 1950s families seem to have been beset with problems that went well beyond patriarchy and separate spheres. For many families the mother-child unit had become increasingly isolated from the kin group, the neighborhood, and community, and even from the father, who worked a long distance away. This was especially true for women who were fully educated and eager to take their place in work and public life. Maternal child rearing under these historically unprecedented circumstances became highly problematic.[39]

Despite such difficulties, the traditional nuclear family is still the family of choice for millions of Americans. They are comfortable with it, and for them it seems to work. It is reasonable, therefore, at least not to place road-blocks in the way of couples with children who wish to conduct their lives according to the traditional family's dictates. Women who freely desire to spend much of their lives as mothers and housewives, outside the labor force, should not be economically penalized by public policy for making that choice. Nor should they be denigrated by our culture as second-class citizens.

The second major proposal for change that has been stressed in national debate is the development of extensive governmental programs offering monetary support and social services for families, especially for the new "non-nuclear" families. In some cases these programs assist with functions that families are unable to perform adequately; in other cases, the functions are taken over, transforming them from family to public responsibilities.

This is the path followed by the European welfare states, but it has been less accepted by the United States than by any other industrialized nation. The European welfare states have been far more successful than the United States in minimizing the negative economic impact of family decline on family members, especially children. In addition, many European nations have established policies making it much easier for women (and increasingly men) to combine work with childrearing.[40] With these successes in mind, it seems inevitable that the United States will (and I believe should) move gradually in the direction of European countries with respect to family policies, just as we are now moving gradually in that direction with respect to medical care.

There are clear drawbacks, however, in moving too far down this road. If children are to be best served, we should seek to make the family stronger, not to replace it. At the same time that welfare states are minimizing some of the consequences of family decline, they may also be causing further decline of the family unit. This phenomenon can be witnessed today in Sweden, where the institution of the family has probably grown weaker than anywhere else in the world.[41] On a lesser scale, the phenomenon has been seen in the United States in connection with our welfare programs. Fundamental to the success of welfare-state programs, therefore, is keeping the ultimate goal of strengthening families uppermost in mind.

A New Social Movement

Although each of the above alternatives has some merit, I suggest a third alternative, which is premised on the fact that we cannot return to the 1950s family, nor can we depend on the welfare state for a solution. Instead, we should strike at the heart of the cultural shift that has occurred, point up its negative aspects, and seek to reinvigorate the cultural ideals of "family," "parents," and "children" within the changed circumstances of our time. We should stress that the individualistic ethos has gone too far, that children are being woefully shortchanged, and that, in the long run, strong families represent the best path toward self-fulfillment and personal happiness. We should bring again to the cultural forefront the old ideal of parents living together and sharing responsibility for their children and for each other.

What is needed is a new social movement whose purpose is the promotion of families and family values within the new constraints of modern life. It should point out the supreme importance of strong families to society, while at the same time suggesting ways that the family can better adapt to the modern conditions of individualism, equality, and the labor force participation of both women and men. Such a movement could build on the fact that the overwhelming majority of young people today still put forth as their major life goal a lasting, monogamous, heterosexual relationship that includes the procreation of children. It is reasonable to suppose that this goal is so pervasive because it is based on a deep-seated human need.

The reassertion of this personal goal as a highly ranked cultural value is not a legislative alternative; politics necessarily must respond to the obvious diversity in American life. But it is an alternative ideally suited to the leadership of broad-based citizens' groups. The history of recent social movements in America provides good reason for hope that such an initiative can make an impact. Witness the recent cultural shifts toward female and minority-group equality and the current move toward environmental protection, each of which has been led by popular movements focusing on fundamental social values. The time seems ripe to reassert that strong families concerned with the needs of children are, under modern conditions, not only possible, but necessary.

Notes

1.   Norval Glenn, ed., "The State of the American Family," *Journal of Family Issues* 8 (No. 4, December 1981), Special Issue.

2.   Sar A. Levitan and Richard S. Belous, *What's Happening to the American Family?* (Baltimore: Johns Hopkins, 1981), pp. 190, 15.
3.   Sar A. Levitan, Richard S. Belous, and Frank Gallo, *What's Happening to the American Family?* (rev. ed.) (Baltimore: Johns Hopkins, 1988), pp. vi, viii.
4.   Carl N. Degler, *At Odds: Women and the Family in America from the Revolution to the Present* (Oxford, England: Oxford University Press, 1980); Lawrence Stone, *The Family, Sex, and Marriage in England* 1500–1800 (New York: Harper and Row, 1977); Steven Mintz and Susan Kellogg, *Domestic Revolutions: A Social History of the American Family* (New York: Free Press, 1988).
5.   Andrew Cherlin and Frank F. Furstenberg, Jr., "The Changing European Family: Lessons for the American Reader," *Journal of Family Issues* 9 (No. 3, 1988), p. 294; John Modell, Frank F. Furstenberg, Jr., and Douglas Strong, "The Timing of Marriage in the Transition to Adulthood: Continuity and Change, 1860–1975," *American Journal of Sociology* 84 (1978), pp. S120–S150.
6.   Susan Cotts Watkins, Jane A. Menken, and John Bongaarts, "Demographic Foundations of Family Change," *American Sociological Review* 52 (No. 3, 1987), pp. 346–358.
7.   Andrew I. Cherlin, *Marriage, Divorce, Remarriage* (Cambridge, MA: Harvard University Press, 1981).
8.   All data are from the U.S. Census Bureau, unless otherwise indicated.
9.   Arthur G. Neal, Theodore Groat, and Jerry W. Wicks, "Attitudes about Having Children: A Study of 600 Couples in the Early Years of Marriage," *Journal of Marriage and the Family* 51 (No. 2, 1989), pp. 313–328; Joseph Veroff, Elizabeth Douvan, and Richard A. Kulka, *The Inner American: A Self-Portrait from 1957 to 1976* (New York: Basic Books, 1981); James A. Sweet and Larry L. Bumpass, *American Families and Households* (New York: Russell Sage Foundation, 1987), p. 400.
10.   David E. Bloom and James Trussell, "What are the Determinants of Delayed Childbearing and Permanent Childlessness in the United States?" *Demography* 21 (No. 4, 1984), pp. 591–611; Charles F Westoff, "Perspective on Nuptiality and Fertility," *Population and Development Review Supplement* (No. 12, 1986), pp. 155–170.
11.   John D'Emilio and Estelle B. Freedman, *Intimate Matters: A History of Sexuality in America* (New York: Harper and Row, 1988).
12.   From a 1987 study sponsored by the National Academy of Sciences reported in the *New York Times*, February 27, 1989, p. B11.
13.   Daniel Yankelovich, *New Rules: Searching for Self-Fulfillment in a World Turned Upside Down* (New York: Random House, 1981), p. 94.
14.   Suzanne M. Bianchi and Daphne Spain, *American Women in Transition* (New York: Russell Sage Foundation, 1986); Victor R. Fuchs, *Women's Quest for Economic Equality* (Cambridge, MA: Harvard University Press, 1988).
15.   Data assembled from U.S. Census reports by Maris A. Vinovskis, "The Unraveling of the Family Wage since World War II: Some Demographic, Economic, and Cultural Considerations," in Bryce Christensen, Allan Carlson, Maris Vinovskis, Richard Vedder, and Jean Bethke Elshtain, *The Family Wage: Work, Gender, and Children in the Modern Economy* (Rockford, IL: The Rockford Institute, 1988), pp. 33–58.
16.   Lenore J. Weitzman, *The Divorce Revolution* (New York: Free Press, 1985).
17.   Paul C. Glick, "Fifty Years of Family Demography: A Record of Social Change," *Journal of Marriage and the Family* 50 (No. 4, 1988), p. 868.
18.   Robert Schoen, "The Continuing Retreat from Marriage: Figures from the 1983 U.S. Marital Status Life Tables," *Social Science Research* 71 (No. 2, 1987), pp.

108–109; Teresa Castro Martin and Larry L. Bumpass, "Recent Trends in Marital Disruption," *Demography* 26 (No. 1, 1989), pp. 37–51.

19.   Sanford M. Dornbusch and Myra H. Strober, *Feminism, Children, and the New Families* (New York: Guilford Press, 1988).

20.   Sandra L. Hofferth, "Updating Children's Life Course," *Journal of Marriage and the Family* 47 (No. 1, 1985), pp. 93–115.

21.   The twenty-year downward spiral of family households came to a (temporary?) halt in the 1986–87 period, when the percentage of family households increased slightly, as documented in Judith Waldrop, "The Fashionable Family," *American Demographics* (March 1988).

22.   Susan Cotts Watkins, Jane A. Menken, and John Bongaarts, op. cit., 1987.

23.   Eugene Smolensky, Sheldon Danziger, and Peter Gottschalk, "The Declining Significance of Age in the United States: Trends in the Well-being of Children and the Elderly since 1939," in John L. Palmer, Timothy Smeeding, and Barbara Doyle Torrey, eds., *The Vulnerable* (Washington, DC: Urban Institute. 1988), pp. 29–54.

24.   Report of House Select Committee on Children, Youth and Families, the *New York Times*, October 2, 1989, p. A12.

25.   Kingsley Davis, ed., *Contemporary Marriage: Comparative Perspectives on a Changing Institution* (New York: Russell Sage Foundation, 1985).

26.   Mary Ann Glendon, *The Transformation of Family Law* (Chicago: University of Chicago, 1989).

27.   Robert N. Bellah, Richard Madsen, William M. Sullivan, Ann Swidler, and Steven M. Tipton, *Habits of the Heart: Individualism and Commitment in American Life* (Berkeley, CA: University of California Press, 1985).

28.   Victor Fuchs, *How We Live* (Cambridge, MA: Harvard University Press, 1983).

29.   Jean Bethke Elshtain, *Public Man, Private Women: Women in Social and Political Thought* (Princeton, NJ: Princeton University Press, 1981).

30.   Francesca M. Cancian, *Love in America: Gender and Self-Development* (Cambridge, England, and New York: Cambridge University Press, 1987).

31.   *U.S. Children and Their Families: Current Conditions and Recent Trends, 1989* (Washington, DC: U.S. Government Printing Office). Nicholas Zill and Carolyn C. Rogers, "Recent Trends in the Well-being of Children in the United States and Their Implications for Public Policy," in Andrew Cherlin, ed., *The Changing American Family and Public Policy* (Washington, DC: Urban Institute, 1988), pp. 31–115; Peter Uhlenberg and David Eggebeen, "The Declining Well-being of American Adolescents," *The Public Interest* (No. 82, 1986), pp. 25–38.

32.   Samuel H. Preston, "Children and the Elderly: Divergent Paths for America's Dependents," *Demography* 21 (No. 4. 1984), p. 443.

33.   Frank F. Furstenberg, Jr., "Good Dads-Bad Dads: Two Faces of Fatherhood," in Andrew Cherlin, ed., *The Changing American Family and Public Policy* (Washington, DC: Urban Institute, 1988), pp. 193–218.

34.   Barbara Ehrenreich, *The Hearts of Men: American Dreams and the Flight from Commitment* (New York: Anchor, 1983).

35.   E. Mavis Hetherington and Josephine D. Arasteh, eds., *Impact of Divorce, Single Parenting, and Stepparenting on Children* (Hillsdale, NJ: Lawrence Erlbaum Associates, 1988); Sara McLanahan and Karen Booth, "Mother-Only Families: Problems, Prospects, and Politics," *Journal of Marriage and the Family* 51 (No. 3, 1989), pp. 557–580.

36.   Urie Bronfenbrenner, *The Ecology of Human Development* (Cambridge, MA: Harvard University Press, 1979).

37.   Alan Wolfe, *Whose Keeper? Social Science and Moral Obligation* (Berkeley, CA: University of California Press, 1989).

38.   Peter L. Berger and Richard J. Neuhaus, *To Empower People: The Role of Mediating Structures in Public Policy* (Washington. DC: American Enterprise Institute, 1977).

39.   Betty Friedan, *The Feminine Mystique* (New York: Laurel, 1983, 1963).

40.   Sylvia Ann Hewlett, *A Lesser Life* (New York: William Morrow, 1986).

41.   David Popenoe, *Disturbing the Nest: Family Change and Decline in Modern Societies* (New York: Aldine de Gruyter, 1988).

2

American Family Decline, 1960-1990:
A Review and Appraisal

Contrary to the view of some academics that the family in America is not declining but just changing, the thesis of this chapter is that family decline since 1960 has been extraordinarily steep, and its social consequences serious, especially for children. Drawing mainly on U.S. Census data, family trends of the past three decades are reviewed. The evidence for family decline is appraised in three areas: demographic, institutional, and cultural. It is argued that families have lost functions, power, and authority, that "familism" as a cultural value has diminished, and that people have become less willing to invest time, money, and energy in family life, turning instead to investments in themselves. Recent family decline is more serious than any decline in the past because what is breaking up is the nuclear family, the fundamental unit stripped of relatives and left with two essential functions that cannot be performed better elsewhere: childrearing, and the provision to its members of affection and companionship.

Family decline in America continues to be a debatable issue, especially in academia. Several scholars have recently written widely-distributed trade books reinforcing what has become the establishment position of many family researchers—that family decline is a "myth," and that "the family is not declining, it is just changing" (Coontz, 1992; Skolnick, 1991; Stacey, 1990). Many academic books (and dozens of articles) have echoed the same theme, including one outspokenly entitled *The Myth of Family Decline* (Dornbusch and Strober, 1988; Gubrium and Holstein, 1990; Kain, 1990; Scanzoni, Polonko, Teachman, and Thompson, 1989). Even Father Andrew Greeley (1991) has weighed in, claiming on the basis of telephone surveys that marriage in America is stronger than ever.

My view is just the opposite. Like the majority of Americans, I see the family as an institution in decline and believe that this should be a cause for alarm—especially as regards the consequences for children. In some sense, of course, the family has been declining since the beginning of recorded history—yet we've survived. But often overlooked in the current debate is the

17

fact that recent family decline is unlike historical family change. It is something unique, and much more serious. The argument for this position, and the evidence to support it, are provided below.

Overview

At the beginning of this century there was a widespread belief that the childrearing functions of the family, coming to full fruition, would stamp the character of our era. In this century's first decade, for instance, the famous Swedish feminist Ellen Key (1909) wrote a book called *The Century of the Child*. Translated into several languages, it quickly became a European best seller. Key maintained that the twentieth century would be focused on the expansion of children's rights, most importantly the right of the child to have a happy, stable home with devoted parents. The American historian Arthur W. Calhoun (1945) reiterated this theme in the first major history of the American family, published in 1917-1919: "On the whole it cannot be doubted that America has entered upon 'the century of the child'.... As befits a civilization with a broadening future, the child is becoming the center of life" (p. 131).

By mid-century a higher proportion of American children were growing up in stable, two-parent families than at any other time in American history (Cherlin and Furstenberg, 1988; Modell, Furstenberg, and Strong, 1978). To this degree these early commentators were prescient. Whatever else it may have been, the decade of the fifties was certainly an era of high birthrates, high marriage rates, low divorce rates, and general family "togetherness" and stability. Children were highly valued by their parents and by their culture. It was also, of course, the heyday of the so-called "traditional nuclear family," the family consisting of a heterosexual, monogamous, lifelong marriage in which there is a sharp division of labor, with the female as full-time housewife and the male as primary provider and ultimate authority.

But since the 1950s the situation for children, far from being the focus of national concern, has in many ways grown progressively worse. In the past thirty years, with remarkable speed, we have moved ever further from the position of a family, and a culture, that places children at the center of life (National Commission on Children, 1991; Select Committee on Children, Youth, and Families, 1989). As we approach the end of the twentieth century, it appears that early prognosticators of a child-centered society were well wide of the mark.

The abrupt and rapid change in the situation of families and children that began in the 1960s caught most family scholars by surprise. At first there was great reluctance to admit that a dramatic change was underway. But, although they may differ about its meaning and social consequences, scholars of all ideological persuasions now view the change as momentous and profound. The liberal authors of a recent history of the American family put it this way:

"What Americans have witnessed since 1960 are fundamental challenges to the forms, ideals, and role expectations that have defined the family for the last century and a half" (Mintz and Kellogg, 1988, p. 204). A conservative family scholar similarly opined: "The social assumptions that had guided human conduct in this nation for centuries were tossed aside with a casualness and speed that were astonishing" (Carlson, 1987, p. 1).

In what ways has the family in America actually changed over the past thirty years? Below, I sketch out the answer to this question with the help of the latest statistics (from the U.S. Census, unless otherwise indicated) and recent social science findings. Data are presented contrasting the American family situation in the late 1980s and early 1990s with that in the late 1950s and early 1960s, a period just prior to the time when the massive family changes began to occur. The data support the thesis, I shall argue, that this period has witnessed an unprecedented decline of the family as a social institution. Families have lost functions, social power, and authority over their members. They have grown smaller in size, less stable, and shorter in life span. People have become less willing to invest time, money, and energy in family life, turning instead to investments in themselves.

Moreover, there has been a weakening of child-centeredness in American society and culture. Familism as a cultural value has diminished. The past few decades have witnessed, for the first time in America history, the rise of adult-only communities, the massive voting down of local funds for education, and a growth in the attitude of "no children allowed." Both in the political process and in the market place, children's issues have been ignored.

What is a "Family"?

What, exactly, is the institutional entity that is declining? Answering such a question may seem a spectacularly unexciting way to begin, but the term "family" has been used in so many ambiguous ways in recent years that the explanation of its use has special importance. Indeed, the term has even become controversial. The struggle over how it should be defined, as is now well known, helped to prematurely end the 1980 White House Conference on Families. Some participants wanted the term to refer to the traditional family; others wanted it to include, for example, a homosexual couple living together. How the term is defined for legislative purposes, of course, makes a significant difference. A unit defined as a family may be in line to receive such special benefits as housing, health care, and sick leave. The controversy over defining the family is very much alive today in classrooms, conferences, and legislatures across the nation.

Family is a "nice" term, one with which we all want to be associated in some way, and therein lies a problem. The term has become a sponge concept, with multiple meanings that can include two friends who live together, the people who work in an office, a local unit of the Mafia, and the family of man. I wish to restrict the term to its most common meaning of a domestic group—a group in which people typically live together in a household and function as a cooperative unit, particularly through the sharing of economic resources, in the pursuit of domestic activities.

Within this meaning of a domestic group, I do not use the term "family" to refer exclusively to parents and their children, as some traditionalists would have it. But neither do I include any two or more people who happen to live together, such as roommates or even adults who merely have an intimate relationship of some kind. I define the family as a relatively small domestic group of kin (or people in a kin-like relationship) consisting of at least one adult and one dependent person. This definition is meant to refer particularly to an intergenerational unit that includes (or once included) children, but handicapped and infirm adults, the elderly, and other dependents also qualify. And it is meant to include single-parent families, stepfamilies, nonmarried and homosexual couples, and all other family types in which dependents are involved.

This definition is not all-purpose, and will not please everyone. Many will doubtless wish that I had included a married couple with no dependents. But it is important to distinguish a mere intimate relationship between adults, no matter how permanent, from the group that results when children or other dependents are present; this is the important point missed by scholars who want us to redefine the family as a sexually bonded or sexually based primary relationship (e.g., Scanzoni et al., 1989). Conservatives will bemoan the fact that the traditional nuclear family is not the focus. Others will object that the definition focuses on a discrete domestic group, arguing that parents need not be living together (as in the case of divorce). And there will be concern that the definition is not broad enough to include many family forms prominent in other cultures, such as that consisting of several kin groups living in a single, complex household. If the definition were more inclusive, however, it would be less meaningful. The domestic group of kin with dependents is its focus; this lies at the heart of most people's meaning of family.

Turning from the question of what a family is to what a family does, the domestic kin groups should be thought of as carrying out certain functions (or meeting certain needs) for society. These functions or needs, as spelled out in almost every textbook of marriage and the family, have traditionally included the following: procreation (reproduction) and the socialization of children; the provision to its members of care, affection, and companionship; economic cooperation (the sharing of economic resources, especially shelter, food, and clothing); and sexual regulation (so that sexual activity in a society is not completely permissive and people are made responsible for the consequences of their sexuality).

Saying that the institution of the family is declining is to say that the domestic kin groups are weakening in carrying out these functions or meeting these societal needs. In other words, for whatever reasons, families are not as successfully meeting the needs of society as they once were (this generalization, of course, does not mean all families). There are many possible reasons for such weakening. It may be that societies are asking less of family members because functions the family has traditionally carried out are no longer as important as they once were, because family members are less motivated to carry out family functions, because other institutions have taken over some of these functions, and so on. These are all matters that must be explored.

American Family Change, 1960-1990

To put the following family trends in perspective, it is important to keep in mind two points. The first is that many of these trends, such as rising divorce and decreasing fertility, had their inception well before 1960; indeed, some have been evident in industrializing nations for centuries. What happened, beginning in the 1960s, is that they either suddenly accelerated, as in the case of divorce, or suddenly reversed direction, as in the case of fertility. The divorce rate had been going up for 100 years, for example, before it rose so precipitously in the sixties (Cherlin, 1992; Inkeles, 1984).

The second point to consider is that the decade of the 1950s was an unusual period, and should be used as a baseline for comparative purposes only with caution. It is a period that requires as much explanation as the period that followed it (Cherlin, 1992). The fertility rate, for example, which had been decreasing for more than 100 years, dramatically reversed its direction in the late 1940s, only to dramatically return again, beginning in the 1960s, to the very low fertility levels of the 1930s.

The Number of Children

Although far from being the most important dimension of family decline, the decline in the number of children in the typical family, and in our society as a whole, is assuredly one of the most carefully studied. Of course a family (and a society) that has fewer children can be just as child-centered, and value children just as much, as a family with more children. The issue of quantity versus quality is real and important. One feature of the traditional nuclear family that arose with industrialization and urbanization was that it had fewer children than prior family types precisely because it valued, and wanted to do more for, each child (Zelizer, 1985). At some point, however, quantity does become an issue. A society needs a certain number of children just to continue from generation to generation.

Since the late 1950s, childbearing among American women, both as an ideal and a practice, has rapidly lost popularity. As a practice, there has been a sharp drop in the total fertility rate. In the late 1950s, the average American woman had 3.7 children over the course of her life. Thirty years later this rate had been cut by nearly one-half. In 1990, the average woman had only 1.9 children, below the figure of 2.1 necessary for population replacement and below the relatively low fertility levels found in the first half of the century.

In the early 1960s, when the trend of lower fertility of the last three decades first became evident, the favored interpretation of demographers was that women's desired family size had dropped; also, mainly because women started having their first child later in life, fewer women ever reached their desired family size (Preston, 1986). In other words, it was not that fewer women were having children but that women were having fewer children. Because child postponement has become so extensive, however, some demographers have predicted that between 20 percent and 25 percent of the most recent cohorts will remain completely childless, and that nearly 50 percent will either be childless or have only one child (Bloom and Trussell, 1984; Westoff, 1986). A far higher percentage of women than this say they want to have children—in fact two children—but the prevailing theory is that they are waiting so long to have them that the desires of many will never be fulfilled (McFalls, 1990). Although the childless estimate of 20 percent to 25 percent has recently been lowered to around 15 percent to 20 percent, it is clear that a substantial portion of young women today will reach the end of their childbearing years never having given birth (Bianchi, 1990; Ryder, 1990).

This change is connected with a dramatic, and probably historically unprecedented, decrease in positive feelings toward parenthood and motherhood. Between 1957 and 1976, the percentage of adults who felt positive about parenthood—that is, who viewed parenthood as a role that could fulfill their major values—dropped from 58 to 44 (Veroff, Douvan, and Kulka, 1981). It has probably dropped still lower today. And between 1970 and 1983, the percentage of women who gave the answer "being a mother, raising a family" to the question, "What do you think are the two or three most enjoyable things about being a woman today?" dropped from 53 to 26 (New York Times Poll, 1983). These attitudinal changes are associated with a remarkable decrease in the stigma associated with childlessness. In less than two decades, from 1962 to 1980, the proportion of American mothers who stated that "all couples should have children" declined by nearly half, from 84 percent to 43 percent (Sweet and Bumpass, 1987; Thornton, 1989).

For all these reasons, children today make up a much smaller proportion of the American population than ever before (a situation that is accentuated by increased longevity). Whereas, in 1960, children under eighteen constituted more than one-third of the population, their proportion has now dropped to only a little over one-quarter. This need not be a cause for concern about the imminent depopulation of America; much of our population growth today comes from immigration, and new immigrants tend to have a higher fertility rate than the native population. Also, in environmental terms, if not economically, it can plausibly be argued that we have become an overpopulated society. Nevertheless, the continuing decline in the number of children has significant ramifications for the priority our society gives to children, and for the cultural attitudes we hold concerning the importance of children in the overall scheme of life.

Marital Roles

Apart from their declining number, a large percentage of children who are born today grow up in a remarkably different family setting than did their forebears of thirty years ago. Major elements of the traditional nuclear family have almost become a thing of the past. First, and in some ways foremost, the marital roles associated with the traditional nuclear family have altered. As a cultural ideal, the doctrine of separate spheres, in which adult women were expected to be full-time housewife-mothers while their husbands were the breadwinners, has virtually ended. In 1960, 42 percent of all families had a sole male breadwinner; by 1988, this figure had dropped to 15 percent. A recent survey found that some 79 percent of adult Americans agreed that "it takes two paychecks to support a family today." And only 27 percent favored a return to "at least one parent raising children full-time" (Mass Mutual American Family Values Study, 1989).

Today, mothers are in the labor market to almost the same extent as nonmothers, with the fastest increases occurring for mothers of young children. In 1960, only 19 percent of married women (husband present) with children under six years of age were in the labor force full- or part-time or were looking for work. By 1990, that figure had climbed to 59 percent. For married women with children six to seventeen years of age, the change has been equally spectacular. In all, 57 percent of women were in the labor force in 1990, up from 38 percent in 1960. (It should be noted that this entry of married women into the labor force has been accompanied by a decline in male labor force participation, especially among older males; between 1960 and 1988, the percentage of males aged sixty-five and over in the civilian labor force declined from 33 to 16; for males aged fifty-five to sixty-four, the decline was from 87 percent to 67 percent [Wilkie, 1991].)

Family Structure and Marital Dissolution

At the same time that our society has disclaimed the role of wives in the traditional nuclear family, it has also heavily discarded the basic structure of that family type—two natural parents who stay together for life. Put another way, we have not only rejected the traditional nuclear family but are in the process of rejecting the nuclear family itself—a sort of throwing out of the baby with the bath water. Although the two trends are not necessarily causally related, they have at least been closely associated temporally. In 1960, 88 percent of children lived with two parents; by 1989, only 73 percent did so.

Even more telling, in 1960, 73 percent of all children lived with two natural parents both married only once. This figure was projected to drop to 56 percent by 1990 (Hernandez, 1988).

One family type that has replaced the intact family of biological parents, and currently is the focus of much social research and public discussion, is the stepparent family. But the fastest growing new family type in recent years has been the single-parent family (almost 90 percent of which are headed by women). In 1960, only 9 percent of all children under eighteen lived with a lone parent. This was about the same percentage as lived with a lone parent in 1900; at that time, however, 27 percent of the single-parent children lived with their father (Gordon and McLanahan, 1991). By 1990, the proportion of single-parent children had jumped to 24 percent, or nearly one-quarter of all children in America (the comparable figures for black children only are 22 percent in 1960 and 55 percent in 1990.)

The above data refer to a snapshot of the population at a single point in time. More dramatic still are the altered chances that children will live in a single-parent family sometime during their lifetimes. Of children born between 1950 and 1954, only 19 percent of whites (48 percent of blacks) had spent some time living in single-parent families by the time they reached age seventeen. But for white children born in 1980, this figure was projected by one estimate to be 70 percent (94 percent for black children). Another way of measuring this phenomenon is the proportion of their childhood that children can be expected to live with both parents. For white children born between 1950 and 1954, that figure is 92 percent (78 percent for blacks). For children born in 1980, the figure drops to 69 percent (41 percent for blacks) (Hofferth, 1985).

One of the main factors accounting for the increase in single-parent families is the growing incidence and acceptance of divorce, especially divorce involving children. Many different divorce rates are in use, and all show striking increases. In number of divorces per 1000 existing marriages, the United States divorce rate in 1960 was nine. That figure by 1987 had more than doubled to twenty-one. In number of divorced persons in the population per 1000 married persons (with spouse present), the 1960 figure was thirty-five. That figure nearly quadrupled by 1988 to 133.

Perhaps the most widely discussed divorce rate is the probability that a marriage will end in divorce. For white females, this probability increased from about 20 percent in 1960 to 45 percent by 1980, leading to the often heard statement that nearly one out of two marriages contracted today will end in divorce (Espenshade, 1985a; Schoen, 1987). With under-reporting taken into account, and including marital separation along with divorce, other scholars have placed the probability of dissolution of a first marriage contracted today at about 60 percent (Bumpass, 1990; Martin and Bumpass, 1989).

It is true that divorce has replaced death as a dissolver of marriages. In times past, the early death of one spouse often ended a union in which children were involved, although single-parent families were never so common as they are today. In 1900, for example, only 2 percent of single-parent children lived with a divorced parent, and 3.4 percent with a never-married parent (Gordon and McLanahan, 1991). A landmark of sorts was passed in 1974, when for the first year in American history more marriages ended in divorce than in death. According to data for the mid-1980s, death now causes only 78 percent as many marital dissolutions as divorce (Glick, 1988).

The causes of the rising divorce rate in modem societies are, of course, multiple (Furstenberg, 1990; Kitson, Babri, and Roach, 1985; Phillips, 1988; White, 1990). They include growing affluence that weakens the family's traditional economic bond, higher psychological expectations for marriage today, secularization, and the stress of changing gender roles. To some extent, divorce feeds upon itself. With more divorce occurring, the more normal it becomes, with fewer negative sanctions to oppose it and more potential partners available. One of the significant changes of recent years is the rising acceptance of divorce, especially when children are involved. Divorces in which children are involved used to be in the category of the unthinkable. Today, children are only a minor inhibitor of divorce, although more so when the children are male than female (Heaton, 1990; Morgan, Lye, and Condran, 1988; Waite and Lillard, 1991). As one measure of the acceptance of divorce involving children, the proportion of persons who disagreed with the statement, "when there are children in the family, parents should stay together even if they don't get along," jumped from 51 percent to 82 percent between 1962 and 1985 (Thornton, 1989). In other words, less than one-fifth of those asked believe that the presence of children should deter parents from breaking up. These data are from a panel study of women born in the Detroit Metropolitan Area; the change in the adult population nationwide could well have been greater.

Another reason for the increase in single-parent families is that many more of today's families start out with just one parent; the children are born out-of-wedlock and the father is absent. In 1960, only 5 percent of all births (22 percent of black births) occurred to unmarried mothers. By 1990, the number had climbed to 24 percent, or nearly a quarter of all children born (62 percent of black births). This is the highest national rate of out-of-wedlock births ever recorded in the United States; it is related to what has been referred to as "a disappearing act by fathers" (Preston, 1984, p. 443).

Clearly, then, family instability has come to be a dominant characteristic of our time. If childhood experiences and adult risks of marital disruption are taken into account, only a minority of children born today are likely to grow up in an intact, two-parent family, and also, as adults, to form and maintain such a family. And because the children of broken homes, compared to the children of intact families, have a much higher chance as adults of having unstable marriages of their own, the future in this regard does not look bright (McLanahan and Bumpass, 1988).

Marriage

A widespread retreat from marriage is another of the major family changes of our time (Espenshade, 1985a, 1985b). In the sense of being postponed, the institution of marriage itself has been in steep decline in recent years. With a median age at first marriage of 24.1 years, young women in 1991 were marrying nearly four years later than their mothers (the median age at first marriage was 20.3 in 1960). Thus, between 1960 and 1990, the proportion of women aged twenty to twenty-four who had never married more than doubled, from 28.4 percent to 62.8 percent; for women aged twenty-five to twenty-nine, the increase was even greater—from 10.5 percent to 31.1 percent.

The proportion ever marrying has also dropped, but not as substantially. For females born in the period from 1938 to 1942, and thus reaching the marital age around 1960, a remarkable 97 percent (of those surviving until age sixteen) could be expected to marry at some time during their lives. For females born in 1983, however, the chances of ever marrying are calculated to be slightly less than 90 percent (Schoen, 1987; Schoen, Urton, Woodrow, and Baj, 1985). For certain segments of the population, the proportion expected eventually to marry is even lower: only about 80 percent for women with a college education, for example, and 75 percent for black women (Glick, 1984).

It is important to point out that both the median age of marriage and the proportion ever marrying have returned to about where they stood at the end of the last century. The 1950s were, therefore, an anomaly in this respect. Also, the older one's age at marriage, the lower the chances of eventual divorce, at least until about age thirty. In this sense, marriage at older ages is beneficial for children and for society. It does not follow, however, that societies with older average ages at marriage have a lower divorce rate. The nation with the oldest average age of marriage today is Sweden, but it also has one of the highest divorce rates (Popenoe, 1987).

The marriage rate is expected to drop further in the future. One reason is that attitudes toward the unmarried adult have changed dramatically in recent decades. In 1957, 80 percent of the population agreed with the statement, "for a woman to remain unmarried she must be sick, neurotic or immoral;" by 1978, the proportion agreeing had dropped to 25 percent (Yankelovich, 1981). Still, the proportion of the population that expects to marry remains very high at 90 percent, and has shown almost no decline since 1960 (Thornton, 1989; Thorton and Freedman, 1982).

The psychological character of the marital relationship has changed substantially over the years (Davis, 1985). Traditionally, marriage has been understood as a social obligation—an institution designed mainly for economic security and procreation. Today, marriage is understood mainly as a path toward self-fulfillment. One's own self-development is seen to require a significant other, and marital partners are picked primarily to be personal companions. Put another way, marriage is becoming deinstitutionalized. No longer comprising a set of norms and social obligations that are widely enforced, marriage today is a voluntary relationship that individuals can make and break at will. As one indicator of this shift, laws regulating marriage and divorce have become increasingly more lax (Glendon, 1989; Jacob, 1988; Sugarman and Kay, 1990).

Apart from the high rate of marital dissolution, there is growing evidence that the quality of married life in America has taken a turn for the worse. There has always been a strong relationship between being married and being relatively happy in life. But an analysis of survey data over the years between 1972 and 1989 indicates that this relationship is weakening. There is an increasing proportion of reportedly happy never-married men and younger never-married women, and a decreasing proportion of reportedly happy married women (Glenn, 1991; Glenn and Weaver, 1988; Lee, Seccombe, and Sheban, 1991). Thus to be happy, men may not need marriage as much as they once did, and fewer women are finding happiness through marriage.

Nonfamily Living

The retreat from marriage has led to sharp increases in residential independence before marriage and in nonmarital cohabitation. Throughout world history, young people, especially women, have tended to live with their parents until they married. (One historical exception was the Northwestern European family pattern of sending adolescents to live and work in the homes of others [Mitterauer and Sieder, 1982], but that is not the situation today.) A survey of the high school class of 1980 found that 70 percent planned to move out of the parental home before marriage (Goldscheider and Goldscheider, 1987). In 1950, only 17 percent of unmarried women in their late twenties headed their own household; by 1980, this figure had jumped to 60 percent. The trend is likely to continue, in part because nonintact family living situations during childhood substantially raise the likelihood of leaving home prior to age eighteen, especially for girls (Aquilino, 1991).

Along with the high divorce rate and the residential independence of the elderly, early home-leaving is a major factor that lies behind the tremendous increase in nonfamily households and nonfamily living. Nonfamily households (defined by the U.S. Census as a household maintained by a person living alone or with one or more persons to whom he or she is not related) amounted to 29 percent of all households in 1990, compared to just 15 percent in 1960. About 85 percent of nonfamily households consist of just one person. The rapid twenty-year upward trend of nonfamily households came to a temporary halt in the period from 1986 to 1987 (Waldrop, 1988).

Also on the rise has been nonmarital cohabitation, or unmarried couples of the opposite sex living together. In part, the declining marriage rate has been offset by the increasing cohabitation rate (Bumpass, Sweet, and Cherlin, 1991). While non-marital couples still make up only a small proportion of all households (3.1 percent in 1990), their numbers are growing. The 1990 figure of 2,856,000 unmarried couple households is more than six times the 1960 figure of 439,000. More importantly, the proportion of first marriages preceded by cohabitation increased from only 8 percent for marriages in the late 1960s to about 50 percent for marriages today (Bumpass and Sweet, 1989).

There is evidence that life for young adults in a nonfamily household may become a self-fulfilling prophecy; not only does it reflect a flight from family life but it may actually promote such a flight. Especially for young women, it has been found that living away from home prior to marriage changes attitudes and plans away from family and toward individual concerns (Waite, Goldscheider, and Witsberger, 1986). Also, living independently may make it more difficult, when marriage finally does take place, to shift from purely individual concerns to a concern for the needs and desires of other family members, especially children (Rossi, 1980). As for nonmarital cohabitation, it has been shown that levels of certainty about the relationship are substantially lower than for marriage (Bumpass et al., 1991).

There is also a growing body of evidence that premarital cohabitation is associated with proneness for divorce (Booth and Johnson, 1988; DeMaris and Rao, 1992; Thompson and Colella, 1992), although the effect may be declining with time (Schoen, 1992). Cohabitation does not seem to serve very well the function of a trial marriage, or of a system that leads to stronger marriages through weeding out those who find that, after living together, they are unsuitable for each other. More likely, a lack of commitment at the beginning may signal a lack of commitment at the end.

Up until the past thirty years, partly due to steadily increasing longevity, Americans had actually spent more years in marriage and as parents with each passing year. But between 1960 and 1980, mainly due to markedly lower fertility and higher divorce rates, the absolute number of years spent in these family statuses declined for the first time in American history. The proportion of adult lives spent as a spouse, a parent, or a member of a conjugal family unit declined even more, reaching the lowest point in history. As early as 1800, the proportion of one's life spent with spouse and children was an estimated 56 percent; it rose to a high of 62 percent in 1960, and reached an all-time low of 43 percent in 1980 (Watkins, Menken, and Bongaarts, 1987). It has been estimated that white women in the period from 1940 to 1945 spent nearly 50 percent of their lives in a marriage (including both first marriages and remarriages); by the period from 1975 to 1980, this figure had dropped to just 43 percent (Espenshade, 1985a, 1985b).

Family Change as Family Decline

To the average American, the family trends of the last thirty years, summarized above, clearly signal the widespread decline of the institution of the family. For example, fewer persons are marrying and they are marrying later, more marriages are broken by divorce, and those marrying are having fewer children. These demographic trends are, in turn, the product of changes in what is culturally accepted in our society. Many surveys have shown a rapidly growing acceptance of divorce, permanent singleness, and childlessness (Thornton, 1989; Thornton and Freedman, 1982).

Despite such seemingly inexorable trends, it has taken a while for many family scholars to comprehend both the magnitude and the negative consequences of the changes that have occurred. At first, there was widespread resistance to the suggestion that the family was weakening or in any kind of trouble. In the mid-1970s, for example, Mary Jo Bane's (1976) influential and widely cited book on family trends appeared, entitled *Here to Stay*. As suggested by the title, it was designed to lay to rest the idea that the family in America was disintegrating or even declining and it contained statements such as: "Demographic materials suggest that the decline of the family's role in caring for children is more myth than fact" (p. 19); "The patterns of structural change so often cited as evidence of family decline do not seem to be weakening the bonds between parents and children" (p. 20); and "The kind of marriage that Americans have always known is still a pervasive and enduring institution" (p. 35).

In keeping with the ideas of many sociologists and other family experts of the time, Bane's book was resolutely upbeat about the family: "As I delved further into the data that describe what Americans do and how they live, I became less sure that the family was in trouble. Surprising stabilities showed up, and surprising evidence of the persistence of commitments to family life" (Bane, 1976, p. x). To be fair to the author, one should note that by the early 1970s the momentous family changes begun in the 1960s had not yet fully become evident. Also, Bane tended to compare the family situation in the early 1970s with that existing at the turn of the twentieth century, when high death rates still caused many families to become broken at an early age.

By the late 1980s, however, this same author took a markedly different and more alarmed tone. In a 1988 article written with a colleague (Bane and Jargowsky, 1988), one finds statements such as: "Family situations of children have changed dramatically since 1970" (p. 222); "The change is astonishing both for its size and for the speed with which it has happened" (p. 222); and "The real force behind family change has been a profound change in people's attitudes about marriage and children" (p. 246).

With the full realization of what has actually happened to the family over the past thirty years now becoming clear, such a change of mind among family scholars has become commonplace. Another example is that of the economist Sar A. Levitan and his colleagues. In their first edition of *What's Happening to the American Family?* (Levitan and Belous, 1981), the authors stressed the family's great resilience; the institution was undergoing "evolution not dissolution," they asserted. "The popular bleak scenario for the family contains a good deal of social instability. Fortunately, a critical analysis of the evidence does not paint such a dire picture, and thus a heartfelt 'hurrah' is in order" (p. 15). They concluded that: "Currently fashionable gloom and doom scenarios miss the essential process of adjustment and change" (p. 190).

In the second edition of this book (Levitan, Belous, and Gallo, 1988), however, the author's complacent mood had strikingly shifted. Now there was apprehensive talk of "radical changes in family structure." "Widespread family breakdown is bound to have a pervasive and debilitating impact not only on the quality of life but on the vitality of the body politic as well" (p. viii). With an apologetic tone, they noted that "the first edition of *What's Happening to the American Family?* envisioned a more sanguine scenario than does the present book...[but] the problems contributing to the erosion of the family have not abated in the 1980s" (p. ix).

In 1987, Norval Glenn, then editor of the influential *Journal of Family Issues*, asked a group of eighteen prominent family sociologists to put in writing how they felt about what was happening to the family in America (Glenn, 1987). Most were scholars who for years had sought to withhold their personal values and beliefs in the interest of scholarly objectivity. Nine of the scholars were "concerned" about family change in America, while only three were "sanguine." (The rest, ever faithful to their social science calling despite being asked explicitly to make a "value judgment," were "not classifiable.") Glenn expressed surprise at the outcome, saying he did not realize, based on their writings, that there was this much concern among family sociologists. The main focus of their concern, incidentally, was children.

As noted at the outset of the present article, however, there is still a reluctance among many scholars of the family to admit that the family is declining. The preferred term is *change*, leading to *diversity*. This may seem to be a mere terminological quibble, but it reflects deep ideological differences.

The problem is not only that the family as an institution has declined, but also that a specific family form—the traditional nuclear family—has declined. And therein lies the basis for much ideological conflict. The 1950s hegemony of the traditional nuclear family helped to fuel the modern women's movement. Reacting strongly to the lingering male dominance of this family form, as well as to its separate-sphere removal of women from the labor market, the women's movement came to view the traditional nuclear family in very negative terms (Friedan, 1963). Today, those who believe in less male dominance and greater equality for women—and that includes most academics and other intellectuals, including myself—share the views of the women's movement in favoring an egalitarian family form, with substantial economic independence for wives. From this perspective, the movement away from the traditional nuclear family is regarded as progress, not decline.

Speaking of family decline under these ideological circumstances, therefore, is seen to be implicitly favoring a discredited family form, one that oppresses women. Indeed, the term *decline* has been used most forcefully by those conservatives who tend to view all recent family change as negative, and who have issued a clarion call for a return to the traditional nuclear family (Dobson and Bauer, 1990). But properly used, the term *decline* should not carry such ideological baggage. To conclude empirically that the family as an institution is declining should not automatically link one to a particular ideology of family forms or gender equality. The two facets of decline—the weakening of the traditional form of the family and the weakening of the family as an institution—must be disaggregated. It is possible after all, at least theoretically, for the family to have become a stronger institution in its shift to a more egalitarian form.

For me, the term decline is important because it provides a "best fit" for many of the changes that have taken place. These changes, in my view, clearly indicate that the family as an institution has weakened. A main cause of this weakening may or may not be the shift of the family away from its traditional nuclear form; that is something requiring further investigation. Those who believe that the family has not declined, on the other hand, must logically hold one of two positions—either that the family has strengthened, or that its institutional power within society has remained unchanged. I believe that one is very hard put, indeed, to find supporting evidence for either of these two positions.

Let us review the evidence supporting the idea of family decline, or weakening. The evidence can be amassed in three broad areas—demographic, institutional, and cultural. In the course of this review I hope that the reader will suspend, for the moment, the automatic reaction of associating decline only with that which is negative. Some of the following aspects of family decline, as discussed below, certainly can be considered beneficial, or positive.

Demographic

Family groups have declined as a demographic reality. They have decreased in size and become a smaller percentage of all households; they survive as groups for a shorter period of time and they incorporate a smaller percentage of the average person's life course. Family groups are being replaced in people's lives by nonfamily groups—people living alone, without children, with an unrelated individual, in an institution, and so forth.

This trend, of course, is not proof, *ipso facto*, that the family institution is declining. Religion does not necessarily decline with a smaller number of churches and synagogues; education does not necessarily decline with fewer schools. But smaller numbers surely, by the same token, do not help to bolster the belief that the family is strengthening.

Institutional

There are three key dimensions to the strength of an institution: the institution's cohesion or the hold that it has over its members, how well it performs its functions, and the power it has in society relative to other institutions. The evidence suggests that the family as an institution has weakened in each of these respects.

First, individual family members have become more autonomous and less bound by the group; the group as a whole, therefore, has become less cohesive. A group or organization is strong (sometimes the phrase used is highly institutionalized) when it maintains close coordination over the internal relationships of members and directs their activities toward collective goals. In a strong group, the members are closely bound to the group and largely follow the group's norms and values. Families have clearly become weaker (less institutionalized) in this sense.

With more women in the labor market, for example, the economic interdependence between husbands and wives has been declining. Wives are less dependent on husbands for economic support; more are able, if they so desire, to go it alone. This means that wives are less likely to stay in bad marriages for economic reasons. And, indeed, some scholars have found a positive correlation between wives' income and the propensity to divorce—that is, the higher the wife's income, the greater the likelihood of divorce (Cherlin, 1981). By the same token, if a wife has economic independence (for example, through state welfare support), it is easier for a husband to abandon her if he so chooses. However one looks at it, and unfortunate though it may be, the decline of economic interdependence between husband and wife (primarily the economic dependence of the wife) appears to have led, in the aggregate, to weaker marital units as measured by higher rates of divorce and separation (for a contradictory view, see Greenstein, 1990).

As the marital tie has weakened in many families, so also has the tie between parents and children. A large part of the history of childhood and adolescence in the twentieth century is the decline of parental influence and authority, and the growth in importance of both the peer group and the mass media (Hawes and Hiner, 1985; Modell, 1989). Typically, the influence of the mass media is conducted through the peer group. There are few parents today who will deny that parental influence over children is on the wane; similarly, there is much less influence today of the elderly over their own children. For example, the proportion of the elderly seeing a child at least once a week declined by 25 percent between 1962 and 1984 (Bumpass, 1990).

The second dimension of family institutional decline is that the family is less able—and/or less willing—to carry out its traditional social functions. This is, in part, because it has become a less cohesive unit. The main family functions in recent times have been the procreation and socialization of children, the provision to its members of affection and companionship, sexual regulation, and economic cooperation. With a birthrate that is below the replacement level, it is demonstrably the case that the family has weakened in carrying out the function of procreation. A strong case can also be made that the family has weakened in conducting the function of child socialization. As Samuel Preston, former president of the Population Association of America, has suggested: "Since 1960 the conjugal family has begun to divest itself of care for children in much the same way that it did earlier for the elderly" (Preston, 1984, p. 443). Quantitative measures of such divestiture are the absenteeism rate of fathers, the decline in the amount of time that parents spend with their children, and the growing proportion of a child's life that is spent alone, with peers, in daycare, or in school (Hewlitt, 1991; Louv, 1990).

A decline in the provision of affection and companionship among adult family members is more difficult to measure, although some data mentioned above seem to suggest that such a decline has taken place. It is difficult to deny, however, that, in sheer number, social ties to nonrelated friends have gained, while social ties to family members have dropped. Measures of this are late marriage, increased single living, high divorce, and fewer family households.

By almost everyone's reckoning, marriage today is a more fragile institution than ever before precisely because it is based mainly on the provision of affection and companionship. When these attributes are not provided, the marriage often dissolves. The chances of that happening today are near a record high.

A decline of the family regulation of sexual behavior is one of the hallmarks of the past thirty years (D'Emilio and Freedman, 1988). Against most parents' wishes, young people have increasingly engaged in premarital sex, at ever younger ages. And against virtually all spousal wishes, the amount of sexual infidelity among married couples has seemingly increased. (Solid empirical support for this proposition is difficult to find, but it is certainly the belief of most Americans.)

Finally, the function of the family in economic cooperation has diminished substantially, as noted above. The family is less a pooled bundle of economic resources, and more a business partnership between two adults (and one that, in most states, can unilaterally be broken at any time). Witness, for example, the decline of joint checking accounts and the rise of prenuptial agreements.

With reference to children, it once was the case that the great majority of households in the nation were family households including children. This meant that most income to households was shared in such a way that children were beneficiaries. Today, households with children make up only 35 percent of the total, a decline from 49 percent in 1960. Income to the great majority of households is not shared with children, and therein lies one of the reasons why children are economically falling behind others, and why 40 percent of the poor in America today are children (Fuchs and Reklis, 1992; Levy and Michel, 1991).

The third dimension of family institutional decline is the loss of power to other institutional groups. In recent centuries, with the decline of agriculture and the rise of industry, the family has lost power to the workplace and, with the rise of mandatory formal education, it has lost power to the school. The largest beneficiary of the transfer of power out of the family in recent years has been the state. State agencies increasingly have the family under surveillance, seeking compliance for increasingly restrictive state laws covering such issues as child abuse and neglect, wife abuse, tax payments, and property maintenance (Lasch, 1977; Peden and Glahe, 1986). The fact that many of these laws are designed to foster the egalitarian treatment of family members, the protection of children, and the advancement of public welfare should not detract from their denial of power to the family unit.

Cultural

Family decline has also occurred in the sense that familism as a cultural value has weakened in favor of such values as self-fulfillment and egalitarianism (Bellah, Madsen, Sullivan, Swidler, and Tipton, 1985; Lasch, 1978; Veroff et al., 1981). In other words, the value placed on the family in our culture, compared to competing values, has diminished. Familism refers to the belief in a strong sense of family identification and loyalty, mutual assistance among family members, a concern for the perpetuation of the family unit, and the subordination of the interests and personality of individual family members to the interests and welfare of the family group.

It is true that most Americans still loudly proclaim family values, and there is no reason to question their sincerity about this. The family ideal is still out there. Yet apart from the ideal, the value of family has steadily been chipped away. The percentage of Americans who believe that "the family should stay together for the sake of the children" has declined precipitously, for example, as noted above. And fewer Americans believe that it is important to have children, to be married if you do, or even to be married, period. In the words of Larry L. Bumpass, another recent president of the Population Association of America, "Profamilial normative pressures have eroded in all areas of the life course" (Bumpass, 1990, p. 492).

Evaluating Family Decline

The net result—or bottom line—of each of these trends is, I submit, that Americans today are less willing than ever before to invest time, money, and energy in family life (Goode, 1984). Most still want to marry and most still want children, but they are turning more to other groups and activities, and are investing much more in themselves. Thus, one can say not only that the family is deinstitutionalizing, but that people are also disinvesting in it. Quite clearly, in this age of the "me generation," the individual rather than the family increasingly comes first.

The increase in individual rights and opportunities is, of course, one of the great achievements of the modern era. No one wants to go back to the days of the stronger family when the husband owned his wife and could do virtually anything he wanted to her short of murder, when the parents were the sole custodians of their children and could treat them as they wished, when the social status of the family you were born into heavily determined your social status for life, and when the psychosocial interior of the family was often so intense that it was like living in a cocoon. Clearly, if the individual rights of family members are to be respected, and a reasonable measure of self-fulfillment is to be achieved, there is such a thing as a family that is too strong. What, therefore, is wrong with the family weakening of recent decades?

Many scholars have noted that the institution of the family could be said to have been in decline since the beginning of mankind. And people of almost every era seem to have bemoaned the loss of the family, even suggesting its imminent demise (Popenoe, 1988). Yet we, as human beings, have made some progress over the centuries. Why, therefore, should we be unduly alarmed about the family decline of our generation? This question is a good one and demands an answer.

Family decline of the past has been of two kinds: functional and structural. Once the only social institution in existence, the family over time has lost functions to such institutions as organized religion, education, work, and government (Lenski and Lenski, 1987). These nonfamily institutions, specialized in certain tasks, have been found to be necessary to the efficient and orderly conduct of human affairs in all but the most isolated and preliterate of social settings. Education and work are the latest functions to be split off from the family unit, the split having occurred for the most part over the past two centuries. Few parents regret that we have public schools, rather than having to teach children themselves. And most are pleased about the higher standard of material living that has resulted, in part, from work being carried out in separate organizations that are better suited to the task. Thus, family decline in this sense—the functional decline that has surely left the family as an institution weaker vis-à-vis other institutions—is not something that is held in disfavor.

From its earliest incarnation as a multifunctional unit, the streamlined family of today is left with just two principal functions: childrearing, and the provision to its members of affection and companionship. Both family functions have become greatly magnified over the years. Once subsidiary functions of the family, they have now become the family's *raison d'etre*.

Turning from function to structure, the family has evolved in a cyclical manner (van den Berghe, 1979). Once presumably organized in terms of nuclear units in nomadic, preliterate groups, the family developed in many cultures over the centuries to become a complex unit consisting of several nuclear families and several generations living together, the so-called "extended family." Although in Northwestern Europe and North America the extended family was never as large or as complex as in much of the rest of the world, nevertheless today's small nuclear family can be thought of as a diminutive form of the larger and more complex households of the past (Kertzer, 1991).

There are more regrets about this structural loss than about the functional changes, and for the most part the structural loss has been a focus of those claiming that there is family crisis. In this view, the nuclear family is becoming too isolated from relatives and left to its own devices; the generations are splitting up. For those who place a strong value on generational continuity, there is a real loss here. Yet few adults today wish to have their parents, their uncles and aunts, and their cousins move back in with them. On the contrary, the movement is in the other direction (Goldscheider and Waite, 1991).

The structural change about which there has been the greatest concern historically, a change associated with both functional decline and the decline of the complex family, is the decline of family authority. In the complex family, authority over members was almost invariably held by the eldest male—the patriarch. Almost all of the family decline alarmists over the years have been males, and their concern has been the decline of male authority in the home. Yet there is obviously another side to this. In the patriarchal family, women by definition were subservient—sometimes highly subservient. The decline of patriarchal authority has not only brought a general decline of authority, but also a rise in the status of women—from being wholly owned appendages of their fathers, husbands, or some other male relative, to being full citizens with equal rights. In this sense, the decline of male authority has meant the rise of female equality. Again, this is a form of family decline about which, to say the least, most members of society today are not very worried (and many no doubt believe, for this reason, that the term "decline" is a highly inappropriate one to use).

So what kind of family decline is underway today that we should be concerned about? There are two dimensions of today's family decline that make it both unique and alarming. The first is that it is not the extended family that is breaking up but the nuclear family. The nuclear family can be thought of as the last vestige of the traditional family unit; all other adult members have been stripped away, leaving but two—the husband and wife. The nuclear unit—man, woman, and child—is called that for good reason: It is the fundamental and most basic unit of the family. Breaking up the nucleus of anything is a serious matter.

The second dimension of real concern regards what has been happening to the two principal functions—childrearing, and the provision to its members of affection and companionship—with which the family has been left. It is not difficult to argue that the functions that have already been taken from the family—government, formal education, and so on—can in fact be better performed by other institutions. It is far more debatable, however, whether the same applies to childrearing and the provision of affection and companionship. There is strong reason to believe, in fact, that the family is by far the best institution to carry out these functions, and that insofar as these functions are shifted to other institutions, they will not be carried out as well.

Discussion of the consequences for children of recent family decline—a cause for alarm—lies beyond the bounds of this paper. On this issue briefly, however, one can do no better than to quote the final report of the bipartisan National Commission on Children (1991) headed by Senator John D. Rockefeller IV:

> Dramatic social, demographic, and economic changes during the past 30 years have transformed the American family. For many children and parents the experiences of family life are different today than a generation ago. Families are smaller. More children live with only one parent, usually their mothers, and many lack consistent involvement and support of their fathers. More mothers as well as fathers hold jobs and go to work each day. Yet children are now the poorest group in America, and if they live only with their mother and she is not employed, they are almost certain to be poor. Moreover, many of the routines of family life have changed; regardless of family income, parents and children spend less time together (p. 15-16).

> By now these changes are quite familiar. Although their causes and consequences are still not fully understood, it is clear that they have had profound effects on family roles and on relationships between fathers, mothers, and children and between families and the communities in which they live. Observers from many quarters worry that these changes have had largely deleterious effects on family life and have caused a dramatic decline in the quality of life for many American children (p. 16).

> Substantial evidence suggests that the quality of life for many of America's children has declined. As the nation looks ahead to the twenty-first century, the fundamental challenge facing us is how to fashion responses that support and strengthen families as the once and future domain for raising children (p. 37).

Conclusion

My argument, in summary, is that the family decline of the past three decades is something special—very special. It is "end-of-the-line" family decline. Historically, the family has been stripped down to its bare essentials—just two adults and two main functions. The weakening of this unit is much more problematic than any prior family change. People today, most of all children, dearly want families in their lives. They long for that special, and hopefully life-long, social and emotional bond that family membership brings. Adults can perhaps live much of their lives, with some success, apart from families. The problem is that children, if we wish them to become successful adults, cannot. (In fact, most young children, other things being equal, would probably prefer to live in the large, complex families of old.) Adults for their own good purposes, most recently self-fulfillment, have stripped the family down to its nucleus. But any further reduction—either in functions or in number of members—will likely have adverse consequences for children, and thus for generations to come.

References

Aquilino, W. S. (1991). "Family Structure and Home-leaving: A Further Specification of the Relationship." *Journal of Marriage and the Family*, 53, 999-1010.

Bane, M. J. (1976). *Here to Stay: American Families in the Twentieth Century*. New York: Basic Books.

Bane, M. J. and Jargowsky, P. A. (1988). "The Links between Government Policy and Family Structure: What Matters and What Doesn't." In A. Cherlin (ed.). *The Changing American Family and Public Policy* (pp. 219-255). Washington, DC: Urban Institute Press.

Bellah, R. N., Madsen, R., Sullivan, W. M., Swidler, A., and Tipton, S. M. (1985). *Habits of the Heart: Individualism and Commitment in American Life*. Berkeley: University of California Press.

Bianchi, S. M. (1990). "America's Children: Mixed Prospects." *Population Bulletin*, 45, 1-43.

Bloom, D. E. and Trussell, J. (1984). "What are the Determinants of Delayed Childbearing and Permanent Childlessness in the United States?" *Demography*, 21, 591-611.

Booth, A. and Johnson, D. (1988). "Premarital Cohabitation and Marital Success." *Journal of Family Issues*, 9, 255-272.

Bumpass, L. L. (1990). "What's Happening to the Family? Interactions between Demographic and Institutional Change." *Demography*, 27, 483-498.

Bumpass, L. L. and Sweet, J. A. (1989). "National Estimates of Cohabitation: Cohort Levels and Union Stability." *Demography*, 26, 615-625.

Bumpass, L. L., Sweet, J. A., and Cherlin, A. (1991). "The Role of Cohabitation in Declining Marriage Rates." *Journal of Marriage and the Family*, 53, 913-927.

Calhoun, A. W. (1945). *A Social History of the American Family* (Vol. 3). New York: Barnes & Noble. (Original work published 1917-1919.)

Carlson, A. C. (1987). "Treason of the Professions: The Case of Home Economics." *The Family in America*, 1, 6.

Cherlin, A. J. (1981). *Marriage, Divorce,Remarriage*. Cambridge: Harvard University Press.

Cherlin, A. J. (1992). *Marriage, Divorce, Remarriage* (rev. ed). Cambridge: Harvard University Press.

Cherlin, A. and Furstenberg, F. F., Jr. (1988). "The Changing European Family: Lessons for the American Reader." *Journal of Family Issues*, 9, 291-297.

Coontz, S. (1992). *The Way We Never Were*. New York: Basic Books.

Davis, K. (ed.). (1985). *Contemporary Marriage: Comparative Perspectives on a Changing Institution*. New York: Russell Sage Foundation.

D'Emilio, J. and Freedman, E. B. (1988). *Intimate Matters: A History of Sexuality in America*. New York: Harper & Row.

DeMaris, A. J. and Rao, K. V. (1992). "Premarital Cohabitation and Subsequent Marital Stability in the United States: A Reassessment." *Journal of Marriage and the Family*, 54, 178-190.

Dobson, J., and Bauer, G. L. (1990). *Children at Risk*. Dallas: Word Publishing.

Dornbusch, S. M. and Strober, M. H. (eds.). (1988). *Feminism, Children and the New Families*. New York: Guilford Press.

Espenshade, T. J. (1985a). "Marriage Trends in America: Estimates, Implications, and Underlying Causes." *Population and Development Review*, II, 193-245.

Espenshade, T. J. (1985b). "The Recent Decline of American Marriage." In K. Davis (ed.). *Contemporary Marriage: Comparative Perspectives on a Changing Institution* (pp. 53-90). New York: Russell Sage Foundation.

Friedan, B. (1963). *The Feminine Mystique*. New York: W. W. Norton.

Fuchs, V. R. and Reklis, D. M. (1992). "America's Children: Economic Perspectives and Policy Options." *Science*, 255, 41-46.

Furstenberg, F. F., Jr. (1990). "Divorce and the American Family." *Annual Review of Sociology*, 16, 379-403.

Glendon, M. A. (1989). *The Transformation of Family Law*. Chicago: University of Chicago Press.

Glenn, N. (ed.). (1987). "The State of the American Family." Special issue of *Journal of Family Issues*, 8 (4).

Glenn, N. (1991). "The Recent Trend in Marital Success in the United States." *Journal of Marriage and the Family*, 53, 261-270.

Glenn, N. D. and Weaver, C. N. (1988). "The Changing Relationship of Marital Status to Reported Happiness." *Journal of Marriage and the Family*, 50, 317-324.

Glick, P. C. (1984). "Marriage, Divorce, and Living Arrangements: Prospective Changes." *Journal of Family Issues*, 5, 7-26.

Glick, P. C. (1988). "Fifty Years of Family Demography: A Record of Social Change." *Journal of Marriage and the Family*, 50, 861-873.

Goldscheider, C. and Goldscheider, F. K. (1987). "Moving Out and Marriage: What do Young Adults Expect?" *American Sociological Review*, 52, 278-285.

Goldscheider, F. K. and Waite, L. J. (1991). *New Families, No Families? The Transformation of the American Home*. Berkeley, CA: University of California Press.

Goode, W. J. (1984). "Individual Investments in Family Relationships Over the Coming Decades." *The Tocqueville Review*, 6, 51-83.

Gordon, L. and McLanahan, S. (1991). "Single Parenthood in 1900." *Journal of Family History*, 16, 97-116.

Greeley, A. M. (1991). *Faithful Attraction: Discovering Intimacy, Love, and Fidelity in American Marriage*. New York: Tor.

Greenstein, T. N. (1990). "Marital Disruption and the Employment of Married Women." *Journal of Marriage and the Family*, 52, 657-676.

Gubrium, J. F. and Holstein, J. A. (1990). *What is Family?* Mountain View, CA: Mayfield.

Hawes, J. M. and Hiner, N. R. (eds.). (1985). *American Childhood*. Westport, CT: Greenwood Press.

Heaton, T. B. (1990). "Marital Stability Throughout the Child-rearing Years." *Demography*, 27, 55-63.

Hernandez, D. J. (1988). "Demographic Trends and the Living Arrangements of Children." In E. M. Hetherington and J. D. Arasteh (eds.), *Impact of Divorce, Single Parenting, and Stepparenting on Children* (pp. 3-22). Hillsdale, NJ: Lawrence Erlbaum.

Hewlett, S. A. (1991). *When the Bough Breaks: The Cost of Neglecting Our Children*. New York: Basic Books.

Hofferth, S. L. (1985). "Updating Children's Life Course." *Journal of Marriage and the Family*, 47, 93-115.

Inkeles, A. (1984). "The Responsiveness of Family Patterns to Economic Change in the United States." *The Tocqueville Review*, 6, 5-50.

Jacob, H. (1988). *Silent Revolution: The Transformation of Divorce Law in the United States.* Chicago: University of Chicago Press.

Kain, E. L. (1990). *The Myth of Family Decline.* Lexington, MA: D.C. Heath.

Kertzer, D. I. (1991). "Household History and Sociological Theory." *Annual Review of Sociology,* 17, 155-179.

Key, E. (1909). *The Century of the Child.* New York: G. P. Putnam's Sons.

Kitson, G. C., Babri, K. B., and Roach; M. J. (1985). "Who Divorces and Why: A Review." *Journal of Family Issues,* 6, 255-293.

Lasch, C. (1977). *Haven in a Heartless World: The Family Besieged.* New York: Basic Books.

Lasch, C. (1978). *The Culture of Narcissism.* New York: W. W. Norton.

Lee, G. R., Seccombe, K., and Shehan, C. L. (1991). "Marital Status and Personal Happiness: An Analysis of Trend Data." *Journal of Marriage and the Family,* 53, 839-844.

Lenski, G., and Lenski, J. (1987). *Human Societies.* New York: McGraw Hill.

Levitan, S. A. and Belous, R. S. (1981). *What's Happening to the American Family?* Baltimore: Johns Hopkins University Press.

Levitan, S. A., Belous, R. S. and Gallo, F. (1988). *What's Happening to the American Family?* (rev. ed.). Baltimore: Johns Hopkins University Press.

Levy, F. and Michel, R. C. (1991). *The Economic Future of American Families.* Washington, DC: Urban Institute Press.

Louv, R. (1990). *Childhood's Future.* Boston: Houghton Mifflin.

Martin, T. C. and Bumpass, L. L. (1989). "Recent Trends in Marital Disruption." *Demography,* 26, 37-51.

Mass Mutual American Family Values Study. (1989). Washington, DC: Mellman & Lazarus.

McFalls, J. A., Jr. (1990). "The Risks of Reproductive Impairment in the Later Years of Childbearing." *Annual Review of Sociology,* 16, 491-519.

McLanahan, S. and Bumpass, L. (1988). "Intergenerational Consequences of Family Disruption." *American Journal of Sociology,* 94, 130-152.

Mintz, S. and Kellogg, S. (1988). *Domestic Revolutions: A Social History of American Family Life.* New York: Free Press.

Mitterauer, M. and Sieder, R. (1982). *The European Family.* Chicago: University of Chicago Press.

Modell, J. (1989). *Into One's Own: From Youth to Adulthood in the United States. 1920-1975.* Berkeley, CA: University of California Press.

Modell, J., Furstenberg, F. F., Jr. and Strong, D. (1978). "The Timing of Marriage in the Transition to Adulthood: Continuity and Change, 1860-1975." *American Journal of Sociology,* 84, S120-S150.

Morgan, S. P., Lye, D., and Condran, G. (1988). "Sons, Daughters, and the Risk of Marital Disruption." *American Journal of Sociology,* 94, 110-129.

National Commission on Children. (1991). *Beyond Rhetoric: A New American Agenda for Children and Families.* Washington, DC: Author.

New York Times poll. (1983, December 4). *New York Times,* p. A-1.

Peden, J. R. and Glahe, F. R. (eds.). (1986). *The American Family and the State.* San Francisco: Pacific Research Institute for Public Policy.

Phillips, R. (1988). *Putting Asunder: A History of Divorce in Western Society.* New York: Cambridge University Press.

Popenoe, D. (1987). "Beyond the Nuclear Family: A Statistical Portrait of the Changing Family in Sweden." *Journal of Marriage and the Family,* 49, 173-183.

Popenoe, D. (1988). *Disturbing the Nest: Family Change and Decline in Modern Societies.* New York: Aldine de Gruyter.

Preston, S. H. (1984). "Children and the Elderly: Divergent Paths for America's Dependents." *Demography*, 21, 435-457.

Preston, S. H. (1986). "Changing Values and Failing Birth Rates." *Population and Development Review*, 12 (Supplement), 176-195.

Rossi, A. S. (1980). "Life Span Theories and Women's Lives." *Signs: Journal of Women in Culture and Society*, 6, 4-32.

Ryder, N. B. (1990). "What is Going to Happen to American Fertility?" *Population and Development Review*, 16, 433-454.

Scanzoni, J., Polonko, K., Teachman, J., and Thompson, L. (1989). *The Sexual Bond: Rethinking Families and Close Relationships*. Newbury Park, CA: Sage.

Schoen, R. (1987). "The Continuing Retreat from Marriage: Figures from the 1983 U.S. Marital Status Life Tables." *Social Science Research*, 71, 108-9.

Schoen, R. (1992). "First Unions and the Stability of First Marriages." *Journal of Marriage and the Family*, 54, 281-284.

Schoen, R., Urton, W., Woodrow, K., and Baj, J. (1985). "Marriage and Divorce in Twentieth Century American Cohorts." *Demography*, 22, 101-114.

Select Committee on Children, Youth, and Families. (1989). *U.S. Children and Their Families: Current Conditions and Recent Trends*. Washington, DC: U.S. Government Printing Office.

Skolnick, A. (1991). *Embattled Paradise: The American Family in an Age of Uncertainty*. New York: Basic Books.

Stacey, J. (1990). *Brave New Families*. New York: Basic Books.

Sugarman, S. D. and Kay, H. H. (eds.). (1990). *Divorce Reform at the Crossroads*. New Haven: Yale University Press.

Sweet, J. A. and Bumpass, L. L. (1987). *American Families and Households*. New York: Russell Sage Foundation.

Thomson, E. and Colella, U. (1992). "Cohabitation and Marital Stability." *Journal of Marriage and the Family*, 54, 259-267.

Thornton, A. (1989). "Changing Attitudes toward Family Issues in the United States." *Journal of Marriage and the Family*, 51,873-893.

Thornton, A. and Freedman, D. (1982). "Changing Attitudes toward Marriage and Single Life." *Family Planning Perspectives*, 14, 297-303.

van den Berghe, P. L. (1990). *Human Family Systems: An Evolutionary View*. Prospect Heights, IL: Waveland Press. (Original work published 1979.)

Veroff, J., Douvan, E., and Kulka, R. A. (1981). *The Inner American: A Self-Portrait from 1957 to 1976*. New York: Basic Books.

Waite, L. J., Goldscheider, F. K., and Witsberger, C. (1986). "Nonfamily Living and the Erosion of Traditional Family Orientations among Young Adults." *American Sociological Review*, 51,541-554.

Waite, L., and Lillard, L. A. (1991). "Children and Marital Disruption." *American Journal of Sociology*, 96, 930-953.

Waldrop, J. (1988, March). "The Fashionable Family." *American Demographics*, pp. 23-26.

Watkins, S.C., Menken, J. A., and Bongaarts, J. (1987). "Demographic Foundations of Family Change." *American Sociological Review*, 52, 346-358.

Westoff, C. F. (1986). "Perspective on Nuptiality and Fertility." *Population and Development Review*, 12 (Supplement), 155-170.

White, L. K. (1990). "Determinants of Divorce: A Review of Research in the Eighties." *Journal of Marriage and the Family*, 52, 904-912.

Wilkie, J. R. (1991). "The Decline in Men's Labor Force Participation and Income and the Changing Structure of Family Economic Support." *Journal of Marriage and the Family*, 53, 111-122.

Yankelovich, D. (1981). *New Rules: Searching for Self-Fulfillment in a World Turned Upside Down.* New York: Random House.

Zelizer, V. A. (1985). *Pricing the Priceless Child: The Changing Social Value of Children.* New York: Basic Books.

Part 2

Marriage and the Family Today

3

The Family Condition of America: Cultural Change and Public Policy

Throughout its history the United States has depended heavily, for both social order and economic success, on the relatively self-sufficient and nurturing family unit—a childrearing unit that is crucial for the survival and development of children, a social unit that attends to its members' socioemotional needs, an economic unit that contains efficiencies derived from the specialization of labor and shared consumption, and a welfare unit that cares for the sick, injured, handicapped, and elderly. Yet in each of these respects the family condition of America has become problematic; by many quantitative measures, American families are functioning less well today than ever before, and less well than in any other advanced, industrialized nation, especially in regard to children. The evidence is strong that today's generation of children and youth is the first in our nation's history to be less well off— psychologically, socially, economically, and morally—than their parents were at the same age. Much of the problem, suggests the evidence, lies with what has happened to the family.[1]

It is hard to conceive of a good and successful society without reasonably strong families—multigenerational, domestic groups of kinfolk that effectively carry out their socially assigned tasks. No socially assigned task is more important than that of raising children to become adults who are able to love and to work and who are committed to such prosocial values as honesty, respect, and responsibility. Successful civilizations heretofore have been based on a family foundation, one that assured that children were taught the values, attitudes, and habits of the culture and became, as adults, reasonably well integrated into society. Indeed, many scholars have viewed civilizational collapse as at least partly a problem of family decline.[2] When a nation's families show signs of disarray, therefore, it surely is reasonable to view these signs as symptoms of a broader social failure.

Biosocial Bases of the Family

Childrearing has long been the family's main biosocial (biological and sociological) function or purpose. The family probably arose because of the paramount need for adults to devote a great amount of time to rearing children. Because human offspring come into the world totally dependent, they must, for a larger portion of their lives than any other species, be cared for and taught by adults. And human childrearing is much more complex than its animal counterpart; without life-guiding instincts, humans must deliberately be taught the "functional alternative" to instincts: culture. To a unique degree, human beings nurture, protect, and educate their offspring.[3]

The mother-child dyad is probably the strongest social bond in the higher animal kingdom, including humans, and it is the typical childrearing structure among most animal species. Certainly the human mother alone can accomplish childrearing; all available evidence shows that children need, at minimum, one adult to care intimately for them. "Survivors" or "resilient children," for example, children from deprived socioeconomic backgrounds who nevertheless grow up successfully, tend to have the common denominator of one adult who gave them inordinate attention.[4]

Yet given the complexities of the task of human childrearing, in all human societies to date the task has been shared by other adults. The institutional bond of marriage between the biological parents, an essential function of which is to tie the father to the mother-child dyad, is a panhuman institution, found in virtually every society; in no society has nonmarital childbirth or the single parent been the cultural norm. In all societies the biological father is identified, and in almost all societies he is important to his children's upbringing, although often indirectly as protector and breadwinner. In most of the world's societies childrearing has involved many more persons than the biological parents; typically members of the broader kinship group share childrearing, but sometimes other community members have participated too.[5] It may well be true, as anthropologist Raoul Naroll has concluded, that "the main point of human social structure in its evolution over the past 5 or 6 million years has been its special care for women and their children."[6]

Cultural Change: Collectivism to Individualism

To fully understand what has happened to the institution of the family in the modern period, one must look at broader cultural change in the values and norms that influence everyday choices. Most societies of the past were highly collectivist (I am using this term with a cultural and not a political meaning); collective goals took precedence over individual ones. "Doing one's duty" was far more important than "self-fulfillment"; or, in the words of Ralf Dahrendorf and Daniel Yankelovich, "social bonds" were more important than "personal choice."[7] The cultures of most developing and developed societies today, however, are moving or have moved toward individualism. Attributes such as strong social hierarchy, in-group harmony, and individual behavior strongly regulated by group norms are giving way to the primacy of personal over social goals, emotional detachment from the group, and an emphasis on self-reliance, personal autonomy, and competitiveness. Indeed, this shift toward individualism seems to be one of the fundamental motivating forces in modern history.[8] This shift has been associated with movement toward a system in which the nuclear family, consisting of parents and their children, becomes structurally separated (sociologists sometimes say isolated) from other social units, including the larger kinship group.[9]

Societies marked by an individualistic culture, with the individualistic nuclear family form, rank higher than collectivist societies in political democracy, individual development, scientific achievement, and (with the important exception of the newly advanced and relatively collectivist Asian societies of the Pacific Rim) economic advancement.[10] Advanced societies accord the highest priority to these goals. Among its many other advantages, the nuclear family is well suited to the development of autonomous individuals and thus to the growth of human freedom—the supreme value of individualistic societies.[11] But the shift from collectivism to individualism entails social costs as well as human gains. Along with political democracy and economic advancement, individualistic societies tend to have high rates of individual deviance, juvenile delinquency and crime, loneliness, depression, suicide, and social alienation. In short, individualistic societies have a greater number of free and independent citizens, but a weaker social order. There is far more social disorder in the United States, for example, than in the relatively more collectivist nations of northwestern Europe, and more disorder in European nations than in the still more collectivist societies of East Asia.

Two factors can be singled out as the dominant generators of the historical trend toward individualism: economic development and cultural complexity, the fundamental components of the master social trend often called modernization. Economic development leads to material affluence, especially personal economic security. Because affluent individuals and families need not directly rely so much on others for economic support, their personal and social autonomy concomitantly increases.[12] Through relying on market goods and services and on state-provided welfare, individuals in affluent societies are able to distance themselves from those intimate social structures and community groupings that have long been the basis for personal security. As these structures of "civil society" thereby weaken, so does the social order.

I will leave to economists any discussion of the sources of economic development. Within a single culture, cultural complexity—the second of the two factors—is generated mainly by the growth of science and technology, mass education, bureaucracy, urban living, and the mass media. Cultural complexity is compounded, of course, when separate cultures based on race, religion, or national origin come together to form a culturally heterogeneous nation or multicultural society. Faced with the weakening of a widely shared and stable culture—with new, different, and often conflicting norms, values, and worldviews—people's decisions about appropriate behavior must be based more strongly on personal attitudes than on traditional cultural standards. This new fact of life in culturally complex societies is reflected in the socialization process: children are taught to rely more on themselves than on the group if they are to adapt successfully to the world around them. One indication of this emphasis is a notable shift from "obedience" to "independence" as a dominant goal of childrearing over recent decades in the United States.[13]

It is important to stress that collectivism is found in many social forms, from huge, totalitarian states to small, isolated groupings of coreligionists. Also, the issue of collectivism generating social order depends greatly on one's geographic perspective. That strong in-group social order can lead to antipathy toward out-groups, resulting in social strife and warfare among groups, is a sociological truism. One very narrow form of collectivism, for example, in which collective social order extends no further than the extended family and local kin group, was labeled "amoral familism" in a classic work by Edward Banfield.[14] In the southern Italian setting of his study, the social world outside the kin group (but still within the local community) was one of general disorder. And, contemporary North Korea—a totalitarian dictatorship and one of the world's last communist nations—has maximized internal order but expresses a powerful military posture toward outsiders.

Indeed, the historical trend toward individualism, although generating some internal disorder, has led to the diminution of disorder among groups and societies—certainly in the form of major world wars This result is partly because group and national allegiances in individualistic societies are weaker, making it more difficult to mobilize people to fight external conflicts. Whatever the reasons, and they are many, the rise of relatively individualistic and economically advanced societies may have put an end to the era—consisting of all recorded human history—when "it was taken for granted that all nations were inherent rivals, seeking to conquer one another unless prevented from doing so."[15]

Individualism comes in many forms. Many people have written of the civic and utilitarian strains of individualism in American life, the individualisms on which this nation was founded.[16] Civic individualism is rooted in the belief in human rights and the sanctity of the individual, with the individual seen as part of a common civic endeavor. Utilitarian individualism is the individualism of personal achievement and the marketplace. Both developed as a reaction to historical forms of collectivism.

A new form of individualism has emerged in advanced, industrial societies—"radical" or "expressive" individualism that is devoted to "self-aggrandizement." In this form of individualism people become narcissistic, hedonistic, and self-oriented, showing concern for groups and for the public good only insofar as these matters directly affect their own well being.[17] In turn, the traditional groupings that make up civil society—neighborhoods, local communities, voluntary associations, religious organizations—become weakened.

Strong elements of radical individualism have been discerned in many highly advanced societies today, but they are especially apparent in the United States. And abundant evidence from many nations shows that the constituent groupings of civil society are in decline.[18]

As a foundation of civil society, the family is by no means exempt from this phenomenon of the deinstitutionalization or decline of civil society. The trend toward radical individualism can be perceived as movement beyond the nuclear family and toward a "postnuclear" family system. The gradual deinstitutionalization of the family, or "family decline" (which in the past has involved the shift from extended to nuclear families and the gradual loss of such family functions as economic production and formal education), consists of an increasing dissociation between pair-bonding, sexual activity, and procreation.[19] These three activities are effectively combined in nuclear family systems, and their dissociation has serious negative social consequences, especially for children.

Family decline highlights the role of affluence in driving individualism. Contrary to the popular notion that economic insecurity is the main cause of family decline, those societies that have moved furthest in a postnuclear family direction are characterized by relative economic security based on some combination of market-distributed personal affluence and welfare state supports. Such societies have high and increasing rates of marital dissolution and nonmarriage, single-parent families, voluntary stepfamilies, single-person households, and nonmarital births. Judged by these measures, the most "postnuclear" societies in the world today are Sweden and the United States, the one having the world's greatest state-generated economic security and the other having the world's greatest market-generated consumer affluence.

Advanced Societies Today: Cultural Trade-Offs

It is useful to examine cultures by scrutinizing the tradeoffs they have made between individualism and collectivism—between emphasizing personal autonomy and self-fulfillment on the one hand, and social order and cultural harmony on the other. A society that has moved too far toward individualism faces problems of personal alienation from the social order, with high rates of depression, eating disorders, suicide, and drug and alcohol abuse, and a breakdown in the social control of individual behavior, with high rates of crime and delinquency. A society that is too collectivist faces problems of political or cultural tyranny, endless warfare with out-groups, and the suppression of individual rights and initiative, all widespread problems that have plagued human history. Neither extreme collectivism nor extreme individualism is socially desirable. The good society is one that strikes a balance between the two poles, providing reasonable personal autonomy, a stable social order, and peace with neighbors.

In the West, my favorite good societies—ones that have struck the best balance between individualism and collectivism—are Iceland and Norway among the Nordic lands, and Switzerland among the nations of continental Europe. These nations are noted for their historical individualism, but at the same time they have highly intact and integrated cultures, strong social orders, economic prosperity, and with the partial exception of Norway, a long history of peace with their neighbors. They also have relatively intact families and communities and low rates of crime and personal pathology. The citizens of these nations, not incidentally, rank very high on cross-national "happiness" surveys.[20]

What is the secret of these societies? In part, they have just been lucky. They are demographically homogeneous (Switzerland is multicultural, but not in the American sense) and geographically in a position of relative isolation from the world around them. And these nations have instituted ways to become wealthy yet minimize the negative consequences of modernization, specifically the trend toward radical individualism. They are less urban than most other advanced nations, for example, and less dominated by the commercialism of the mass media. Culturally, these nations combine individualism with a moderate collectivism; we can refer to them with the phrase "communitarian individualism."[21] Individual goals are important, but they are blended with strong communal concerns and feelings of national solidarity. Self and community are in better balance than in other highly developed nations, especially the United States.

The advanced society today that has shifted least in the direction of radical individualism and postnuclear familism is Japan. Of the advanced societies, Japan ranks highest on "doing one's duty" collectivism and lowest on "self-fulfillment" individualism; in turn, Japan has the highest degree of internal social order and Japanese citizens have the lowest degree of personal autonomy.[22] This cultural situation can be attributed mainly to Japan's tremendous cultural homogeneity and very recent affluence, and because Asian cultures have traditionally been much more collectivist than Western cultures. Nevertheless, by all indications Japan is moving in the individualistic, postnuclear direction, showing signs of both growing personal autonomy and increased social disorder, including family breakup.

And the recent experience of Japan and other Pacific Rim nations has put to rest one proposition long held in the West—that a high degree of cultural individualism is necessary for economic advancement. This proposition certainly was validated by much of the Western experience, the classic example being individualistic England's (and later America's) pioneering role in the Industrial Revolution. Most of the great scientific and technological discoveries and inventions associated with that revolution came from relatively individualistic nations. Recent events suggest, however, that even in strictly economic terms the trend toward cultural individualism can proceed too far. The most economically successful nations today, and probably in the future, are those that are able to maintain a fairly cohesive social order through the collectivist attribute of a group identity and commitment that encourages honesty, respect for authority, and a sense of personal responsibility. One thinks of nations like Japan, Taiwan, Singapore, and Korea, but it is also likely that—partly because of their relatively stronger collectivism—most European nations will come to overshadow the economic achievements of the United States.

The Problem of America: Overindividualism

The United States has long been known as the world's most individualistic society. Yet in its heyday, over most of the past 150 years, a strong belief in the sanctity and importance of social units, such as local communities, religious organizations, voluntary associations, and the nation as a whole, tempered this individualism.[23] People's identities were rooted in such social units, and their lives were directed toward social goals that these units espoused. At the same time a cultural hegemony existed, dominated by a mostly Anglo-Saxon elite. Newcomers to the nation quickly assimilated, for the most part, to the norms and values that had been brought by the founding settlers (albeit somewhat modified in the new surroundings). Thus the United States has been marked for much of its history by a strong communitarian individualism, precisely the balance that has led to social success in other Western societies.

As the nation has become more affluent and the culture ever more diverse, however, and as self-expression and self-development have become life's dominant purposes, this situation has changed dramatically. People's faith and trust in social institutions, and their willingness to have their identities linked to them, have weakened enormously. Social units of all types, including the family, are increasingly viewed, with skepticism, as somewhat "illegitimate."[24] Especially since the 1950s, significant informal relationships, social networks, and social supports have been declining. There has been a decline in people being married, visiting informally with others, and belonging to voluntary associations, and an increase in living alone.[25] Nationally, the sense of cultural solidarity has become a pale shadow of its former being; it still can be activated through jingoist appeals in brief wars like that in the Persian Gulf but seemingly can no longer be invoked to solve such outstanding social problems as those of the inner city.

America today has all the earmarks of an overly individualistic society, with failing families, rising crime, declining interpersonal and political trust, growing personal and corporate greed, deteriorating communities, and increasing confusion over moral issues. These are all dimensions of what is increasingly felt to be "social decline." The average American seemingly has become more fearful, anxious, and unsettled. Tempers have become shorter, life's little satisfactions less frequent, and the emotional feel of life less secure. These trends are a recipe for social disaster. The push for self-fulfillment, when carried to the extreme, leads not to personal freedom and happiness but to social breakdown and individual anguish.[26]

By no means, it is important to add, has every aspect of America deteriorated in recent decades; in several key areas, indeed, this nation has seen rapid social progress. For instance, we are a much more inclusive society today—segregation and racism have substantially diminished, and blacks and other minority groups are now more fully accepted into the mainstream. The legal, sexual, and financial emancipation of women has become a reality as never before in history. With extraordinary advances in medicine, the end of many infectious diseases, and changes in lifestyle, we have greater longevity and, on the whole, better health. And our average material standard of living, especially in the possession of consumer durables, has increased significantly.

America's fundamental problem today is cultural disintegration, a weakening of the ties that bind. The tendency toward individualism and self-fulfillment has become too powerful; we have become, in David Riesman's phrase, an "over-optioned" society.[27] Postnuclear family decline is heavily implicated in this trend, but of course the family reflects changes in the larger sociocultural environment. To make matters worse, this cultural trend is now associated with relative economic decline and the likely deterioration in our status as a world political power.[28]

What has generated this overindividualistic social breakdown? In accordance with the theoretical propositions presented above, two factors stand out: our extreme cultural heterogeneity and our great personal wealth. Of all the advanced nations, the United States is by far the most culturally heterogeneous and complex on virtually all measures. Like Canada, Australia, and New Zealand, we were originally a nation centrally made up of immigrants from various European nations. But in two aspects of cultural complexity we are unique among advanced nations: our close proximity to the third world nations of Latin America and the originally involuntary presence of a large number of African Americans. Ours is a grand social experiment, and cultural pluralism has greatly enriched American life. Yet it has also fostered, over time, a weakening sense of common culture and national identity, and accelerated the trends toward radical individualism. When people cannot agree about what values they share and which social authorities they recognize and respect, they naturally fall back on more individualistic attitudes and patterns of living.

The United States may no longer be the world's wealthiest nation on a per capita basis, but it is probably still the wealthiest nation measured by the average material living standard of households, as determined by such indices as size of domicile and ownership of consumer durables. Personal wealth is high because more of our wealth remains in private hands; we rank lowest among the advanced nations, for example, in government receipts as a percentage of gross domestic product.[29] Such personal wealth enhances the ability of Americans to pursue an individualistic, privatized lifestyle, apart from the larger community. (Our heavy reliance on the market distribution of wealth, relatively untempered by government regulation, creates additional problems through generating inequalities; income and wealth are more un-equally distributed in America than in other advanced nations, and our tax structure is relatively regressive.)

Restoring Civil Society in America

If overindividualism is the problem, and it is caused fundamentally by affluence and cultural complexity, what could possibly be the solution? There is no way to undo our affluence and cultural complexity; nor would that necessarily be desirable. But ways do exist by which the negative consequences of affluence and complexity can be minimized. In general, people require two essential things for their social well being: close personal attachments and good community relationships. To have a society in which these are enhanced, we must seek to restore a cultural balance between individual autonomy and community needs.[30] With an ideology of communitarian individualism, our goal should be to promote families that can perform their assigned tasks, communities that can provide support to such families, and a larger society bound together by a culture of shared values. In the remainder of this chapter I will deal mainly with strategies that could alleviate the problem of family decline. But because all of the dimensions of social decline are so interrelated, it is useful briefly to share some thoughts on the strengthening of local communities and the promotion of national solidarity.[31]

A major deterrent to selfish individualism is the "natural communities" that exist throughout human life, communities based on free association and sets of relational networks, on primary groups and voluntary associations, on families and local neighborhoods—communities where people have both a sense of cultural identity and a feeling of belonging. These are the locale of civility—courtesy, politeness and decency toward others, cooperation and self-restraint—on which so much of "the good life" depends. Unfortunately, such fundamental and essential social formations can readily be upset and displaced by both the market and the state. Indeed, the social environment in this respect should be thought of as every bit as fragile, and as worth preserving, as the natural environment, with its similarly intricate and easily damaged ecological network. Despite the many benefits they generate in economic growth and in social justice, both the market and the state reduce our direct reliance on others and thus tend to weaken the community fabric.[32]

State displacement of civil society has most painfully been evident in the history of the formerly communist states of Eastern Europe,[33] but it can also be seen to some degree in the strong welfare states of Western Europe. (The decline of the institution of the family in these nations has been comparable to the decline in America, although—owing to welfare measures—without such devastating consequences.) In America, contrary to what most conservatives argue, it is the untrammeled market and not the state that has done the most damage to civil society. We have the weakest state sector by far among the advanced nations, and the most unregulated market. Through advocating a social structure in which consumer choice and pleasurable consumption are the highest values, through promoting high rates of mobility, a gambler's mentality, income inequality, and materialism, the market is certainly no friend of civil society. Daniel Bell was probably right when he noted the "cultural contradiction of capitalism," that capitalism tends to undermine the very values—such as honesty and hard work—on which its ultimate success depends.[34]

The reinvigoration of civil society in America depends in part on shifting away from our current preoccupation with individual rights. Strong local communities necessarily set a framework within which people will live, which involves making fundamental moral judgments about how they should live. The assumptions that all rights rest with the individual, and that local government should be morally neutral, are antithetical to the continued existence of such communities. A new agenda of "group rights" is not what is called for; few agendas are better suited to intergroup conflict to say nothing of group tyranny—the oppression of the individual by the majority. "What we need," as Mary Ann Glendon says, "is not a new portfolio of 'group rights' but a fuller concept of human personhood and a more ecological way of thinking about social policy."[35]

We are clearly at an early stage of development in our public policy thinking about how best to support positively (and avoid damaging) viable natural communities, while protecting the fundamental rights of individuals. There are the obvious concerns about racial and ethnic discrimination. And our impulses to support community can sometimes run awry, as was the case with the "community action" programs of the 1960s. Many community development efforts of that time, aimed at ending the War on Poverty, are considered to have been a failure.[36] But just as we now require environmental and family impact statements for pending legislation, so should we be thinking in similar terms about the impact of public policies on functioning local communities and civil society in general. An important caveat is that many existing communities in America could hardly be called natural. They are artificial, market-generated, income, and lifestyle enclaves that function mainly to preserve property values; or depressed areas, found in both urban and rural settings, from which everyone who could afford to has long since fled. The issue of which communities should garner public support is a profound one. Nevertheless, in general, public policies should seek to protect local neighborhoods against the unnecessary intrusion of outsiders, promote community identity and solidarity through local social, educational, cultural, and religious organizations, and deeply respect the wishes and concerns of each subcultural grouping.

While we are shoring up natural communities, however, we must be equally concerned about maintaining national solidarity. No nation can survive without a framework of common values.[37] A "natural-communities policy" is a different strategy than the one followed successfully for the first two hundred years of our nation, which typically was oriented to promoting rapid assimilation to the dominant European-based culture. Because the dark side of strong, in-group solidarity tends to be bigotry, prejudice, and violence against out-groups, the community strategy, if carried to the extreme, could lead to the tribalization and breakdown of America as we have known it. Utmost care will be necessary, therefore, to avoid the furtherance of moral exclusiveness in local communities. A natural-communities policy must be counterbalanced by strongly fostering those common values and traditions that have held us together at the national level. If these shared values and traditions were to be lost, we as a nation would be bound together solely by the market and its ally, the mass media. What could be called amoral communalism would then reign supreme over the land.

This concern for national solidarity is all the greater because of the new conditions under which we now live. As a culturally heterogeneous society from the beginning, the United States has been profoundly fortunate in having had a great amount of uninhabited space. If Americans did not wish, or were not able, to fit into the cultural mainstream, they could go off and live somewhere by themselves. Although many such isolated subcultures still exist in this country, the possibility today of geographic and cultural isolation has greatly diminished. Not only is usable space a diminishing resource, but modern transportation and communication technologies and economic forces bind the nation ever closer together in a network of interaction. And the widespread and continuing growth of metropolitan areas, despite the attempts of suburbanites to isolate themselves, compounds the connections that we all have. It is no longer possible or feasible for natural communities to exist in splendid isolation.

Apart from our governmental and legal institutions, the social institution that has played the most important role in enabling the nation to remain somewhat unified over the past centuries is probably education. The schools have taught patriotism, common values, and most importantly, a common language. Although local schools must remain, under a natural-communities policy, as strong, community-led institutions, they should also continue to heavily promote national identity and solidarity. I suggest, for example along the lines advocated by Chester Finn, that a strong, uniform national curriculum be incorporated into our primary and secondary schools not only in such fundamental subjects as math, science, and writing, which are so necessary for economic success in the modern world, but also in our Western traditions.[38] I suggest further that our colleges and universities, which draw in a larger percentage of citizens than in any other world nation, should also heavily stress our common Western values.

Just as moral exclusiveness is an issue at the local level, so also must it be a concern at the national level. Americans have gradually been developing a more cosmopolitan and global frame of mind. Efforts to promote national solidarity should not impede that development. While the society and the polity remain national in scope, the economy is increasingly international. It would be especially counterproductive if national solidarity were to be promoted in the age-old fashion of jingoism—through focusing attention on some presumed external threat, either political or economic. With the end of the Cold War and the globalization of the economy, maintaining national solidarity without inventing a new enemy will become a national test of character.[39]

Nuclear Families: The Vital Factor

At the heart of civil society lies the family.[40] In 1973, Margaret Mead told a Senate committee, "as families go, so goes the nation."[41] She might have been more precise. The market and the state seem to go on despite everything, but it is increasingly clear that "as families go, so goes civil society." A symbiotic relationship exists between the family and civil society. The family in an unfriendly surrounding culture is precarious; the stresses can be overwhelming. And civil societies depend on families to inculcate those civic values—honesty, trust, self-sacrifice, personal responsibility—by which they can thrive. In this sense, families can be thought of as "seedbeds of civic virtue." Such civic values are taught in the home, or they virtually are not taught at all. The school can try to teach these values—as it must—but if they are not taught within the home, early in a child's life, it is usually too late.

What family structure, under the conditions of industrial, liberal-democratic nations, is best able to produce offspring who grow up to be both autonomous and socially responsible, while also meeting the adult needs for intimacy and personal attachment that become ever more compelling in an increasingly impersonal world? Based on all available empirical evidence, as well as the lessons of recent human experience, the family structure that unquestionably works best is the nuclear family. I do not necessarily mean the traditional nuclear family, characterized by male dominance and a stay-at-home wife, which has been the predominant family form of the past 150 years (historians often refer to this as the modern family). I refer instead to the nuclear family in more general terms—consisting of a male and female living together, apart from other relatives, who share responsibility for their children and for each other.

Consider the fate of other family forms. There is no advanced, Western society where the three-generation extended family is very important, and where it is not also on the wane. Among advanced, industrial societies, Japan is the exception, but with the passing of the pre-World War II generation and the movement of women into the labor force, the days of the extended family there appear numbered. In the United States, it is the hope of some of my female college students that their mothers will come to live with them at the birth of their child, enabling these young women happily to stay on in the workplace. But such an arrangement on a widespread basis is hardly in the offing; for one thing, the mothers in question are now themselves in the labor force. Some scholars suggest that a new extended family is to be found in the trend toward step and blended families. "Isn't it nice," they say, "that we now have so many new relatives around!" The final verdict is not yet in on stepfamilies, but preliminary evidence from the few empirical studies that have been done sends quite the opposite message, and it is a chilling one. The National Child Development Study in Great Britain, a longitudinal analysis of 17,000 children born in 1958, found that the chances of stepchildren suffering social deprivation before reaching twenty-one are even greater than those left living after divorce with a lone parent. Similar findings are turning up in the United States.[42]

Another alternative, somewhat similar to extended families, is the bunching together of mostly unrelated individuals in a group setting. This was the dream of the 1960s flower children, and the ideal of some of their scholarly allies. But virtually all of the communes have been notoriously unsuccessful (where are they today?). And even in their heyday, one of their most distinguishing characteristics was few or no children. Their main purpose was adult fulfillment, not generational continuity.

At the other extreme from the extended family are such postnuclear alternative family forms as the single-parent family. Here, accumulating evidence on the personal and social consequences of this family type paints a grim picture indeed. A recent survey found, for example, that children from single-parent families are two to three times more likely to have emotional and behavioral problems than children from intact families, and by no means is reduced family income the sole factor involved.[43]

If we rule out these family alternatives, we are left with the nuclear family—children raised by their biological parents. Just as the international emergence and growth of liberal democracy may proclaim the "end of history," or at least the "end of ideology," I suggest that the nuclear family proclaims something similar in the family field. Family history comes to an end in this elemental, essential unit of human procreation.[44] As liberal democracy does the best job of resolving what Hegel referred to as peoples' "struggle for recognition," so the nuclear family is best at producing the kind of adults who can both promote and benefit from liberal democracy. Other family forms are not only possible but optimal in other cultural settings, but in advanced societies the nuclear family best combines the nurture of children with the strong need for emotional intimacy and the sexuality of parents. It is the family form for the modern world and, moreover, the family form that people in modern societies favor. The overwhelming majority of young people today put forth as their major life goal a lasting, monogamous, heterosexual relationship that includes the procreation of children.[45]

Let us explore more fully the benefits that strong nuclear families bring to an affluent and high-achieving, individualistic, democratic society, the reasons why nuclear families are worth tremendous social efforts to support and maintain. First, monogamous marriage—the basis of the nuclear family—brings enormous benefits to the adults involved. It is ironic in this age of self-fulfillment, when people are pulling themselves away from marriage, that a happy marriage seems to provide a powerful source of self-fulfillment. By virtually every measure, married individuals are better off than single individuals; quite clearly, marriage is good for one's physical and mental health.[46] Based on the evidence, nothing would benefit the nation more, perhaps, than a national drive to promote strong marriages. Studies of depression, probably the most pervasive mental health problem in America today (particularly among young people) and one that by some estimates has increased as much as tenfold in the past two generations, indicate this point. These studies make clear that having an emotional confidant is probably the single best inhibitor of (unipolar) depression—not just any emotional confidant, but especially one that involves a stable relationship with the opposite sex. By the same token, "happiness" and "subjective well-being" have also been shown to depend, more than anything else, on ties with spouse, family, and friends.[47]

Whichever sex personally gains the most from being married, and scholars are in conflict about that issue, society certainly gains enormously from having a high percentage of men who are married. Unmarried women can take pretty good care of themselves, but unmarried men have difficulty in this regard. In general, as James Q. Wilson has stressed, every society must be wary of the unattached male, for he is universally the cause of numerous social ills.[48] The good society is heavily dependent on men being attached to a strong moral order centered on families, both to discipline their sexual behavior and to reduce their competitive aggression. Men need the moral and emotional instruction of women more than vice versa; and family life, especially having children, is a considerable civilizing force for men.[49] (It is not uncommon to hear men say that they will give up certain deviant or socially irresponsible patterns of life only when they have children, for then they feel the need to set a good example.)

Yet men today spend more time apart from family life than at probably any other time in American history. About a quarter of all men ages twenty-five to thirty-four (18.6 percent of all men aged eighteen or older) live in nonfamily households, either alone or with an unrelated individual. Indeed, for Americans as a whole, just as the 1950s was a high watermark of family involvement, today is a low watermark. The proportion of the average American's adult life spent with spouse and children in 1960 was 62 percent, the highest in our history; today it is about 43 percent, the lowest in our history.[50] This trend alone probably helps to account for the high and rising crime rates over the past thirty years, a period in which the number of violent crimes per capita, as reported to authorities, increased by 355 percent. (And it should at least give us pause before wholeheartedly endorsing such movements as "single parents by choice," with its message that "women should not have to marry men to have babies."[51])

Many recent empirical studies and investigations by social scientists have focused on those elements of nuclear family childrearing that produce autonomous yet socially responsible adults. Of fundamental importance for the child, as Urie Bronfenbrenner has long pointed out, is the presence of "one or more persons with whom the child develops a strong, mutual, irrational, emotional attachment and who is committed to the child's well-being and development, preferably for life."[52] There can be little doubt that the biological parent, usually the mother, is best suited to this role, although many other kinds of people obviously have had success in special situations.

The principal issue is what is called attachment. Most of the voluminous literature on attachment theory focuses on the need for a child to have a strong, emotional attachment with an adult. The theory has garnered solid empirical support. A growing body of findings indicates that infants who do not have a strong attachment, especially in the first year of life but probably longer than that, have intellectual, emotional, social, and moral problems in later childhood. Moreover, according to recent evidence, these problems may carry over to adulthood.[53] Adult attachments (especially sustained pair-bonding), as already noted, seem to be as important to personal well being as child attachments, and they are shaped to a significant degree by the attachment experiences of childhood. For example, in a recent study of middle-aged adults who had satisfying marriages, maintained close friends, and were happily engaged in their work, the most important single explanatory factor was having had warm and affectionate parents when they were very young. In fact, the much-discussed decline of trust in American life today, especially in interpersonal relationships, could well be related to childhood attachment-type problems, including the distrust and loss of confidence in parents that often is a consequence of divorce.[54]

It is highly relevant that the traditional family role of men in almost all societies has been that of protector and provider, precisely so that mother and infant could be closely attached. In the absence of a husband or other helping relative, mother-infant attachment obviously becomes problematic. Today, however, childrearing women are more isolated from others than at any other time. Some American men are directly involved in childrearing, others are providing more help to mothers than their own fathers did, but many men, through the avenues of out-of-wedlock births or divorce, have abandoned their children entirely. The state and the market can give some help to the abandoned mothers, as they should, but they cannot provide the emotional attachment that is the basis of good childrearing.

An inescapable benefit of high male involvement in childrearing concerns the resource of time. Good childrearing takes time, and two parents can devote more attention to a child than a single parent. The significance of time in childrearing is highlighted by empirical findings on the promotion of "prosocial behavior" in children. The development of prosocial behavior—which includes helping, sharing, and concern for others—has been shown to stem from early attachment experiences, from the modeling by children of their parents' prosocial behavior, and from good nurturing, especially the way children are disciplined. At heart, prosocial behavior is based on strong feelings of empathy for other people. The type of discipline that best promotes the development of empathy in children is that which involves reasoning with the child, clearly pointing out the consequences of the child's actions on others. Discipline that relies on physical punishment, in contrast, often fails to develop empathy and, in any event, mainly teaches what is wrong rather than what is right.[55] (It has often been noted that families who have prosocial children, yet rarely use physical punishment, do not have to rely on punishment; as the result of lengthy interaction between parent and child, the child knows just what the parent is thinking and will adjust his or her behavior accordingly.) Discipline with reasoning and explanation is time intensive, especially compared with physical punishment. Today, when the time devoted to parent-child interaction is decreasing, especially in the father-absent family, it is likely that the teaching of empathy correspondingly suffers.

To make matters worse, no discipline at all—permissiveness—takes even less time. Parents who lack time and who also disavow physical punishment—a typical combination today—are shifting their childrearing techniques in the permissive direction. This path may be the worst of all, leading at best to a nation of anxious, aimless, and depressed youth who become troubled, self-indulgent adults.

Rebuilding the Nest

For all of the above reasons, our nation is well advised to establish as a paramount national goal the promotion of intact, nuclear families that can successfully raise children. If we had such a goal, what would be the most worthwhile public policies to achieve it? Two broad efforts should be uppermost: the promotion of long-term, monogamous marriages, especially when children are involved; and the provision of additional resources to the parents of young children so that parents will be able to do a better job of childrearing.

The marriage question is the most difficult one. A massive cultural decline has occurred in the ideal of marital permanence, even when children are involved. For example, while 51 percent of Americans in 1962 said that "parents who don't get along should not stay together because there are children in the family," in 1985 the figure was 82 percent.[56] Social stigma against divorce has all but disappeared, and with the divorce rate remaining very high (latest estimate: 60 percent probability of divorce for first marriages; higher for second marriages),[57] it is likely that any remaining stigma against divorce will be further diminished. A recent study found that individuals who have experienced parental divorce as children, or who have experienced divorce in their own marriages, have more favorable attitudes toward divorce than do those persons who have not had such experiences.[58] This could change, however, as the children of the "divorce revolution"—who are painfully aware of the consequences of divorce—become adults.

With the United States having the industrial world's highest divorce rate, one might have expected a national commission, or at least a congressional investigation, to study the problem. But, unlike the case with almost every other national social problem, no such national study or investigation has ever been undertaken. Nor is there much likelihood of one. The basic reason is that it would step on too many toes; divorce has become a legal and moral right, and in most states divorces can be secured today with little cost or effort and no moral disapproval. Moreover, often led by the cultural and intellectual elite, national sentiment tends to accept a high rate of divorce as inevitable. As Frank F. Furstenberg. Jr. and Andrew Cherlin concluded in their book on the consequences of divorce, "we are inclined to accept the irreversibility of high levels of divorce as our starting point for thinking about changes in public policy."[59]

Few wish to return to the era of no divorce; some divorces are clearly desirable. The central problem is the so-called individualistic divorce when children are involved—typically one partner departs in order to achieve self-fulfillment, leaving the children in the lurch. The number of such divorces has greatly increased. Neither the state nor the market probably can do very much to remedy the problem; at best, they should avoid exacerbating the situation. Longer waiting periods for divorcing couples with children would probably help, combined with mandatory marriage counseling. Perhaps we should institute a two-tier system of divorce law; marriages between adults without minor children would be relatively easy to dissolve, but marriages between adults with children would not. Properly conceived family life and sex education in the schools might help. Rigorously enforcing economic child support from divorced fathers and stigmatizing "deadbeat dads" would probably yield more male responsibility, as well as marginally more money for children.

But the problem is at heart cultural, not political or economic. Married couples must increasingly come to believe that they live in a society where marriage and marital permanence are valued, and where divorce is to be undertaken only as a very last resort. And for that to occur, our cultural values must change. It is hard to imagine, for marriage and divorce, the kind of attitudinal and value changes that have occurred in recent decades with respect to gender roles, minority rights, the environment, and smoking, but changes in those areas certainly point out that rapid and relatively deep cultural change is possible. In our overmedicalized society, perhaps it would help to cast divorce as a health problem.[60] Data could probably be gathered easily showing that divorce is a more serious threat to public health than, for example, smoking.

How to get men to marry the mothers of their children in the first place is no less daunting a task than lowering the divorce rate. It rests on a combination of having fewer unplanned births through widespread birth control, and finding ways to lock the father into the union (at least when the child is young). The message to men must be loud and clear: if you father a child, you are obligated to provide economic, social, and emotional support both to the child and to the child-caring mother.

One of the few institutions still pushing today for strong nuclear families is religion, but even there the message has become compromised to appear more sensitive to "nontraditional" and "alternative" family forms. Liberals and especially feminists often support such compromises, partly in fear that society will shift back to the traditional nuclear family, with all of its rejected moral baggage. But there need be little fear of that; the real fear is how to prevent our society from culturally deconstructing into a sea of individualistic chaos, for that is the direction in which the trends of the past few decades have been carrying us.

Even when fathers and mothers marry and remain together, however, their problems may have just begun. Children are no longer valued by our culture at the highest level of priority, as they have been for most of our history. Parents are economically falling behind nonparents; they have enormous problems meshing their family and work lives and are faced with a local environment that is hardly conducive to childrearing. So effectively has the children-first cultural message been suppressed in favor of a do-your-own-thing individualism for adults, especially by the advertising and entertainment industries, that many parents speak of their own lifestyles today in countercultural terms; it is them against the rest of the world.[61]

The income of families with young children has remained relatively stagnant for almost two decades, despite a doubling of women in the labor force. Whatever economic gains have been achieved for children stem mostly from having two parents at work and from the decrease in family size, both of which have now about reached their limits.[62] At the same time, the economic situation of the elderly has markedly improved. This anomaly is largely because the elderly have been handsomely rewarded through income redistribution (especially Social Security and Medicare), while children have not. According to Peter Peterson and Neil Howe, who estimate that eleven times more benefit dollars per capita go to those over sixty-five than to those under eighteen, Americans have decided to socialize much of the cost of growing old, but very little of the cost of raising children.[63] By another estimate, 22.9 percent of the federal budget in 1987 went to support the elderly, while only 4.8 percent supported children.[64] Any serious consideration of equity or national interest underlines the need of childrearing families for economic assistance, and several ways to provide such assistance are currently on the national table. Many proposals involve a child allowance or tax credit/exemption for children, such as the $1,000 refundable child tax credit proposed by the bipartisan National Commission on Children, headed by Governor John D. Rockefeller IV.[65]

Parents of young children need time, however, even more than money. For children in America today there is a national time famine, brought about mainly by father absence and by both husband and wife being in the labor force. Moreover, the arrival of a new baby instigates the most stressful period in the life course of most marriages. Having more time to adjust to the radically changed family situation would be beneficial not only to the child but to the marriage.[66]

Contrary to the predictions made earlier in this century, new evidence suggests that adults in their prime work years are spending more time on the job than ever before.[67] Estimates of the thirty-year decline in the time that parents spend with their children run as high as 40 percent.[68] As the working world currently is organized, a fundamental problem is the assumption that someone is home taking care of the kids. We should enact policies that make work more family-friendly, including parental leave, flexible hours, compressed work weeks, more part-time work (with benefits), job sharing, and home-based employment opportunities. Another possibility is more "career sequencing" in which parents deliberately postpone careers to provide more time for young children.[69]

Finally, many of the local environments in which children are being raised today are saturated with crime, materialism, and the loss of neighborliness, leading parents to despair.[70] Such problems can only be resolved, in the final analysis, by a reinvigoration of civil society.

The New Familism: A Hopeful Trend

One bright spot on the national scene is what some of us have called "the new familism," a growing belief by Americans that, yes, the family really is of central importance and worth preserving.[71] There are two groups primarily involved in this cultural minishift: the maturing baby boomers, now at the family stage of the lifecycle and family oriented as never before, and the "baby boom echo" children of the divorce revolution, now coming into adulthood with a troubled childhood to look back on and a new resolve not to go down the same path their parents took. Spurred by growing evidence that recent family changes have hurt children, the middle-aged, childrearing baby boomers clearly have shifted the media in a more profamily direction. Only time will tell, however, about the echo-children of the 1970s. Some evidence suggests that the will to change is there: they tend to favor marital permanence more than their parents did, for example, perhaps because they do not take the family as much for granted as their parents (the children of the familistic 1950s) did.[72] But do they also have the psychological wherewithal to change, or will their insecure childhood remain personally damaging to them for the rest of their lives? Studies of the long-term effects of divorce and other recent cultural changes on children and adolescents provide no solace in regard to this question.[73]

A few other sociocultural factors and trends seem to be working in a profamily direction. One is AIDS, which has now demonstrably slowed the sexual revolution. As one entertainment figure recently said (with obvious dismay), "dating in Hollywood just isn't what it used to be." Neither is dating on the college campus, but the changes so far have not been remarkable. Possibly a more important factor, working paradoxically in a profamily direction, is the economic downturn. Just as affluence breeds marital breakup, so moderate economic decline may generate more family solidarity. The problem is that economic decline has two conflicting consequences on the family. One is the hunker-down attitude that is good for marital permanence; people look to their social ties for support, and they have fewer options to break apart from those ties. But the other is unemployment and the misery it brings, no one's prescription for a happy marriage.

Social theorists might add another explanation for the profamily trend. Cultural change is often dialectical and cyclical, and some cycles of change are patterned in generational terms.[74] Not all cultural values can simultaneously be maximized, and one generation comes to value, because they have less of it, what their parents' generation rejected. This may be happening today in the family, a shift away from individualism and choice and toward family and other social bonds. Pessimists might say that the new shift, if it really exists, will be short-lived. The long-run effects of affluence and cultural complexity on the promotion of individualism seem highly compelling. But the fact is, no one is able to predict the future, even something as relatively simple as foretelling the collapse of communism a year before it occurs.[75]

The strong belief that a cultural shift is occurring, away from radical individualism and toward collective values, might become a "culture-fulfilling prophecy." Certainly, public policy should posit such a shift as an overriding goal and do everything possible to encourage it. If my analysis is correct, this encouragement would mean measures to curtail the negative effects of affluence and cultural complexity, programs to foster nuclear families and natural communities while protecting them from unnecessary incursions of both the market and the state, and efforts to maintain national solidarity and a common culture. This is a tall order, to be sure, but one that is rooted in the fundamental nature of our predicament.

Notes

1.   National Commission on Children, *Beyond Rhetoric: A New American Agenda for Children and Families* (Washington, DC: U.S. Government Printing Office, 1991); National Commission on America's Urban Families, *Families First* (Wash-

ington, DC: U.S. Government Printing Office, 1993); Select Committee on Children, Youth, and Families, *U.S. Children and Their Families: Current Conditions and Recent Trends, 1989*, 101 Cong. 1 Sess. (Washington, DC: Government Printing Office, 1989); Isabel V. Sawhill, "Young Children and Families," in Henry J. Aaron and Charles L. Schultze, eds., *Setting Domestic Priorities* (Washington, DC: Brookings, 1992), pp. 147-84.

2. See for example, Pitirim A. Sorokin, *Social and Cultural Dynamics* (New York: American Books, 1941).

3. Pierre L. van den Berghe, *Human Family Systems: An Evolutionary View* (Prospect Company Heights, IL: Waveland Press: 1990/1979); Jane B. Lancaster and Chet S. Lancaster, "The Watershed: Change in Parental-Investment and Family Formation Strategies in the Course of Human Evolution," in J. B. Lancaster et al., eds., *Parenting Across the Life Span: Biosocial Dimensions* (Hawthorne, NY: Aldine de Gruyter, 1987), pp. 187-205.

4. Urie Bronfenbrenner, "Discovering What Families Do," in David Blankenhorn, Steven Bayme, and Jean Bethke Elshtain, eds., *Rebuilding the Nest* (Milwaukee: Family Service America, 1990), pp. 27-38; on survivors, see Emmy E. Werner, "Children of the Garden Island," *Scientific American* 206 (April 1989), pp. 106-08; and Emmy E. Werner and Ruth S. Smith, *Overcoming the Odds: High-Risk Children from Birth to Adulthood* (Ithaca, NY: Cornell University Press, 1992).

5. Kingsley Davis, ed., *Contemporary Marriage: Comparative Perspectives on a Changing Situation* (New York: Russell Sage Foundation, 1985); Martin Daly and Margo Wilson, *Sex, Evolution, and Behavior*, 2d ed., (Belmont, CA: Wadsworth, 1983); Mary Maxwell Katz and Melvin J. Konner, "The Role of the Father: An Anthropological Perspective," in Michael E. Lamb, ed., *The Role of the Father in Child Development* (New York: John Wiley, 1981), pp. 155-85; and Ruth Busch, *Family Systems: A Comparative Study of the Family* (New York: Peter Lang, 1990).

6. Raoul Naroll, *The Moral Order: An Introduction to the Human Situation* (Beverly Hills, CA: Sage, 1983), p. 343.

7. Ralf Dahrendorf, *Life Chances: Approaches to Social and Political Theory* (Chicago: University of Chicago Press, 1979); and Daniel Yankelovich, "How Changes in the Economy are Reshaping American Values," in Henry J. Aaron et al., eds. *Values and Public Policy* (Washington, DC: Brookings Institution, 1994), pp. 16-53.

8. Francis Fukuyama, *The End of History and the Last Man* (New York: Free Press, 1992), emphasizes this point, drawing on Hegel's notion that history is driven by "a struggle for recognition"—the intense desire of human beings to have their inherent worth acknowledged and respected.

9. A cross-cultural analysis by Harry C. Triandis et al. found that a family measure accounted for more variance between collectivism and individualism than any other. "The Measurement of the Etic Aspects of Individualism and Collectivism," *Australian Journal of Psychology* 38 (1986), pp. 257-67.

10. Harry C. Triandis. "Cross-Cultural Studies of Individualism and Collectivism," in John J. Berman, ed., *Nebraska Symposium on Motivation*, 1989, vol. 37 (Lincoln, NE: University of Nebraska Press, 1990), pp. 41-133.

11. Brigitte Berger and Peter L. Berger, *The War Over the Family: Capturing the Middle Ground* (New York: Anchor Press/Doubleday, 1983); C. C. Harris, *The Family and Industrial Society* (London: George Allen and Unwin, 1983); Lawrence Stone, *The Family, Sex and Marriage in England 1500-1800* (New York: Harper and Row; 1979); Emmanuel Todd, *The Explanation of Ideology* (Basil Blackwell, 1985); and Emmanuel Todd, *The Causes of Progress: Culture Authority and Change* (New York: Basil Blackwell, 1987).

12. Margaret Mooney Marini, "The Rise of Individualism in Advanced Industrial Societies," University of Minnesota, 1991.
13. Duane F. Alwin, "From Obedience to Autonomy: Changes in Traits Desired in Children, 1924-1978," *Public Opinion Quarterly* 52 (Spring 1988), pp. 33-52.
14. Edward C. Banfield, *The Moral Basis of a Backward Society* (New York: Free Press, 1958).
15. Ronald Ingelhart, *Culture Shift in Advanced Industrial Societies* (Princeton, NJ: Princeton University Press, 1990), p. 424.
16. Robert N. Bellah et al., *Habits of the Heart: Individualism and Commitment in American Life* (Berkeley, CA: University of California Press, 1985); and Robert N. Bellah et al., *The Good Society* (New York: Alfred J. Knopf, 1991).
17. This is not the same as Ronald Ingelhart's well-known concept "postmaterialism," which involves the rejection of materialism. See *The Silent Revolution: Changing Values and Political Styles Among Western Publics* (Princeton, NJ: Princeton University Press, 1977) and Inglehart, *Culture Shift*.
18. Christopher Lasch, *The Culture of Narcissism: American Life in an Age of Diminishing Expectations* (New York: W.W. Norton 1987); Bellah et al., *Habits of the Heart*, and Herbert Hendin, *The Age of Sensation* (New York: Norton, 1975). On the decline of civil society, see Allan Wolfe, *Whose Keeper? Social Science and Moral Obligation* (Berkeley, CA: University of California Press, 1989); Amitai Etzioni, *The Spirit of Community: Rights, Responsibilities, and the Communitarian Agenda* (New York: Crown, 1993); and Philip Selznick, *The Moral Commonwealth: Social Theory and the Promise of Community* (Berkeley, CA: University of California Press, 1992).
19. David Popenoe, *Disturbing the Nest: Family Change and Decline in Modern Societies* (Hawthorne, NY: Aldine de Gruyter, 1988), chapter 13.
20. Based on quantitative "quality of life" measures, Raoul Naroll determined Norway to be the world's best society. Naroll, *The Moral Order*, chapter 3. On happiness surveys, see Fritz Strack, Michael Argyle, and Norbert Schwarze, eds., *Subjective Well-Being: An Interdisciplinary Perspective* (Pergamon Press, 1991).
21. Triandis, "Cross-Cultural Studies," p. 105.
22. See, for example. Robert J. Smith, *Japanese Society: Tradition, Self and the Social Order* (New York: Cambridge University Press, 1983).
23. America's civic individualism was stressed by the first analyst of American individualism, Alexis de Tocqueville, *Democracy in America*, ed. Richard D. Heffner (Toronto: Penguin, 1956).
24. Louis Harris, *Inside America* (New York: Vintage Books/Random House, 1987).
25. James S. House, "Social Support and the Quality of Life," in Frank M. Andrews, ed., *Research on the Quality of Life* (Ann Arbor: University of Michigan Press, 1986), p. 267, comparing adults in the 1950s with those in the 1970s.
26. Andrew Oldenquist, *The Non-Suicidal Society* (Bloomington: Indiana University Press, 1988).
27. David Riesman, "Egocentrism," *Encounter* 55 (August-September 1980), pp. 19-28.
28. Paul Kennedy, *The Rise and Fall of the Great Powers: Economic Change and Military Conflict from 500-2000* (New York: Vintage Books/Random House, 1987); and Bennett Harrison and Barry Bluestone, *The Great U-Turn: Corporate Restructuring and the Polarizing of America* (New York: Basic Books, 1988).
29. The 1989 data from the Organization for Economic Cooperation and Development show the U.S. figure to be 30.9 percent in 1989, compared with 38.5 percent in Britain, 47.8 percent in France, and higher still in the Nordic countries. *OECD Economic Outlook* 53 (June 1993), p. 216.

30. This is the credo of communitarians. See Michael Sandel, *Liberalism and the Limits of Justice* (New York: Cambridge University Press, 1982); Etzioni, *The Spirit of the Community*; and the journal *The Responsive Community*.

31. This issue is explored more fully in David Popenoe, "The Roots of Declining Social Virtue: Family, Community and the Need for a 'Natural Communities' Policy" in Mary Ann Glendon and David Blankenhorn, eds., *Seedbeds of Virtue* (Lanham, MD: Madison Books, 1995), pp. 71-104, and in this volume.

32. The "natural communities" concept is closely related to the concept of protecting "social capital" in James S. Coleman, *Foundations of Social Theory* (Cambridge, MA: Belknap Press, 1990), and of protecting "mediating institutions" advanced by Peter L. Berger and Richard J. Neuhaus, *To Empower People: The Role of Mediating Structures in Public Policy* (Washington, DC: American Enterprise Institute for Public Policy Research, 1977).

33. Zbigniew Rau, "Human Nature, Social Engineering, and the Reemergence of Civil Society," *Social Philosophy and Policy* 8 (1991), pp. 159-79.

34. Daniel Bell, *The Cultural Contradictions of Capitalism* (New York: Basic Books, 1976).

35. Mary Ann Glendon, *Rights Talk: The Impoverishment of Political Discourse* (New York: Free Press, 1991), p. 137.

36. Nathan Glazer, *The Limits of Social Policy* (Cambridge, MA: Harvard University Press, 1988).

37. Arthur M. Schlesinger, Jr., *The Disuniting of America: Reflections on a Multicultural Society* (New York: W.W. Norton, 1992).

38. Chester E. Finn, Jr., *We Must Take Charge: Our Schools and Our Future* (New York: Free Press, 1991). The difficulties in reaching agreement on "American values," of course, are considerable. See James Davison Hunter, *Culture Wars: The Struggle to Define America* (New York: Basic Books, 1991).

39. Robert B. Reich, *The Work of Nations: Preparing Ourselves for 21st-Century Capitalism* (New York: Alfred A. Knopf. 1991).

40. Moira Eastman, *Family, the Vital Factor: The Key to Society's Survival* (North Blackburn, Victoria: CollinsDove, 1989).

41. Cited in Walter F. Mondale's foreword to Edward F. Zigler, Sharon Lyn Kagan, and Edgar Klugman, eds., *Children, Families, and Government* (New York: Cambridge University Press, 1983), p. xi.

42. Kathleen E. Kiernan, "The Impact of Family Disruption in Childhood on Transitions Made in Young Adult Life," *Population Studies* 46 (1992), pp. 213-34. See also National Commission on Children, *Speaking of Kids: A National Survey of Children and Parents* (Washington, 1991).

43. Nicholas Zill and Charlotte A. Schoenborn, "Developmental, Learning, and Emotional Problems: Health of Our Nation's Children, United States, 1988," in National Center for Health Statistics, *Advance Data*, no. 190, November 16, 1990.

44. Family history comes to an end just about where it started. As sociologist Pierre L. van den Berghe has noted, "Advanced industrial societies have recreated, through a long evolutionary path, much the same kind of mobile, seminomadic, nuclear, bilateral family...as existed in the simplest, smallest societies." *Human Family Systems: An Evolutionary View* (Prospect Heights, IL: Waveland Press, 1990/1979), p. 132.

45. Richard A. Easterlin and Eileen M. Crimmins, "Recent Social Trends: Changes in Personal Aspirations of American Youth," *Social Science Research* 72 (July 1988), pp. 217-23.

46. Walter R. Gove, Carolyn Briggs Style, and Michael Hughes, "The Effect of Marriage on the Well-Being of Adults: A Theoretical Analysis," *Journal of Family*

Issues 11 (March 1990), pp. 4-35; and R. H. Coombs, "Marital Status and Personal Well-Being: A Literature Review," *Family Relations* 40 (January 1991), pp. 97-102.

47.   On the health effects of the nuclear family, see Leonard A. Sagan, *The Health of Nations* (New York: Basic Books, 1987). On depression, see Gerald L. Klerman and Myrna M. Weissman, "Increasing Rates of Depression," *Journal of the American Medical Association* 261 (April 1989), pp. 2229-35. On social supports, see Nan Lin, Alfred Dean, and Walter M. Ensel, *Social Supports, Life Events and Depression* (Academic Press, 1986). On subjective well-being, see Fritz Strack, Michael Argyle, and Norbert Schwarze, eds., *Subjective Well-Being*.

48.   James Q. Wilson, "Culture, Incentives, and the Underclass," in Henry J. Aaron et al., eds., *Values and Public Policy* (Washington, DC: Brookings Institution, 1994), pp. 54-80.

49.   George Gilder, *Men and Marriage* (Gretna, LA: Pelican, 1986).

50.   Susan Cotts Watkins, Jane A. Menken, and John Bongaarts, "The Demographic Foundations of Family Change," *American Sociological Re*view 52 (June 1987), pp. 346-58.

51.   See Barbara Dafoe Whitehead, "Dan Quayle was Right," *Atlantic* (April 1993) pp. 47-84.

52.   Urie Bronfenbrenner, "Discovering What Families Do," in Blankenhorn, Bayme, and Elshtain, *Rebuilding the Nest*, pp. 27-38.

53.   John Bowlby, *Attachment and Loss*, 3 vols. (New York: Basic Books, 1969, 1973, 1977); and Willard W. Hartup. "Social Relationships and Their Developmental Significance," *American Psychologist* 44 (February 1989), pp. 120-26; Cindy Hazan and Phillip R. Shaver, "Love and Work: An Attachment-Theoretical Perspective," *Journal of Personality and Social Psychology* 59 (1990), pp. 270-80; Mary D. Salter Ainsworth, "Attachments beyond Infancy," *American Psychologist* 44 (April 1989), pp. 709-16; Robert S. Weiss, "The Attachment Bond in Childhood and Adulthood," in Colin Murray Parkes, Joan Stevenson-Hinde, and Peter Maris, eds., *Attachment across the Life Cycle* (London: Tavistock/Routledge, 1991), chapter 4; Phillip R. Shaver and Cindy Hazan, "Adult Romantic Attachment: Theory and Evidence," in D. Perlman and W. Jones, eds., *Advances in Personal Relationships* (London: Jessica Kingsley, 1993), chapter 4.

54.   Carol E. Franz, David C. McClelland, and Joel Weinberger, "Childhood Antecedents of Conventional Social Accomplishment in Midlife Adults: A 36-Year Prospective Study," *Journal of Personality and Social Psychology* 60 (1991), pp. 585-95; and John Nordheimer, "For Lovers, No. 1 Activity These Days is Worrying," *New York Times*, February 12, 1992, p. C10.

55.   Nancy Eisenberg and Paul H. Mussen, *The Roots of Prosocial Behavior in Children* (New York: Cambridge University Press, 1989).

56.   Norval D. Glenn, "The Family Values of Americans," Working Paper 2 (New York: Council on Families in America, Institute for American Values, 1991), p. 6.

57.   Larry L. Bumpass, "What's Happening to the Family? Interactions between Demographic and Institutional Change," *Demography* 27 (November 1990), pp. 483-98.

58.   Paul R. Amato and Alan Booth, "The Consequences of Divorce for Attitudes toward Divorce and Gender Roles," *Journal of Family Issues* 12 (September 1991), pp. 306-22.

59.   Frank F. Furstenberg. Jr., and Andrew Cherlin, *Divided Families: What Happens to Children When Parents Part* (Cambridge, MA: Harvard University Press 1991), p. 105.

60.   Thanks to Barbara Dafoe Whitehead for making this observation.

61. Barbara Dafoe Whitehead, "Maryland Focus Group Report on Family Time," Working Paper 6 (New York: Council on Families in America, Institute for American Values, 1991).
62. "Families on a Treadmill: Work and Income in the 1980s," A staff study prepared for the use of members of the Joint Economic Committee of the U.S. Congress, January 17, 1992; Frank Levy and Richard C. Michael, *The Economic Future of American Families: Income and Wealth Trends* (Washington, DC: Urban Institute Press, 1991); Frank Levy, *Dollars and Dreams: The Changing American Income Distribution* (New York: Basic Books, 1987); and Diane J. Macunovich and Richard J. Easterlin, "How Parents Have Coped: The Effect of Life Cycle Demographic Decisions on the Economic Status of Pro-School Age Children, 1964-87," *Population and Development Review* 16 (June 1990), pp. 301-25.
63. Peter G. Peterson and Neil Howe, *On Borrowed Time: How the Growth in Entitlement Spending Threatens America's Future* (San Francisco, CA: ICS Press, 1988), p. 11.
64. Sylvia Ann Hewlitt, *When the Bough Breaks: The Costs of Neglecting Our Children* (New York: Basic Books. 1991), p. 14.
65. National Commission on Children, *Beyond Rhetoric: A New American Agenda for Children and Families* (Washington, DC: Government Printing Office, 1991); and Elaine Ciulla Kamarck and William A. Galston, *Putting Children First: A Progressive Family Policy for the 1990s* (Washington, DC: Progressive Policy Institute, 1990).
66. Carolyn Pape Cowan and Philip A. Cowan, *When Partners Become Parents: The Big Life Change for Couples* (New York: Basic Books, 1992).
67. Juliet B. Schor, *The Overworked American: The Unexpected Decline of Leisure* (New York: Basic Books, 1992).
68. William Mattox. Jr., "Running on Empty: America's Time-Starved Families with Children," Working Paper 5 (New York: Council on Families in America, Institute for American Values, 1991).
69. For a wide range of useful child policies, see Hewlitt, *When the Bough Breaks*. For sequencing, see Arlene Rossen Cardozo, *Sequencing* (New York: Collier Books, 1986); and Felice N. Schwartz, *Breaking with Tradition: Women, Management, and the New Facts of Life* (New York: Warner, 1992).
70. See Richard Louv, *Childhood's Future* (Boston, MA: Houghton Mifflin, 1990).
71. David Popenoe, "Fostering the New Familism," *Responsive Community* 2 (Fall 1992), pp. 31-39, and this volume.
72. Kristin A. Moore and Thomas M. Stief, "Changes in Marriage and Fertility Behavior: Behavior Versus Attitudes of Young Adults," Washington, Child Trends, 1989.
73. Judith S. Wallerstein and Sandra Blakeslee, *Second Chances: Men, Women, and Children a Decade after Divorce* (New York: Ticknor and Fields, 1989); and Peter Wilson, "The Impact of Cultural Changes on the Internal Experience of the Adolescent," *Journal of Adolescence* 11 (1988), pp. 271-286.
74. Zvi Namenwirth and Robert Weber, *Dynamics of Culture* (London: Allen and Unwin, 1987); and William Strauss and Neil Howe, *Generations* (New York: William Morrow, 1991).
75. Timur Kuran, "'Now Out of Never,' The Element of Surprise in the East European Revolution of 1989," *World Politics* (December 1991), pp. 7-48.

4

Family Values: A Communitarian Position

Most Americans now agree that the past three decades have not been kind to the American family. During this period—one in which many observers were proclaiming with great insistence that "the family is just changing not declining"—the social institutions of marriage and the family, in fact, have weakened more, as measured by a variety of indicators, than during any other period of similar length in the history of our nation (Popenoe, 1993a). In view of today's sky-high divorce rates, burgeoning nonmarital pregnancy rates, and nearly a quarter of all American children still living below the poverty line, even archprotagonists of "family diversity" are now muting their efforts to retire the concept dear to the hearts of each generation's conservatives: family decline.

Despite growing agreement that the family is declining and not just changing, however, many Americans have great difficulty coming to grips with the moral dimensions of this contemporary family trend. Perhaps we should merely acquiesce to it, as for the most part we have been doing. Times do change after all, and maybe we need the family less than we used to. And anyway, has not one's family become a strictly private matter, something that should not be the business of the rest of us?

Unfortunately, the "family values debate" in this nation has become heavily politicized and polarized between conservatives and liberals. On the right, the self-avowed "profamily" forces have taken moral positions—such as the prohibition of homosexuality, premarital sex, pornography, and abortion—that are thoroughly unacceptable those who stress individual rights. To save the family, they argue, we must try to stamp out many undesirable patterns of individual behavior. The forces of the left, in their turn, have tended to denigrate or dismiss the family, often perceiving it to be an institution that is inherently patriarchal, inegalitarian, detrimental to women, and a bulwark of derided "bourgeois values." Even the simple phrase "the family" is a negative to many liberals, as they sense in its use a moral absolutism and threatened social straightjacket. The much-preferred term is "families," which implies that everyone should have freedom of choice in family matters.

What is the reasonable person to believe? Which of the many family-value issues in the national debate today should command our greatest attention and concern? A communitarian perspective can help to provide the answer. In a national sociocultural movement led by Amitai Etzioni, communitarians call for a reawakening of our allegiance to the shared values and institutions—most of all the family—that sustain us in a way that balances individual rights with social responsibilities. Communitarians argue that if we keep our eye on the central issue—the strengthening of the social order and the welfare of children—neither the position of the right nor the left is very helpful in coming to grips with what ails the American family. And, surprisingly, the most important family concern has barely been mentioned in the public debate.

As I shall document in this chapter, there is much social science evidence to support the middle-of-the-road communitarian position. A close look at recent social trends and at the accumulating social science evidence on matters concerning the family find that the case for the various right-wing "prohibitions" is not very compelling; these prohibitions are at best peripheral to the goal of shoring up family life in America. Yet, in sharp contrast to the left-wing emphasis on family diversity, the evidence also suggests that a very high value should be placed on what communitarians advocate: the two-parent, child-centered nuclear family.

Communitarian advocacy for the intact nuclear family, however, should not imply support for continuing the traditional form of the nuclear family—male-dominated and with women restricted to the mother/housewife role. This is a critical distinction, one typically lost in the current debate. Maintaining the traditional nuclear family, as some conservatives demand, is socially impossible, if not also morally unwise. But disowning the nuclear family so as to cleanse ourselves of its traditional form—the disturbing message of much leftist thought—is surely a classic case of throwing out the baby with the bathwater.

Family Change and Communitarian Values

What does it actually mean to say that the family is an institution in decline? Let us consider first what a social institution is: a way of organizing human behavior in such a way that society's needs are best served. A social institution consists essentially of normative, accepted codes that indicate how people should act in a certain area of life. As a socially sanctioned unit of childrearing, the family was probably the first social institution in evolutionary terms, and it is one of the few social institutions that is universal—found in some form in every known society.

One reason that the institution of the family is universal is that every society has a paramount need to raise children. Children come into this world totally dependent, and they must, for a longer portion of their lives than for any other species, be taken care of and taught by adults. Almost all societies have assigned this task to the biological parents (assuming they exist), or at least to the biological mother. In all societies the biological father is identified where possible, and in most societies he plays an important role in his children's upbringing. Beyond this, family form varies considerably, ranging from the nuclear form, with the two parents living apart from their relatives, to families where the grandmother or other relatives play a major role.

Until recent centuries, however, adult family members did not necessarily consider childrearing to be their primary task. As a unit of rural economic production the family's main focus was economic survival. Rather than the family existing for the sake of the children, it could be said that the children, as needed workers, existed for the sake of the family. One of the monumental family transitions in history, therefore, was the rise in industrial societies of what we now refer to as the traditional nuclear family—husband away at work, wife taking care of the home and children, and the family unit living apart from relatives. The primary focus of this historically new family form was indeed the care and nurturing of children, and parents dedicated themselves to this task. It was within this family form that western egalitarian democracy, with its emphasis on the relatively autonomous yet socially responsible individual, came to full fruition. And it was this family form that generated the individuals who were responsible for the tremendous intellectual and economic achievements of the industrial era (Berger and Berger, 1983; Sagan, 1987).

In the past thirty years modern societies have been witness to another major family transformation: the beginning of the end of the traditional nuclear family. Three important changes have occurred. First, many parents voluntarily have broken their nuclear family ties (at a rate currently estimated to be over 50 percent), and many mothers have decided voluntarily to forgo marriage, with the consequence that, for the first time in history, a surprisingly large number of children are being raised in single-parent households, apart from other relatives (Organization for Economic Cooperation and Development, 1990). Second, women in large numbers have left the role of full-time mother and housewife to go into the labor market. And, third, the main focus of the family has shifted away from both economic production and childrearing to a paramount concern for the psychological well being and self-development of its adult members. As one indication of the strength of this new focus, parents increasingly tend to break up—even when they still have children at home to raise—if their needs for psychological stability and self-fulfillment are not met in the marriage relationship.

Through all of these recent shifts, the family has lost tremendous social power in society. Once the only social institution in existence, it is now small, fragile, and overshadowed by both the state and the market. People today spend a smaller portion of their lives actually living in families than at probably any other time in history (Watkins, Menken, and Bongaarts, 1987). This trend of family decline, of course, is strongly associated with such concurrent cultural trends as increasing individual autonomy, choice of lifestyles, material affluence, social power for women, and tolerance of individual and cultural diversity. It reasonably can be said that, in many respects, the family's decline is the adult individual's gain.

One thing that has not changed through all the years and all the family transformations, however, is the need for children to be raised by adults, the raison d'être of the family in the first place. Especially in modern, complex societies, in which children need an enormous amount of education and psychological security in order to succeed, active and nurturing relationships of adults to children are critical. Yet today's children probably spend less time with adults, including their parents, than in any other period of history. Absent fathers, working mothers, distant grandparents, anonymous schools, and transient communities are all indicators of a dramatic decrease in child-centeredness, not only within the family but within society as a whole. (Even the speed of modern life is anti-child; children thrive at a much more patient, casual pace of living.)

Underlying this decrease in child-centeredness is the radical individualism of modern societies: the preoccupation with personal expression, occupational success, and material gain (Bellah et al., 1985, 1991). Except insofar as they represent means of personal expression for adults, and thus the enhancement of adult self-development, children increasingly are seen as a hindrance to leading "the good life" (Hewlett, 1991). This is a fundamental reason why the birth rate is now below that necessary even for the replacement, much less the growth, of the population.

In summary, the trends of modern living—most of all within the family—are leaving children stranded and isolated in their wake. The condition of the family is probably the single most important factor accounting for today's record-high, and in many cases increasing, rates among juveniles and adolescents of delinquency and violence, suicide, depression, obesity/anorexia, drug abuse, and nonmarital pregnancies (National Commission on Children, 1991; Select Committee on Children, Youth and Families, 1989). High rates of these personal and social problems are found at all class levels and among all sectors of our population.

How should we as a society respond to this socially destructive situation, one that augurs so poorly for the future? Government programs of various sorts may help. But the only long-run solution is a shift in the cultural values by which we live, a shift from family-demeaning to family-supportive communitarian values.

With respect to the universal moral choice between individual autonomy and social obligation, between promoting individual development and fostering social order, societies historically have tended to suppress the individual in favor of strengthening the social. But today, the United States is at the opposite end of the continuum. Individuals have more autonomy than ever before in history, and it is the social that has become problematic. What is problematic is not only that normally interpreted as social breakdown—for example, the extraordinarily high rates of crime—but also the fact that the social order has become less able to nourish individual development. If the social sciences have taught us anything it is that for maximum personal growth, individuals must live in a reasonably cohesive and stable social order. Yet increasingly, and despite the high value we place on self-development, people are seemingly more fearful, anxious, and stressed (Myers, 1992; Oldenquist, 1986). Their self-development is being inhibited.

A cohesive, stable, and nourishing social order, communitarians believe, is based on each member's fulfilling his or her social obligation and commitments. But what is a social obligation? What commitments do individuals have to society as a whole? Beyond pursuing one's self-interest, how should one's social duties be fulfilled? There is the obvious, albeit minimal answer to these questions involving a "live and let live" principle. In pursuing one's own self-interest one should not unduly impair the ability of others to pursue their self-interest. To this minimal answer can be added another obvious yet fundamental principle: One should be a "good citizen" and vote, take an interest in public issues, and participate in community activities.

Yet, by far the most important social obligation that each individual can fulfill is to responsibly and successfully raise a child to adulthood. It is clearly in everyone's best interest that adults raise their offspring to be healthy, happy, and productive members of society. On such an obligation, the next generation's character, and thereby the future of society, depends.

The Key Moral Issues

This brings us to the central question of taking a communitarian position in regards to current family trends. Communitarians believe that the highest social value should be placed on parent-child relationships and the fostering of a child-centered society. It is essential to proclaim that children are a society's most important asset, and that once born, they should be loved and valued at the highest level of priority. A "secure base," in the words of John Bowlby (1988), should be a part of every child's birthright.

This moral priority evinces the unequivocal affirmation of monogamous, procreative marriages and of strong, enduring families whose members have time for each other, do many things together, communicate well with one another, and mutually foster the social values on which the good society depends: sharing, cooperation, commitment, and social responsibility. Each of the specific moral positions outlined below stems from this overriding focus on the social importance of strong families and child-centeredness.

Marital Dissolution

The first issue to be considered is the most important of all to the promotion of strong families and child-centeredness. Yet surprisingly, of the moral issues taken up in this chapter, it is the least widely discussed. There are no national antidivorce movements like those for antiabortion, no national commissions examining the problem of divorce like those for pornography, and few indignant outcries from the pulpit about marital dissolution of the kind heard frequently about premarital sexuality.

The results of ongoing research in the social sciences strongly confirm the negative effects of a high divorce rate, especially on children (Dawson, 1991; Emery, 1988; McLanahan and Sandefur, 1994; Wallerstein and Blakeslee, 1989). Indeed, few bodies of social research have had such consistent findings. But with the well-founded statistical expectation that at least one marriage in two contracted today will end in divorce or separation, moral (and legal) restraints on divorce have obviously weakened enormously (Martin and Bumpass, 1989). To be divorced was once a highly stigmatized status; today it has almost become the norm (Glendon, 1987; Jacob, 1988; Phillips, 1988). We have had a divorced president, most religious congregations now contain a large number of divorced members, and even many religious leaders are in second marriages.

A reinstated moral (to say nothing of legal) prohibition against divorce would be an unreasonable intrusion on personal liberty. Especially when children are not involved—the case in many marriages today—there is little social benefit in trying to keep two people together who are miserable in each other's company. Companionship has become the main reason for marriage, and when this is no longer obtainable, people should have the right to move on (Cancian, 1987). A society that values companionate marriages with strong emotional ties must at the same time expect a relatively high divorce rate.

Yet from the perspective of children and the stability of family life, divorce has become too easy, too accepted. There is a new mindset that divorce is now an acceptable possibility in each person's life. People enter marriages realizing that if things do not work out, there is a quick remedy. Indeed, some lawyers now tell people when they marry that they should spend as much time planning for their divorce as they spend planning for their marriage. Worst of all, having children is no longer a compelling reason not to divorce; couples with children divorce at a rate only slightly lower than couples without children (Waite and Lillard, 1991). In a momentous change of opinion over the last twenty-five years, the great majority of Americans today believe that "a married couple should not necessarily stay together for the sake of the children" (Thornton, 1989; Thornton and Freedman, 1983).

The new attitude toward divorce strikes at the very heart of the family institution. If all families consisted of nothing but an intimate relationship between two adults, society could probably survive a relatively high breakup rate. But when children are the involuntary victims of the breakup, we are all losers. Greater moral concern about the dissolution of families when children are involved, therefore, is absolutely essential. Making divorce involving children somewhat more difficult in legal terms provides one answer. But constant moral reaffirmation of the importance of lasting marriages and some cultural re-stigmatization of divorce when children are involved are more important in the long run. This moral position draws support from the fact that two family-related conditions in life are still deeply desired by almost all young people: a divorce-free home in which to grow up and a stable marriage of their own as adults.

With such a moral position about family dissolution comes a correlate— one in favor of the intact, nuclear family. Not all intact two-parent families are successful at raising children. And single-parent families and stepparent families, which today are typically the product of divorce, can often be very successful at this task. Many social scientists have worked diligently to document these facts. Yet the statistical evidence is overwhelming that an intact family is the better vehicle for childrearing (Angel and Angel, 1993; Garfinkel and McLanahan, 1986; Hetherington and Arasteh, 1988). Moreover, it is what children want. For people living in alternative family forms, real sensitivity and often material assistance from others are indispensable. But to waver on the fundamental importance of the intact family in the interest of, for example, promoting "diversity" or "tolerance" is to weaken a moral message on which the vary future of society depends.

Gender Roles

At the heart of the breakdown of the modern family are changing gender roles. More than anything else, strengthening the modern family involves finding ways to improve intimate, long-term relationships between men and women and ways of assisting them in their joint task of childrearing. Unfortunately, partly because the moral issues involved are so complex and difficult to unravel, the gender-role debate is not often cast in moral terms.

Let us begin with the gender-role issue of married women in the labor force, for it is one of the most widely discussed but easiest to resolve. Most men of late middle age and older look back with nostalgia to the era of the traditional nuclear family. But social conditions unquestionably have changed. In what represents a tremendous historical shift, only about one-third of the adult life of the average married woman today will be spent as the mother of at-home children. Even if one were to assume that a woman's main purpose in life was to be a mother and housewife, it is clearly unreasonable for most married women to devote their entire adult lives to these two roles because of later ages at first marriage, average family sizes of less than two children, and much longer life spans (Bergmann, 1986; Bianchi and Spain, 1986; Davis and van den Oever, 1982; Filene, 1986; McLaughlin et al., 1988).

If for no other reason then (other reasons are discussed below), the family era of economically dependent, full-time housewives should be regarded as a thing of the past. Women today are socialized and educated, as are men, to enhance their personal development, make an economic contribution, and contribute fully to public life. For women, as well as for men, the central problem in the organization of adult life is not work versus children but how best to encompass both paid work and raising children.

Dramatic though the demographic and economic changes have been, however, the issue of married women in the workforce and the demise of the separate-sphere family is only the tip of the iceberg in the gender-role debate. The heart of the matter is the way in which men's and women's "inherent nature" is perceived and the expectations we have about their "proper" roles and behavior within the family and within society at large. Again, the debate about male-female similarities and differences has become so polarized between right and left and has taken on so many ideological-political overtones that reasoned discussion is difficult. Also, the position at which one comes into the debate depends on the cultural context. In many contexts, one might emphasize male-female similarities. But in America today, communitarians can reasonably say, it is important to consider more carefully some differences.

The view of the extreme right is that men and women are biologically and irrevocably different in so many fundamental respects that they necessarily should inhabit separate spheres of life, with women taking domestic roles and meeting the emotional-expressive needs of society and men taking work and public roles and thus meeting society's instrumental needs. Man at work and woman at the hearth, it is argued, is not only in the best interest of society but is how the world has always been and ever shall be.

One problem with this viewpoint, as noted above, is that the conditions of life have changed markedly, making such traditional gender roles now largely obsolete whether one supports them or not. Another problem is that differences between men and women have been so exaggerated and distorted throughout history that much of social life has been unfavorable to women. Men have frequently used their public power to the detriment of women. Also, because a wide range of emotions and behaviors is found within both females and males, with much overlap between the two groups, the locking of each sex into separate spheres retards personal development and violates personal liberty.

Some evidence suggests that, at least in modern societies, those members of each sex who have the highest levels of self-esteem and self-confidence tend to exhibit a balance of "male" and "female" characteristics and virtues, so-called psychological androgyny (Cook, 1985; Spence and Helmreich, 1978; Kaplan and Sedney, 1980). For this and other reasons, the notion that men and women ought to be socialized to be more alike is worthy of support. It is in society's best interest to promote more sensitive and caring men who take a greater interest in domestic roles, especially childrearing, and more self-confident and assertive women who are active in work and public life. Indeed, the successful experiences of the Scandinavian nations, where this has been a goal of public policy, indicate that such socialization is clearly possible (Moen, 1989).

In contrast to the extreme right, the extreme left takes the view that there are no socially important biological differences between men and women other than childbearing. It is asserted that virtually all male-female differences in psychology and behavior are culturally determined and therefore subject to the human will to change. The implicit (and sometimes explicit) goal of such change is social androgyny—the social identity of men and women. In the utopian society of the extreme left, one would never be able to predict by sex alone what social roles a person will play in life (Okin, 1989). Such androgyny-oriented intellectuals see the perfect society as one in which men would do 50 percent of the domestic work, including childrearing, and women would do 50 percent of the public work.

While the right-wing view of male-female differences is detrimental to women, the left-wing view is detrimental to the family. The well-functioning family has always been based on a division of labor that reflects the different abilities and motivations of each sex in childrearing; motherhood and fatherhood have never been thought of as the same. Universally, women have cared for very young children, and men have typically played the childcare roles of provider, protector, and backup assistant. No research has demonstrated that men and women, who obviously reflect the sexual dimorphism found throughout the higher animal kingdom that is related to the biology of reproduction, are not also fundamentally different in other ways, such as in the ability to nurture infants. Without substantial evidence to the contrary, we cannot assume that men and women, given their radically different reproductive roles, could ever be psychologically and behaviorally the same. Many communitarians believe (myself of course included), therefore, that we should think about gender roles and male-female equality more in terms of complementarity, symmetry, and equivalency than in terms of identity (Popenoe, 1993b; Rossi, 1985).

Although it has brought many benefits to men well as to women, the gender-role revolution of recent decades has not been kind to families (Friedan, 1981; Mintz and Kellogg, 1988). The negative effects on the family probably stem mostly from the rapid pace at which the revolution has taken place. But the extraordinary emphasis on gender similarities and workplace equality between men and women, although necessary to counteract the kinds of social distortions still reflected in the views of conservatives, has downplayed women's reproductive role and thus tended to denigrate motherhood (Gallagher, 1989; Hewlett, 1986; Mason, 1988). And the desirable efforts to change the role expectations for "husband" and "wife" so as to reduce male dominance and female subordination in the home have tended to undermine the more socially important roles of "father" and "mother" (Johnson, 1988).

The gender-role revolution is implicated in today's historically high marital dissolution rates (Blumstein and Schwartz, 1983; Cherlin, 1992). Gender roles within marriage have become increasingly ambiguous and are thus a frequent cause of marital discord (Hochschild and Machung, 1989). This may be particularly true of economic roles: There is some evidence that the closer a wife's income gets to that of her husband's, the higher the probability of divorce (Cherlin, 1979; Ross and Sawhill, 1975).

The consequences of the gender-role revolution on women have received the bulk of scholarly attention, but equally important have been the consequences, mostly unintended, on men. Men, for example, seem increasingly reluctant to commit to a relationship. And when they do commit, they are less likely to stay committed. In addition to the fear of failure in a high-divorce era, one broad reason for the decline in marital commitment among men is that men's traditional reasons for getting married have been weakened. Through the removal of the double standard of sexual behavior, for instance, women have gained most of the sexual freedoms that men have long held. But this change has also diminished one of the main reasons why men marry—to obtain regular, legitimate sex. Men can now get as much legitimate sex as they want outside of marriage.

Another reason men traditionally have married is to become an economic provider. One important factor in the positive correlation between a wife's income and the chances of divorce, noted above, has been labeled "the independence effect." Because women are more able to maintain themselves economically, they are less likely to stay in an unhappy marriage. But the other side of the coin is that because women are more able economically to maintain themselves, men have less reason for marrying and less compunction about breaking up a marriage once they are in it.

A fundamental problem these few examples point out is the failure to recognize that men and women are in many ways different. They have different sexual drives, different propensities toward children, different perspectives on relationships, different conceptions of morality, and perhaps even speak a different language (Gilligan, 1984; Moir and Jessel, 1991; Pool, 1994; Tannen, 1990). They also have different reasons for marrying. A major social task that lies ahead, therefore, is how better to organize the modern family in recognition of these differences without retracting the positive benefits of the gender-role revolution. This is no easy task. But one starting point is to view marriage not as a tie between persons with identical roles but as a complementary relationship between persons who will each bring different outlooks and abilities to the union

It is both significant and hopeful that in modern societies today the emergence of a new realism about family matters has appeared, one that bodes well for the future of the family and the needs of children. The gender-role debate is turning more in the direction of frankly discussing gender differences. A growing number of women has begun to rethink their lives and their careers along lines different from those of men, with a new interest in "sequencing" work and family pursuits, for example, in a way that enables them to spend more time with very young children (Cardozo, 1986). In view of the new work roles of women, many men are becoming more actively involved in childrearing. And the structure of the workplace is becoming more supportive of families and children, with the emergence of parental leave, flexible hours, and other measures that enable both parents to better combine paid work with childcare. All of these trends, most communitarians believe, should vigorously be encouraged.

The Subsidiary Moral Issues of the Right

Strong positions on four other moral issues—the prohibition of homosexuality, pornography, premarital sex, and abortion—have been forcefully put forth by the right in America as part of a "profamily" agenda. Although these issues have an obvious family-relatedness, they are much less important to the promotion of strong families and child-centeredness, as we shall see, than the issues considered above. They are also highly controversial. Few communitarians, including Amitai Etzioni, have taken a public position on all of them. But I shall nevertheless sketch out a possible communitarian position, while recognizing that not all who claim the mantle of communitarianism will agree with me entirely.

Homosexuality

Homosexuality is probably second only to abortion in being the most controversial social issue in America today. Yet the controversy over homosexuality greatly overemphasizes its moral significance as a threat to families. On this issue, and several of those discussed below, the distinction between prohibition, tolerance, and affirmation is important. The debate over homosexuality has tended to be between those who favor outright prohibition and those who favor unequivocal affirmation. The position advocated here is that society should, in support of personal liberty, tolerate a wide range of sexual practices, including homosexuality. In support of the family, however, society should not necessarily affirm every aspect of homosexuality and the homosexual lifestyle as the moral or social equivalent of heterosexuality. As the basis of family life, and thus the key to both social order and societal continuation, heterosexuality should continue to command a high status as a social value.

Moral positions on homosexuality often rest on whether homosexuality is seen as biologically or culturally determined. Many homosexuals have striven in recent years to document that homosexuality is entirely biological, or "essentialist," in character. Like left-handedness or color blindness, it is argued, a person is born either homosexual or heterosexual, and little cultural conditioning, to say nothing of personal or social choice, is involved. In keeping with this assumption, a common (and almost certainly erroneous) assertion is that homosexuals make up "about 10 percent" of every population.

As I read the available evidence, it does not support the essentialist position. A biological proclivity may be a necessary, but it is not a sufficient, cause of most homosexuality. Homosexuality is most likely the result, as John Money (1988) has concluded, of (still undetermined) biological factors in combination, at certain critical stages of individual development, with a social learning or conditioning component. The same holds true for almost all human behavior.

That societies differ greatly in both the prevalence of homosexuality and in their acceptance of homosexual practices supports the proposition that homosexuality is a partly learned (culturally induced) phenomenon. Some societies appear to be almost entirely free of overt homosexual practices. Others, such as some American Indian tribes, have sequential bisexuality built into their cultures. (Typically, immediately after puberty boys go through a culturally approved stage involving homosexual practices but as adults become exclusively heterosexual.) Another societal variation is the bisexual practice in Ancient Greece in which adult males would have sex both with their wives and with boys. Further support for the proposition that homosexuality is a cultural phenomenon comes from the fact that societies, such as our own, have changed greatly over time in the prevalence of, and attitudes toward, homosexual practices (Greenberg, 1988).

It is also important to stress that the term homosexuality refers to a wide spectrum of phenomena, ranging from casual and one-time sexual encounters between persons of the same sex, through bisexuality, to persons who believe that they were born homosexual and have never been erotically attracted to the opposite sex. This suggests that the mix of biology and culture in the creation of homosexuality can be quite variable.

Humans are a remarkably sex-oriented species, and we engage in far more sexual activity than is necessary for procreation. Not only does much of our sexual activity have pure pleasure as its goal, but many people seem fully capable of having other than heterosexual interests. The sex drive can manifestly be focused on a wide variety of objects: people of the same sex, inanimate objects, animals, and one's own manipulations. Indeed, a sizable number of males in our society are presumed to have engaged in some nonheterosexual practices at some time during their life.

In the Judeo-Christian tradition, a strong moral stand has been taken against all nonheterosexual sex practices: masturbation, bestiality, and homosexuality (as well as "kinky" heterosexual practices). Yet on scientific grounds it is difficult to make the case that any of these practices, on their own, have a sufficiently negative social or personal impact to warrant moral, much less legal, prohibition. We should be tolerant of these practices when they are engaged in voluntarily, in private, and do no harm to others.

Such tolerance, however, needs to be distinguished from full affirmation. Societies that place a high value on individual rights and freedoms should tolerate a wide array of homosexual practices, but societies dedicated to the promotion of strong families and child-centeredness should not at the same time advocate or affirm all of the values associated with homosexuality as it is expressed today.

Much of the homosexuality we see about us today goes well beyond occasional or even regular homosexual practice. In recent decades and apparently for the first time in world history on anything like the present scale, many homosexuals are pursuing a separate and exclusive homosexual lifestyle. Indeed the label "homosexual" to refer to a particular social status was not even invented until modern times. Throughout history many people have engaged in homosexual practices, but there seem to have been very few exclusive homosexuals of the type that see themselves (and are often seen by others) as a special status apart from heterosexuals. Today's exclusive homosexuals increasingly live apart from heterosexuals and espouse a subculture in which families and children have little place and homosexuality is put forth as the social and moral equivalent of heterosexuality. In the male homosexual world, this subculture is also relatively promiscuous and disparaging of monogamy.

If the exclusive homosexuality and homosexual subcultures becoming so prevalent in the modern world are largely constructed socially, and the evidence strongly suggests that they are, moral questions may properly be raised. Society can reasonably examine the nature of the social construction, for example, and, if necessary, seek changes. If certain political goals of the organized homosexual community are not in society's best interest, it is reasonable that they be challenged. Society can also proscribe certain homosexual practices if they are socially destructive, just as it proscribes some heterosexual practices.

Nuclear familism and homosexualism as lifestyles incorporate contradictory values and views of the world. It would be a moral contradiction for society to affirm and promote the nuclear family, with its basis in heterosexuality and its generation and nurturance of children, while at the same time affirming and promoting all of the values of the homosexual subculture. Fully aware of this contradiction, the homosexual community has assumed a leading role in attempts to redefine the family under the banner of "family diversity" and to cast doubt on the validity and importance of heterosexuality. If they are really concerned about the well being of the family, the moral agents of society should oppose these attempts.

As a case in point, one of the interesting moral questions that has arisen in recent years concerns the granting of legal and church marriages to homosexual couples. Through legal and religious marriage, many homosexual couples wish both to fall under the jurisdiction of family law (with its legally enforceable rights and duties) and to be provided with the spiritual blessing of the church. In considering this issue one should keep in mind that the main social purpose for the institution of marriage is the insurance of family stability for children (Davis, 1985; Houlgate, 1988). This institutional purpose, and therefore the importance of the social institution in general, would surely be compromised by incorporating the marriage of same-sex couples.

It is important to add, however, that society has a stake in the promotion of monogamous relationships among homosexuals and in protecting weaker partners in homosexual relationships from exploitation. For this reason, it seems reasonable to establish for homosexual couples marriage-like "domestic partnership" laws, along with their religious equivalents, that could extend to such couples some of the rights and responsibilities of the institution of marriage.

Pornography

Commercial pornography, mainly consumed by men, is pervasive in modern societies. Recently, the prohibition of pornography has become a burning issue that allies strange bedfellows—radical conservatives and radical feminists. Conservatives believe that it is helping to destroy marriage, while radical feminists hold that it promotes rape and sexual violence and is inherently degrading to women. Evidence to support these positions is limited (Zillman and Bryant, 1989). Some experimental evidence suggests that the repeated viewing of sexual violence on the screen desensitizes and disinhibits men and fosters attitudes that at least trivialize rape. There is much less evidence that a moderate use of nonviolent "erotica" pornography weakens marriages. Relevant to this issue is the fact that Japan, a very low-rape and strong-family country, has a thriving market for pornography, much of which is extremely violent, and that the pornography industry has flourished in Sweden and Denmark, where women have a higher status than probably anywhere else in the world.

It is important to distinguish between the different kinds of pornography. Much current pornography, for example that available in the friendly local video store, merely portrays sex acts in which people morally and legally may engage in private. Such a portrayal of common reality (albeit in a distorted, exaggerated, and sleazy way) is certainly not everyone's cup of tea, but in this liberal age the case for its strict prohibition due to some overriding social reason is not an easy one to make (Hawkins and Zimring, 1988; Randall,

1989). At the other extreme is pornography that portrays, purely for the purpose of perverse titillation, patently offensive and illegal acts, for example sex with children and physical violence against women. The case for banning such obscene pornography is compelling.

The social problem of pornography is in some ways similar to that of alcohol. Like alcohol, pornography is something many people (men) desire and, when used strictly in moderation, it appears to be relatively innocuous from both a personal and social standpoint. As in the case of the public management of alcohol, the moral or legal prohibition of all forms of pornography is not the answer. In addition to the virtually insuperable difficulties of enforcing such a prohibition, it would probably do little to promote strong families. Yet all pornography should be kept out of the hands of children, and the availability of even legalized pornography to adults should be controlled.

Premarital Sex

One of the most prominent norms of the Victorian era was the stricture concerning sex before marriage. It applied mainly to women, however, and was part of the now-infamous double standard. In this regard we have truly been through a social revolution in the past thirty years: Few people today, women or men, marry as virgins or even desire their spouse to be a virgin (D'Emlio and Freedman, 1988). Yet the "profamily" right still seeks to morally enforce this norm of sexual behavior.

If there were evidence to show that waiting until marriage to have sex would significantly strengthen marriages, a case could perhaps be made for continuing the moral prohibition of premarital sex—though for egalitarian reasons it should apply to both men and women. But I know of no such evidence. To the contrary, members of fundamentalist and conservative Protestant denominations, for example, who almost surely practice premarital sexual continence more than the rest of the population, have a relatively high divorce rate (Kitson, Babri, and Roach, 1985). Indeed, it is a plausible proposition that some premarital sexual experience actually enhances the institution of marriage.

In any event, two features of modern life suggest that it is highly unrealistic to continue to expect premarital sexual abstinence. First, the time period between puberty and marriage has lengthened dramatically (Modell, 1989). Average first-marriage ages today are about twenty-four for women and twenty-six for men. This is some ten to fifteen years after puberty, which in turn comes at an earlier stage of life than ever before in history. Second, our culture and mass media have become highly charged with sexually oriented material.

We might be able to make some modifications in our culture, but we cannot do much about the long period of time between sexual awakening and the marital state. Marriages at younger ages might be a solution, but such marriages are ill advised on other grounds. Victorian norms prohibiting premarital sex, therefore, seem clearly outmoded.

Moral concern should be focused not on the prohibition of premarital sex but on sexual promiscuity, teenage sex, and unprotected sex. Society does have an important stake in seeking to limit all three of these phenomena. Sexual promiscuity, the frequent and indiscriminate changing of sex partners, may well endanger marriages by establishing behavior patterns that are antithetical to stable, long-term relationship. Teenage sex, in the sense of sexuality engaged in by immature individuals, is an important moral issue because it involves individuals who are not yet mature enough to successfully envelop sexuality within a loving relationship. And the vast social problems of abortion, unwanted children, and teenage parents, to say nothing of contagious disease, dictate that all premarital sexuality that is unprotected by the use of safe and effective contraceptives should be considered morally out of bounds.

Abortion

Finally, a very brief word about what is undoubtedly the most divisive domestic issue in America today (and one of the most divisive in our nation's history) (Luker, 1984; Rosenblatt, 1991). This is obviously not the place to engage the terribly thorny moral questions that have dominated the abortion debate, such as at what point a fetus becomes a human life and whether or not abortion should be included under a woman's right to privacy (Tribe, 1990). Many reasonable moral grounds exist for limiting, if not prohibiting, the practice of abortion, and almost no society morally condones abortion under any and all circumstances (Glendon, 1987). Yet as a threat to the institution of the family, the practice of abortion as it exists in America does not appear to be a serious concern.

From a moral perspective focusing strictly on strong, child-centered families, abortion is best viewed in connection with birth control. With current technological knowledge, there is no way to have a satisfactory birth-control system without the possibility of using abortion as a backup when other methods of birth control fail, a not-infrequent occurrence given the current level of contraceptive technology. To oppose abortion is to oppose having a satisfactory birth-control system.

Of course, one can argue that any form of birth control is antichild, and in the sense that it prevents children from being conceived, that is true. Yet the world hardly needs more unplanned children. What it needs is more wanted children, whose parents are able to rear them to become healthy, happy, and self-reliant adults.

At least in a comparison of nations, there is no evidence that tolerance of abortion is associated with antichild attitudes. In fact, quite the opposite appears to be the case. Japan, for example, which typically receives very high marks for child-centeredness, has since World War II been highly tolerant of abortion. And many European nations in which abortion has not generated the controversy found in the United States have stronger commitments to children than does our nation. It is important to add, however, that in most of these nations restrictions on abortion—and general moral concern about abortion—are considerably greater than what is advocated by radical American prochoicers (Glendon, 1987).

Conclusion

In trying to decide what positions to take in today's family-values debate, the reasonable person faces an agonizing quandary. Not only are firm cultural guidelines weakening, but the moral stands advocated by the right and the left are highly contradictory. The extreme right advocates a policy of return to the family form of an earlier era, while the extreme left advocates what often seems a virtual abandonment of the nuclear family in favor of alternatives.

The communitarian position lies between the two extremes. Our principal concern, according to communitarians, should be for strong and successful nuclear, child-rearing families. Evidence from the social sciences convincingly supports the view that such families are a fundamental social necessity with no adequate substitutes. Once this moral focal point is established, positions on such family related issues as divorce, homosexuality, and abortion tend to fall into place.

There is no going back to the traditional male-dominated, separate-sphere nuclear family of an earlier era. Changes in values and in the structure of society have made that family form obsolete. What we should be fostering instead are nuclear families in which women and men are equal partners—equal in power and decision-making and providing complementary and equivalent contributions. Two key characteristics of the traditional nuclear family, however, should be preserved at all costs: an enduring sense of family obligation and the desire to put children first.

References

Angel, Ronald I., and Angel, Jacqueline L. (1993). *Painful Inheritance: Heath and the New Generation of Fatherless Families*. Madison: University of Wisconsin Press.

Bellah, Robert N., Madsen, Richard, Sullivan, William M., Swidler, Ann, and Tipton, Steven M. (1985). *Habits of the Heart*. Berkeley: University of California Press.

Bellah, Robert N., Madsen, Richard, Sullivan, William M., Swidler, Ann, and Tipton, Steven M. (1991). *The Good Society*. New York: Alfred A. Knopf.

Berger, Brigitte and Berger, Peter L. (1983). *The War Over the Family: Capturing the Middle Ground*. Garden City, NY: Anchor.

Bergmann, Barbara R. (1986). *The Economic Emergence of Women*. New York: Basic Books.

Bianchi, Suzanne M. and Spain, Daphne (1986). *American Women in Transition*. New York: Russell Sage Foundation.

Blumstein, Philip and Schwartz, Pepper (1983). *American Couples*. New York: Pocket Books.

Bowlby, John (1988). *A Secure Base: Parent-Child Attachment and Healthy Human Development*. New York: Basic Books.

Cancian, Francesca M. (1997). *Love in America*. Cambridge: Cambridge University Press.

Cardozo, Arlene Rossen (1986). *Sequencing*. New York: Collier Books.

Cherlin, Andrew (1979). "Work Life and Marital Dissolution." In G. Levinger and O. C. Moles (eds.). *Divorce and Separation* (pp. 151–66). New York: Basic Books.

Cherlin, Andrew (1992). *Marriage, Divorce, Remarriage*. Cambridge, MA: Harvard University Press.

Cook, Ellen Piel (1985). *Psychological Androgyny*. New York: Pergamon.

Davis, Kingsley (ed.) (1985). *Contemporary Marriage: Comparative Perspectives on a Changing Institution*. New York: Russell Sage Foundation.

Davis, Kingsley and van den Oever, Pietronella (1982). "Demographic Foundations of New Sex Roles." *Population and Development Review* 8 (3), 495–511.

Dawson, Deborah A. (1991). "Family Structure and Children's Health and Well-Being: Data from the 1988 National Health Interview Survey on Child Health." *Journal of Marriage and the Family* 53 (3), 573–84.

D'Emilio, John and Freedman, E. (1988). *Intimate Matters: A History of Sexuality in America*. New York: Harper and Row.

Emery, Robert B. (1988). *Marriage, Divorce, and Children's Adjustment*. Newbury Park, CA: Sage.

Filene, Peter G. (1986). *Him/Her Self: Sex Roles in Modern America*. Baltimore: Johns Hopkins University Press.

Friedan, Betty (1981). *The Second Stage*. New York: Summit.

Gallagher, Maggie (1989). *Enemies of Eros*. Chicago: Bonus Books.

Garfinkel, Irwin and McLanahan, S. S. (1986). *Single Mothers and Their Children: A New American Dilemma*. Washington, DC: The Urban Institute.

Gilligan, Carol (1984). *In a Different Voice*. Cambridge, MA: Harvard University Press.

Glendon, May Ann (1987). *Abortion and Divorce in Western Law*. Cambridge, MA: Harvard University Press.

Greenberg, David F. (1988). *The Construction of Homosexuality*. Chicago: University of Chicago Press.

Hawkins, Gordon and Zimring, Franklin E. (1988). *Pornography in a Free Society*. Cambridge: Cambridge University Press.

Hetherington, E. Mavis and Arasteh, Josephine D. (eds.) (1988). *Impact of Divorce, Single Parenting, and Stepparenting on Children*. Hillsdale, NJ: Lawrence Erlbaum.

Hewlett, Sylvia Ann (1986). *A Lesser Life*. New York: William Morrow.

Hewlett, Sylvia Ann (1991). *When the Bough Breaks*. New York: Basic Books.

Hochschild, Arlie, with A. Machung (1989). *Second Shift: Working Parents and the Revolution at Home*. New York: Viking.

Houlgate, Laurence D. (1988). *Family and State: The Philosophy of Family Law*. Totowa, NJ: Rowman and Littlefield.

Jacob, Herbert (1988). *Silent Revolution: The Transformation of Divorce Law in the United States*. Chicago: University of Chicago Press.

Johnson, Miriam M. (1988). *Strong Mothers, Weak Wives: The Search for Gender Equality*. Berkeley: University of California Press.

Kaplan, A. G. and Sedney, M. A. (1980). *Psychology and Sex Roles: An Androgynous Perspective*. Boston: Little, Brown.

Kitson Gay C., Babri, K. B., and Roach, M. J. (1985). "Who Divorces and Why?" *Journal of Family Issues* 6 (3), 255-93.

Luker, Kristin (1984). *Abortion and the Politics of Motherhood*. Berkeley: University of California Press.

McLanahan, Sara S. and Sandefur, Gary (1994). *Growing Up with a Single Parent.* Cambridge, MA: Harvard University Press

McLaughlin, Steven D. et al. (1988). *The Changing Lives of American Women.* Chapel Hill, NC: University of North Carolina Press.

Martin, Teresa Castro and Bumpass, L. L. (1989). "Recent Trends in Marital Disruption." *Demography* 26 (1), 37-51.

Mason, Mary Ann (1988). *The Equality Trap.* New York: Simon and Schuster.

Mintz, Steven and Kellogg, Susan (1988). *Domestic Revolutions: A Social History of Family Life.* New York: Free Press.

Modell, John (1989). *Into One's Own: From Youth to Adulthood in the United States 1920–1975.* Berkeley: University of California Press.

Moen, Phyllis (1989). *Working Parents: Transformations in Gender Roles and Public Policies in Sweden.* Madison: University of Wisconsin Press.

Moir, Anne and Jessel, David (1991). *Brain Sex.* New York: Lyle Stuart.

Money, John (1988). *Gay, Straight and In-Between: The Sexology of Erotic Orientation.* New York: Oxford University Press.

Myers, David G. (1992). *The Pursuit of Happiness.* New York: William Morrow.

National Commission on Children (1991). *Beyond Rhetoric: A New American Agenda for Children and Families.* Washington, DC: U.S. Government Printing Office.

Okin, Susan Moller (1989). *Justice, Gender, and the Family.* New York: Basic Books.

Oldenquist, Andrew (1986). *The Non-Suicidal Society.* Bloomington: University of Indiana Press.

Organization for Economic Cooperation and Development (1990). *Lone-Parent Families.* Paris: Organization for Economic Cooperation and Development.

Phillips, Roderick (1988). *Putting Asunder: A History of Divorce in Western Society.* Cambridge: Cambridge University Press.

Pool, Robert (1994). *Eve's Rib: Searching for the Biological Roots of Sex Differences.* New York: Crown.

Popenoe, David (1988). *Disturbing the Nest: Family Change and Decline in Modern Society.* New York: Aldine de Gruyter.

Popenoe, David (1993a). "American Family Decline: 1960–1990: A Review and Appraisal." *Journal of Marriage and the Family* 55 (3), 525-42.

Popenoe, David (1993b). "Parental Androgyny." *Society* 30 (6), 5-11.

Randall, Richard S. (1989). *Freedom and Taboo: Pornography and the Politics of a Self Divided.* Berkeley: University of California Press.

Rosenblatt, Roger (1991). *Life Itself: Abortion in the American Mind.* New York: Random House.

Ross, Heather L. and Sawhill, I. V. (1975). *Time of Transition: The Growth of Families Headed by Women.* Washington. DC: The Urban Institute.

Rossi, Alice S. (1985). "Gender and Parenthood," In A. S. Rossi (ed.). *Gender and the Life Course* (pp. 161–92). New York: Aldine de Gruyter.

Sagan, Leonard A. (1987). *The Health of Nations.* New York: Basic Books.

Select Committee on Children, Youth and Families (1989). *U.S. Children and Their Families: Current Conditions and Recent Trends, 1989.* Washington, DC: U.S. Government Printing Office.

Spence, J. T. and Helmreich, R. L. (1978). *Masculinity and Femininity: Their Psychological Dimensions, Correlates, and Antecedents.* Austin: University of Texas Press.

Tannen, Deborah (1990). *You Just Don't Understand: Woman and Men in Conversation.* New York: William Morrow.

Thornton, Arland (1989). "Changing Attitudes Toward Family Issues in the United States." *Journal of Marriage and the Family* 51 (4), 873-93.

Thornton, Arland and Freedman, D. (1983). "The Changing American Family." *Population Bulletin* 38 (4). Washington, DC: Population Reference Bureau.

Tribe, Laurence H. (1990). *Abortion: The Clash of Absolutes.* New York: W.W. Norton.

Waite, Linda and Lillard, Lee A. (1991). "Children and Marital Disruption." *American Journal of Sociology* 96 (4), 930-53.

Wallerstein, Judith S. and Blakeslee, S. (1989). *Second Chances: Men, Women and Children a Decade after Divorce.* New York: Ticknor and Fields.

Watkins, Susan Cotts, Menken, Jane A., and Bongaarts, John. (1987). "Demographic Foundations of Family Change." *American Sociological Review* 52 (3), 346-58.

Zillmann, Dolf and Bryant, Jennings (eds.) (1989). *Pornography: Research Advances and Policy Considerations.* Hillsdale, NJ: Lawrence Erlbaum.

5

The Evolution of Marriage and the Problem of Stepfamilies: A Biosocial Perspective

One of the fastest growing family types in every advanced industrial nation has been the stepfamily. A stepfamily occurs when a two-biological-parent family is not formed or breaks up and the custodial parent mates with a new partner, or when both biological parents die and the custody of a child is assumed by a new family. Using a simple definition, a *stepfamily* is a family in which at least one member of the adult couple is a stepparent (Beer, 1989, p. 7). To better understand the nature of stepfamilies, the reasons for their increase in number, and the problems they pose, this chapter examines the biological and social (biosocial) bases of human families, how marriage and family life have evolved in human history, and recent family change.

In 1990, 11.3 percent of U.S. children under age eighteen lived with two parents married to each other, one of whom was their stepparent, while 21.6 percent lived with their mother only, 3.1 percent lived with their father only, 57.7 percent lived with both their biological parents, and the remaining 6.3 percent lived with neither parent or were "unknown or unaccounted for" (U.S. Bureau of the Census, 1992).[1] Demographer Paul C. Glick (1989) estimated that about one third of all children today may be expected to become stepchildren before they reach age eighteen. Looking at the picture more broadly, he suggested that one out of every three Americans is now a stepparent, a stepchild, a stepsibling, or some other member of a stepfamily and "more than half of Americans today have been, are now, or will eventually be in one or more step situations during their lives" (Larson, 1992, p. 36).

Stepfamilies have been present throughout world history, owing mainly to the high death rate of parenting adults. In the early seventeenth century in colonial Virginia, for example, only an estimated 31 percent of white children reached age eighteen with both parents still alive.[2] Yet, although historical data are scarce, stepfamilies were probably never so common as they are today. In most stable agrarian societies, widespread opposition to remarriage was prevalent, especially for women with children (Macfarlane, 1986.) When stepfamilies did occur, they typically involved close relatives of the deceased parents. Even in premodern England, where remarriage appears to have been tolerated and even encouraged, data from nineteen English villages during the period 1599-1811 indicate that only 4.3 percent of all children lived in stepfamilies at any given time (Laslett, 1977). It is important to add that in many premodern societies, children were raised as much by relatives and by the larger community as by the nuclear family, and the structure of the nuclear family was probably of considerably less importance for childrearing than is the case today.

Although historical data on stepparenting in the United States are lacking, relatively good data exist on changes over time in the percentage of children living in other than intact, two-parent families for all reasons, including divorce, desertion, and nonmarital births. During the late nineteenth and early twentieth centuries, an estimated one third of children spent some part of their childhood living in other than intact families (Hernandez, 1993). By the middle of the twentieth century the situation had improved substantially, due largely to steeply diminishing death rates and relatively low marital dissolution rates. The chances that a child born in the late 1940s and early 1950s would not be living at age seventeen with both biological parents were, by one estimate, only about 20 percent (Bumpass and Sweet, 1989). This was probably an all-time historical high point in the prevalence of the intact two-biological-parent family.

Since 1960, however, the chances of spending part or all of one's childhood outside an intact family have grown dramatically. According to various estimates, the chances that a child born around 1980 will not be living at age seventeen with both biological parents have increased to over 50 percent (Hernandez, 1993). Thus, we have rapidly gone from an intact-family apogee to what is probably an historical nadir. In 1960, an estimated 83 percent of all children were living with their two married, biological parents; by 1990, this figure was 58 percent.[3] During this three-decade period, the percentage of stepchildren under age eighteen living with a stepparent has climbed from 6.7 percent to 11.3 percent.[4] More than nine out of ten stepchildren live with their biological mother and a stepfather.

Accounting for this recent increase in family fragmentation are two main factors: voluntary marital dissolution and nonmarital births. The chances today that a first marriage will end in divorce or separation stand at over 50 percent, following a gradual increase in the divorce rate over the past 150 years. About three out of five divorcing couples have at least one child (Bumpass, 1990). The growth of nonmarital births is more recent and more dramatic; nonmarital births as a percent of all births increased from 5.3 percent in 1960 to 28 percent today. In contrast, the death of parents has become an insignificant factor in family fragmentation. Well over 90 percent of children reach age eighteen with both parents still alive.

The Problem of Stepfamilies

Many, and perhaps most, stepfamilies today lead contented home lives and produce happy and successful children. But a growing body of evidence suggests that the increase of stepfamilies has created serious problems for child welfare (Ihinger-Tallman, 1988). Virtually all of the children of nonmarital births and marital dissolution end up in one of two family types: single-parent families (usually mother-headed) or stepfamilies. Contrary to the view of some social scientists in recent years who believed that the effects of family fragmentation on children were both modest and ephemeral, there is now substantial evidence to indicate that the child outcomes of these alternative family forms are significantly inferior to those of families consisting of two biological parents. Compared to those in intact families, children in single-parent and stepfamilies are significantly more likely to have emotional and behavioral problems, to receive the professional help of psychologists, to have health problems, to perform poorly in school and drop out, and to leave home early (Bray, Berger, Boethel, Maymi, and Touch, 1992; Dawson, 1991; Hetherington and Jodl, 1994; Zill, 1988; Zill and Schoenborn, 1990). Moreover, some of these negative effects have been shown to persist into adult life.

Social scientists used to believe that, for positive child outcomes, stepfamilies were preferable to single-parent families. Today, we are not so sure. Stepfamilies typically have an economic advantage, but some recent studies indicate that the children of stepfamilies have as many behavioral and emotional problems as the children of single-parent families, and possibly more (e.g., Kiernan, 1992).

Stepfamilies apparently have been regarded as problematic at all times and in all societies, perceived as a family form that is sometimes necessary, but to be avoided if possible. The stepmother in Western societies, for instance, has long been a focus of scorn in nursery rhymes and folk tales (Collins, 1991). In folk literature from around the world, stepparents commonly appear in a highly unfavorable light. Today, stepfamilies may have become even more problematic than in the past because they are created mostly by divorce and nonmarital births rather than by the death of a parent. Many studies have verified that children whose birth families have been disrupted by divorce show more emotional and behavioral problems than those whose families have been disrupted by the death of a parent (e.g., Kiernan, 1992; Timms, 1991; Zill, 1988). For stepchildren, the continuing existence of a biological parent can create additional problems due to the complexity of relationships and the possibility for increased interpersonal conflict.

Certain problems are more prevalent in stepfamilies than in other family forms. A common finding is that stepparents provide less warmth and communicate less well with their children than do biological parents (Thomson, McLanahan, and Curtin, 1992). A number of studies have found that a child is far more likely to be abused by a stepfather than by the biological father (Daly and Wilson, 1985; Gordon, 1989; Russell, 1983, 1984; Wilson, Daly, and Weghorst, 1980). One Canadian investigation found that "preschoolers in Hamilton [Ontario] living with one natural and one stepparent in 1983 were 40 times as likely to become child abuse statistics as like-aged children living with two natural parents" (Wilson and Daly, 1987; p. 228). On the basis of this and other studies, these investigators concluded that "stepparenthood per se remains the single most powerful risk factor for child abuse that has yet been identified" (Daly and Wilson, 1988, pp. 87-88). Compared to children in intact and single-parent households, they suggest, "stepchildren are not merely 'disadvantaged,' but imperiled" (Wilson and Daly, 1987, p. 230).

As in single-parent families, a major problem of the stepfamily phenomenon is the net loss of fathering in children's lives. Some 80 percent of divorced fathers remarry, and a large portion of these fathers transfer their parenting to stepchildren; this has been described as a "transient father" syndrome or a system of "child swapping" (Furstenberg, 1988). Many studies have shown that stepfathering acts to diminish contact between original fathers and their biological children (Furstenberg and Nord, 1985; Furstenberg, Nord, Peterson, and Zill, 1983; Man, 1990; Seltzer and Bianchi, 1988; White, 1994).[5] In their turn, stepfathers take a considerably less active role in parenting than do custodial biological fathers, according to many studies, and frequently become disengaged from their stepchildren following the establishment of a stepfamily (Bray, 1988; Hetherington, 1987; White, 1994). "Even after two years," it is reported, "disengagement by the stepparent is the most common parenting style" (Hetherington, Stanley-Hagan, and Anderson, 1989, p. 308).

Another problematic aspect of stepfamilies is their high breakup rate, higher than that of two-biological-parent families. According to the most recent census data, more than 62 percent of remarriages among women under age forty will end in divorce, and the more that children are involved, the higher the redivorce rate. Thus, not only is the quality of family life in stepfamilies typically inferior to that of biological-parent families but the children of stepfamilies face a greater chance of family breakup than they did in their original families (White and Booth, 1985). By one estimate, about 15 percent of all children born in recent decades will go through at least two family disruptions before coming of age (Furstenberg, 1990).

In summary, according to the available evidence, stepfamilies tend to have less cohesive, more problematic, and more stressful family relationships than intact families, and probably also than single-parent families. Put more strongly by a recent article in *Psychology Today*, stepfamilies "are such a minefield of divided loyalties, emotional traps, and management conflicts that they are the most fragile form of family in America" ("Shuttle Diplomacy," 1993).

Biosocial Bases of Family Life

In order to better understand the special problems that stepfamilies pose, it is necessary to delve into the fundamental biosocial nature of human family life. Even though family life today is heavily shaped by a massive layer of culture, the predispositions of our biological makeup are ever present. It is almost certainly the case that families are more than just arbitrary social constructs that can be redesigned at will; they are partly rooted in biology, especially because they intimately concern what is most basic to life—the reproduction of the species.[6]

Human beings have evolved as biological organisms through the process of natural selection generated by differential reproduction. The Darwinian explanation of evolution is accepted by virtually all biologists; there are no competing theories that have any evidential support (Barkow, 1989; Goldsmith, 1991; Hinde, 1987). From a Darwinian perspective, all living things are motivated by a "drive" to survive and reproduce, and the nature of human beings today is partly the result of the expression of this drive throughout the millions of years of our species' development. The distinctive qualities of the human species were heavily shaped in what is referred to as the environment of evolutionary adaptedness (EEA), which consisted of small tribal groupings of hunter-gatherers in a wood and grasslands (Savanna) ecology, and was organized around relatively tight-knit nuclear families designed for food procurement and the procreation and socialization of the young.[7] Those human beings best adapted to this environment were more likely to survive, reproduce, and produce successful offspring (Leakey and Lewin, 1992).

One of the most distinctive traits of the human species is our family system—a nuclear family grouping in which the biological father is not only identified, but is also normally involved in the upbringing of his children. The human family was probably the first of our social institutions, and was a major factor in enabling us to become the dominant species on earth. Within the rest of the animal kingdom, the fatherless mother-child family unit largely prevails. There are few animal species in which the male plays much of a role in childrearing beyond that of sperm donor.[8] But owing to the pronounced and lengthy dependence of human offspring on adults (partly the result of having such large and complex brains), human mothers required significant help from others in order to survive, and the biological father was the most highly motivated to provide that help. Anthropologists Jane and Chet Lancaster (1987) put the matter as follows:

> In the course of evolution, the keystone in the foundation of the human family was the capturing of male energy into the nurturance of young, most specifically for the collaborative feeding of weaned juveniles. The human family is a complex organizational structure for the garnering of energy to be transformed into the production of the next generation, and its most essential feature is the collaboration of the male and female parent in the division of labor (p. 192).

In the words of biosociologist Pierre L. van den Berghe (1988), "the human family is, very simply, the solution our hominid ancestor evolved over three to five million years to raise our brainy, slow-maturing...highly dependent, and, therefore, very costly (in terms of parental investment) babies" (p. 43).

From the perspective of evolutionary biology, the organization of the human nuclear family is based on two inherited biological predispositions that confer reproductive success, one that operates between parent and child, and the other between parent and parent. The first is a predisposition to advance the interests of genetic relatives before those of unrelated individuals, so-called inclusive fitness, kin selection, or nepotism (Hamilton, 1964). With respect to children, this means that men and women have likely evolved to invest more in children who are related to them than in those who are not (Smith, 1988). The world over, such biological favoritism tends to be the rule.

The second biological predisposition is for males and females to have some emotional affinity for each other beyond the sexual act, and to establish pair bonds (Hamilton, 1984; Lovejoy, 1981). We tend to fall in love with one person at a time. Although we think of love attachments as being highly social in character, they also have a strong biological component (Hinde, 1987). There exists an "affective attachment" between men and women that causes us to be infatuated with each other, to feel a sense of well being when we are together with a loved one, and to feel jealous when others attempt to intrude into our relationship. Around the world today, almost all adults pair-bond with someone of the opposite sex for at least a portion of their lives, and monogamous relationships are the rule (even in the 85 percent of known societies that permit or prefer polygyny). All known human societies have recognized the existence of the pair-bond, and have given it formal sanction through the institution of marriage (van den Berghe, 1990). In summary, as Dobash, Dobash, Wilson, and Daly (1992) wrote:

> It is a cross-culturally and historically ubiquitous aspect of human affairs that women and men form individualized unions, recognized by themselves and by others as conferring certain obligations and entitlements, such that the partners' productive and reproductive careers become intertwined (p. 84).

Yet, the human family is not an especially stable institution. It exists in a delicate balance between the centripetal bonding forces and centrifugal forces that operate in the opposite direction—to pull family members apart. One fundamental reason for family instability is that, at heart, human beings are probably more self-interested than truly altruistic, even toward our own relatives and intimates. We act, first and foremost, in the interest of self-survival. But another reason is that the male-female bond, especially when compared to the mother-infant bond, is notoriously fragile. Although marriage is universal, divorce has also been a central feature of human social life. It has recently been suggested that, in the EEA, the practice of monogamy may have meant that a man only stayed with a women until their child was out of infancy, a period of about four years (Fisher, 1992).

Possibly the most disintegrating force acting on the human pair bond is the male sexual drive. Can anyone really believe that the male sex drive was designed to ensure lifelong sexual fidelity to one mate? As anthropologist Donald Symons (1985) summarized, "human sexuality, especially male sexuality, is by its very nature ill-designed to promote marriage, and gender differences in sexuality do not seem to be complementary" (p. 151). Universally, men are the more sexually driven and promiscuous, while women are more relationship-oriented. Sex researcher Alfred Kinsey once said, "Among all peoples, everywhere in the world, it is understood that the male is more likely than the female to desire sexual relations with a variety of partners" (Daly and Wilson, 1983, p. 281).

Sexual and Reproductive Strategies

To understand the male difference, and why human pair bonds are in many ways so fragile, we must consider the radically dissimilar sexual and reproductive strategies of males and females (Trivers, 1972). Biologically, the primary reproductive function for males is to inseminate, and for females is to harbor the growing fetus. Because male sperm are numerous and female eggs are relatively rare (both being the prime genetic carriers), a distinctive sexual or reproductive strategy is most adaptive for each sex. Males, much more than females, have the capacity to achieve vast increases in reproductive success by acquiring multiple mates. One man with 100 mates could have hundreds of children, but one woman with 100 mates could not have many more children than she could have with just one mate. Males, therefore, have more incentive to spread their numerous sperm more widely among many females, and females have a strong incentive to bind males to themselves for the long-term care of their more limited number of potential offspring.

The woman's best reproductive strategy is to ensure that she maximizes the survivability of the one baby she is able to produce every few years through gaining the provision and protection of the father (or, today, the government!). The man's best strategy, however, may be twofold. He wants his baby to survive, yes, and for that reason he may provide help to his child's mother. But, at the same time, it is relatively costless to him (if he can get away with it) to inseminate other women, and thereby help to further insure that his genes are passed on. Using the popular terms suggested by evolutionary scientists Patricia Draper and Henry Harpending (1982), male reproductive strategy can range from the promiscuous and low paternal-investment "cad" approach, in which sperm is widely distributed with the hope that more offspring will survive to reproduce, to the "dad" approach, in which a high paternal investment is made in a limited number of offspring.

Why aren't all men promiscuous cads? Because, in addition to the pull of the biological pair-bonding and parenting predispositions discussed previously, virtually all human societies have established strong cultural sanctions that seek to limit male promiscuity and protect the sanctity of the family. Some anthropologists have suggested that the chief function of the culturally elaborated kinship structures that human beings have devised, and which provide the social basis of premodern societies, is to "protect the mother-infant bond from the relative fragility and volatility of the male-female bond" (Tiger and Fox, 1971, p. 71). The famous anthropologist Bronislaw Malinowski, in *Sex, Culture and Myth* (1930), pointed out the way in which kinship structures perform this function (cited in Moynihan, 1986):

> In all human societies the father is regarded by tradition as indispensable. The woman has to be married before she is allowed legitimately to conceive... An unmarried mother is under a ban, a fatherless child is a bastard. This is by no means only a European or Christian prejudice; it is the attitude found amongst most barbarous and savage peoples as well... The most important moral and legal rule concerning the physiological side of kinship is that no child should be brought into the world without a man—and one man at that—assuming the role of sociological father, that is, guardian and protector, the male link between the child and the rest of the community (pp. 169–170).

Paternal Certainty

If a man is to stay with one woman rather than pursue many different women, according to sociobiologists, the "paternal certainty" of his offspring is extremely important. A woman can be certain about her own offspring, but a man cannot be. Because the biological goal is to pass on one's genes, it would be genetic folly for a man to spend his life with one woman unknowingly raising someone else's child in place of his own. For this reason, some evolutionists believe that monogamy arose first, and that high paternal investments evolved only after monogamy had produced a decrease in uncertainty concerning the paternity of offspring (Peck and Feldman, 1988).

The likely impact of the paternal certainty issue can be seen throughout the world today. Studies have shown that family systems in which paternity tends not to be as acknowledged or is downplayed relative to maternity, and systems in which paternal investments are minimal, are those in which confidence of paternity is low (Flinn, 1992, p. 80). In other words, a male tends to invest in his mate's children only when his paternal confidence is high. As anthropologists Steven Gaulin and Alice Schlegel (1980) put it, "cultural patterns leading to heavy male investment in wife's children are common only where mating patterns make it likely that such investment benefits bearers of the male's genes" (p. 308).

Paternal certainty may be an important, and is certainly a relatively unexamined, evolutionary insight to bear in mind when analyzing social conditions in modern societies. The evidence suggests that paternal certainty is diminishing in our time, with these same predicted consequences of unacknowledged paternity, the downplaying of fatherhood, and decreasing paternal investment.

The predominance of the primordial hunter-gatherer lifestyle began to decline some 10,000 years ago with the rise of horticultural societies and a more settled way of life. With the warming of the earth and the end of the Ice Age, plant food resources increased and big game hunting declined in importance. Rudimentary technologies of agriculture and the domestication of animals were put into widespread use. Since then (an extremely short period of time in the history of the species), human social life has changed dramatically, with enormous increases in population densities and in the scale and technological sophistication of societies (Lenski, Lenski, and Nolan, 1991). Over time, the emergence of plow agriculture and food surpluses led to the rise of agrarian societies. With the development of class hierarchies and, eventually, the state, cooperation and trust among kinfolk as the main bases of social order gave way to power and domination by the few, leading to the endless tribal conflicts, wars, and the many other violent forms of struggle for the control of resources that have characterized recorded human history.[9]

During the most recent stages of the development of the human species, rapidly paced cultural evolution has overtaken slow-moving biological evolution as the main force of social change (Hallpike, 1986; Scott, 1989). One result is that family structures around the world today are widely variable, determined more by cultural differences than by biological predispositions. Cultural differences, in turn, are strongly related to levels of economic and social development, and to ecological circumstance.

Associated with the rise of horticultural and agrarian societies was a fundamental shift in people's attitudes toward reproduction (Lancaster and Lancaster, 1987). When people perceive that the resources necessary to sustain life and reproductive success are abundant and generally available to all, as was presumably the case among our hunter-gatherer ancestors, the reproductive strategy is to have as many children as possible and share and share alike. Reproduction is limited only by the need of parents to sustain themselves, which in hunter-gatherer societies may have caused women to bear children only about once every four years. This strategy still prevails today in remote parts of the world.

But with increased density of population and wealth, people came to perceive that resources were limited, that major differentials existed between who survived and who did not, and that survival was very much dependent on who controlled the most resources. It was no longer sufficient merely to rear as many offspring as possible and hope that they would survive to reproduce. Reproductive strategies became individually tailored to maximize the use and control of resources. It was necessary to try to guarantee children access to resources in the form of education or inheritance, for example, so that they would have an advantage over other parents' children.

Marriage and Divorce in Premodern Societies

The new perception of resource scarcity in complex societies generated a dramatic transformation in family life and kinship relations, including concern for the "legitimacy" of children, the rise of inheritance laws, and the careful control of female sexuality. The nuclear family gave way to the complex, extended family; the conjugal unit became imbedded in an elaborate kinship network. The father role of authority figure and head of household grew in importance, whereas the status of women deteriorated. Sociologist Martin King Whyte (1978) found, in a comparative analysis of data on ninety-three preindustrial societies drawn from the Human Relations Area Files, that "in the more complex cultures, women tend to have less domestic authority, less independent solidarity with other women, more unequal sex restrictions...and fewer property rights" (p. 172).

Through the institutionalization of cultural norms and sanctions, complex societies have become heavily devoted to socially controlling male and female sexual strategies. The most important social institution serving this purpose is marriage. Marriage can be defined simply as "a relationship within which a group socially approves and encourages sexual intercourse and the birth of children" (Frayser, 1985, p. 248). As this definition suggests, marriage as an institution is best thought of in terms of group norms rather than individual pursuits. The norms of marriage include some degree of mutual obligation between husband and wife, the right of sexual access (usually, but not inevitably exclusive), and persistence in time. Throughout most of recorded history, until recently, most marriages were arranged (although the principals typically had a say in the matter); they were less alliances of two individuals than of two kin networks, typically involving an exchange of money or goods.

Various theories have been put forth to explain the fundamental purposes of marriage. But certainly one purpose is, as noted previously, to hold men to the pair-bond, thereby helping to ensure high quality offspring and, at the same time, helping to control the open conflict that would result if men were allowed unlimited ability to pursue the "cad" strategy with other men's wives. As demographer Kingsley Davis (1985) stated:

> The genius of the family system is that, through it, the society normally holds the biological parents responsible for each other and for their offspring. By identifying children with their parents, and by penalizing people who do not have stable reproductive relationships, the social system powerfully motivates individuals to settle into a sexual union and take care of the ensuing offspring (pp. 7-8).

Margaret Mead is purported to have said, with male biology strongly in mind, that there is no society in the world where men will stay married for very long unless culturally required to do so. Although biology may pull men in one direction, culture has sought to pull them in another. The cultural pull can be seen in the marriage ceremony. Reinforced by ritual and public acknowledgment, the ceremony stresses the long-term commitment of the male, the durability of the marital relationship, and the importance of the union for children. A major intent of the ceremony is to solidify a strong social bond in addition to the sexual tie.

Marriages around the world are not necessarily monogamous, however. In about 85 percent of the world's premodern societies, marital polygyny (one man, several women) is condoned, and in many of these societies it is actually preferred and practiced to the extent possible. Yet, even in these societies, the great majority of men (and all women) live monogamously. Why do some premodern societies prefer or permit (simultaneous) polygyny, while others do not? There is no definitive answer to this question, although many researchers have investigated it (Betzig, 1986; Lee and Whitbeck, 1990). Polygyny may have been quite limited in the EEA, as it is among hunter-gatherer societies today. Due to the generation of great wealth and economic inequalities, polygyny probably increased with the rise of agriculture. Wealth is essential for securing mates in all polygynous societies; the well-to-do men are most likely to have polygynous marriages.

Divorce is almost as universal as marriage. Societies differ greatly in the degree to which divorce actually occurs, but there are few societies in which it is totally absent or absolutely forbidden. Low divorce societies tend to be those in which women have little relative autonomy, especially in the economic sphere. The growing economic autonomy of women is a principal factor accounting for increased divorce in modern societies over the past 150 years (Goode, 1993; Phillips, 1988). The leading causes for divorce around the world, however, are drawn directly from the realm of evolutionary biology—adultery (especially women's) and infertility (Betzig, 1989).

Marriage and Divorce in Urban-Industrial Societies

Just a couple of hundred years ago, after people had been living for many millennia in agrarian societies, a relatively few societies shifted to an urban and industrial way of life. This is the way of life to which most societies in the world today appear to be headed (Goode, 1970). Urban-industrial societies, of course, have created their own, new problems. But they have dramatically reduced poverty and, through the associated rise of liberal democracy, eased those conditions in complex agrarian societies that generated gross inequalities of income and status. Women, for example, are in the process of regaining the relatively equal status they presumably had in early hunter-gatherer societies.

In urban-industrial societies, reproductive concerns about the quantity of children have largely given way to concerns about quality. Children in these societies require massive parental investments if they are to succeed, and childrearing has become extraordinarily expensive in terms of time and money. The low birth rates and small average family sizes found in these societies, therefore, may be considered an adaptive reproductive strategy.

Simultaneous polygyny is not permitted in any society that, to date, has achieved urban-industrial status. Among the many reasons for mandating monogamy is that it is fairer to both women and men, equality being one of the supreme values of the modern period. In the United States today, we take for granted that monogamy is the natural and preferred form of marriage although, increasingly, the high marital breakup rate suggests that "serial monogamy" or "successive polygamy" is the actual institutional form of our time.

In the preindustrial West, at least in northwest Europe, a relatively nuclear family structure existed for many centuries prior to the Industrial Revolution, unlike the situation in most of the rest of the world where complex, extended families predominated. The modern nuclear family that accompanied the emergence of urban-industrialism and cultural modernity in the West was distinctly different from its preindustrial predecessor, however. The rise of this new family form, in the words of historian Lawrence Stone (1977), was "one of the most significant transformations that has ever taken place, not only in the most intimate aspects of human life, but also in the nature of social organization" (p. 687). In structure, the modern family was smaller, even more nuclear in the sense of being split off from relatives, and more stable because there were fewer early deaths of husbands and wives (Kertzer, 1991). But it was in the tone or quality of family life that the modern family was truly unique. The new family form was emotionally intense, privatized, and child-oriented; in authority structure, it was relatively egalitarian; and it placed a high value on individualism in the sense of individual rights and autonomy.

Today, the modern nuclear family—what we now call the "traditional nuclear family"—is denigrated by some scholars in the belief that it dreadfully oppresses women. Yet, the nuclear family that predominated in the United States from the early 1800s through the 1950s probably represented, for most married women, a significant life improvement. As historian Carl N. Degler (1980) noted: "the marriage which initiated the modern family was based upon affection and mutual respect between the partners, both at the time of family formation and in the course of its life. The woman in the marriage enjoyed an increasing degree of influence or autonomy within the family" (pp. 8-9). Lawrence Stone (1977) suggested that this was "the first family type in history which was both long-lasting and intimate" (p. 679).

The big winners from the emergence of the modern nuclear family, however, were not women, but children. In preindustrial Europe, parental care of children does not seem to have been particularly prominent, and such practices as infanticide, wet nursing, child fosterage, and the widespread use of lower status surrogate caretakers were common (Draper and Harpending, 1987). According to evidence assembled by demographer Sheila Ryan Johansson (1987), "malparenting in the form of extreme parental neglect (or even abuse) must have been wide-spread" (p. 68). Draper and Harpending (1987) suggested that one of the greatest achievements of the modern nuclear family was the return to the high-invest-ment nurturing of children by their biological parents, the kind of parenting characteristic of our hunter-gatherer ancestors. As appraised by Degler (1980):

> The attention, energy and resources of parents in the emerging modern family, were increasingly centered upon the rearing of their offspring. Children were now per-ceived as being different from adults and deserving not only of material care but of solicitude and love as well. Childhood was deemed a valuable period in the life of every person and to be sharply distinguished in character and purpose from adult-hood. Parenthood thus became a major personal responsibility, perhaps even a burden (pp. 8–9).

Family stability during this era, together with parental investments in chil-dren, may have been greater than at any other time in history. Cultural sanc-tions concerning marriage were powerfully enforced, and thanks to ever low-ering death rates and low divorce rates, both parents were typically able to see their children through to adulthood. This remarkably high family stability helps to explain why the family situation in the United States today appears so troubled, particularly in the minds of the older generation.

Recent Family and Cultural Change in America

In the past half century, the U.S. family has been on a social roller coaster. The ups and downs have been quite astonishing. Following World War II, the United States entered a two-decade period of extraordinary economic growth and material progress. Commonly referred to as simply "the 50s," it was the most sustained period of prosperity in U.S. history. Together with most other industrially developed societies of the world, this nation saw improvements in the levels of health, material consumption, and economic security that had scant historical precedent. For most Americans, the improvements included striking increases in longevity, buying power, personal net worth, and govern-ment-sponsored economic security.

The 1950s was also an era of remarkable familism and family togetherness, with the family an institution undergoing unprecedented growth and stability within the middle and working classes. The marriage rate reached an all-time high, the birth rate returned to the high levels of earlier in the century, gener-ating the baby boom, and the divorce rate leveled off. Home, motherhood, and child-centeredness reigned high in the lexicon of cultural values. A higher proportion of children were growing up in stable, two-parent families than ever before in U.S. history (Cherlin and Furstenberg, 1988, p. 294; Modell, Furstenberg, and Strong, 1978).

Beginning in the 1960s, however, a series of unanticipated social and cul-tural developments took place that shook the foundations of the modern nuclear family. As the authors of a recent history of the U.S. family (Mintz and Kellogg, 1988) said, "what Americans have witnessed since 1960 are fundamental challenges to the forms, ideals, and role expectations that have defined the family for the last century and a half" (p. 204). Men abandoned their families at an unprecedented rate, leaving behind broken homes and single-parent, female-headed households. Women relinquished their traditional mother/housewife roles in unexpectedly large numbers and entered the labor force. The percentage of births taking place outside of marriage skyrocketed. Highly permissive sexual behavior became acceptable, accompanied by the widespread dissemination of pornography.

Not only did the modern nuclear family become fragmented, but participation in family life went into a precipitous decline (Popenoe, 1993). A calculation by demographers indicates that while the proportion of one's adult life spent living with spouse and children was 62 percent in 1960, the highest in our history, in just twenty-five years this figure dropped to 43 percent, the lowest in our history (Watkins, Menken, and Bongaarts, 1987).

Underlying these family-related trends was an extraordinary shift in cultural values and self-definition. An abrupt acceleration occurred in the long-run cultural shift, associated with the rise of modernity, from communitarian or collectivist values to the values of individualism. Trust in, and a sense of obligation toward, the larger society and its institutions rapidly eroded; the traditional moral authority of social institutions such as schools, churches, and governments withered. What emerged, instead, was a new importance given by large segments of the population to the personal goal and even moral commandment of expressive individualism or "self-fulfillment" (Bellah, Madsen, Sullivan, Swidler, and Tipton, 1985). In public opinion polls, Daniel Yankelovich (1994) found that people today place a lower value on what we owe others as a matter of moral obligation, on self-sacrifice, on social conformity, and on restraint in matters of physical pleasure and sexuality, and we place a higher value on self-expression, individualism, self-realization, and personal choice.

The institution of marriage was particularly hard hit. "At no time in history, with the possible exception of Imperial Rome," Kingsley Davis (1985) said, "has the institution of marriage been more problematic than it is today" (p. 21). Davis may only have been thinking of Western history, but his point is probably still valid. Many marriages, those involving close companionship and intimacy between well-matched people, may provide more personal satisfaction than marriages ever have before. But marriage has also been deinstitutionalized on a scale that is unprecedented. The distinguished French sociologist Louis Roussel (1989) suggested, in fact, that a double deinstitutionalization has occurred: Individuals are more hesitant to enter or commit themselves to institutional marriage roles, and societies have weakened their normative sanctions over such roles.

The marriage rate has steadily declined over the past few decades, from 76.7 marriages per 1,000 unmarried women in 1970, to 54.2 in 1990. The divorce rate, although it has leveled off, remains at a historically high level. Marriage has become a voluntary relationship that individuals can make and break at will. As one indicator of this shift, the legal regulation of marriage and divorce has become increasingly lax (Glendon, 1989; Jacob, 1988; Sugarman and Kay, 1990). In summary, fewer people ever marry, those who marry do so at a later age, a smaller proportion of life is spent in wedlock, and marriages are of a shorter duration (Espanshade, 1985).

The underlying causes for the decline of marriage and the high divorce rate are numerous and not fully understood (Goode, 1993; Phillips, 1988). Widely recognized causal factors include material affluence (it weakens the family's traditional economic bond), higher psychological expectations for marriage, secularization, and rapidly changing gender roles. Much of the evidence, however, points to the fact that the recent changes in marriage and divorce are fundamentally rooted in the cultural shift from a collectivist to an individualist ethos, and are related to the decline of social institutions in general.

Divorce feeds upon itself, and today we have what can be called a "divorce climate." The more divorce there is, the more "normal" it becomes, with fewer negative sanctions to oppose it and the more potential remarriage partners become available. One of the significant attitudinal changes of recent years is the rising acceptance of divorce, especially when children are involved. Divorces involving children used to be in the category of "unthinkable." Today, children are only a minor inhibitor of divorce, slightly more so when the children are male than female (Heaton, 1990; Morgan, Lye, and Condran, 1988; Waite and Lillard; 1991). As one measure of the acceptance of divorce involving children, the proportion of persons answering "no" to the question, "should a couple stay together for the sake the children?" jumped from 51 percent to 82 percent between 1962 and 1985 (Thornton, 1989). In other words, less than one fifth of the population today believes that the presence of children should deter parents from breaking up.

The high voluntary dissolution of marriages might not be a serious problem if only adults were involved although, even then, it certainly generates considerable instability and anxiety. The problem is that young children, if they are to grow up successfully, still need strong attachments to parents. The evidence strongly suggests that parental bonds with children have suffered in recent years; and that the tremendous parenting advantages of the modern nuclear family are on the wane. As Samuel Preston (1984), former president of the Population Association of America, suggested, "Since 1960 the conjugal family has begun to divest itself of care for children in much the same way that it did earlier for the elderly" (p. 443). Quantitative measures of such divestiture are the absenteeism rate of fathers, the decline in the amount of time that parents spend with their children, and the growing portion of a child's life that is spent alone, with peers, in daycare, in school, and watching television (Hewlett, 1991; Louv, 1990).

The Social Response to Stepfamilies

The decline of marriage and the increase of divorce are, of course, the major contributors to the recent growth of stepfamilies. Because childrearing is such a time- and energy-consuming activity, it has always been a difficult activity for a lone parent to successfully accomplish. On this ground alone, in addition to the parent's desire to have a new partner for his or her own sake, it seems entirely reasonable for the custodial parent of minor children following a death or divorce, and for the woman who has a nonmarital birth, to seek to replace the missing biological parent. Yet, as is now evident, this action generates serious problems of its own.

One approach to addressing these problems is to provide more collective assistance to stepfamilies. It is surely the case, especially in view of the diminution of kinship and neighborhood groupings, that stepfamilies need our collective help and understanding more than ever. But we should not confuse short-run actions aimed at helping stepfamilies with long-run solutions. If the argument presented in this chapter is correct, and the family is fundamentally rooted in biology and at least partly activated by the "genetically selfish" activities of human beings, childrearing by nonrelatives is inherently problematic. It is not that unrelated individuals are unable to do the job of parenting; it is just that they are not as likely to do the job well. Stepfamily problems, in short, may be so intractable that the best strategy for dealing with them is to do everything possible to minimize their occurrence.

Unfortunately, many members of the therapeutic and helping professions, together with a large group of social science allies, now take the view that the trend toward stepfamilies cannot be reversed. In a recent book on stepfamilies, for example, sociologist William R. Beer (1989) began, "For better or worse, the stepfamily is the family of the future" (p. 1). Just as the nuclear family was adapted to the industrial society, he suggested:

> [T]he stepfamily is a family form well matched to post-industrial society. This kind of society is typified by an emphasis on personal freedom and emotional fulfillment, sexual experimentation and egalitarianism, a reduced importance of kinship and consequent salience of nonfamily agencies that care for and educate the young, nurture the elderly, and carry on almost all economic activity (p. 7).

A close companion to this belief in stepfamily inevitability and optimum fit with a changing society is the view that we should now direct most of our attention toward understanding the familial processes of stepfamilies, and seek to develop social policies and interventions that will assist children's adjustment to them. In turn, the problems of stepfamilies are seen to be ones of "incomplete institutionalization" and "role ambiguity" (Cherlin, 1978; Giles-

Sims, 1984; Giles-Sims and Crosbie-Burnett, 1989). Once stepfamilies become more common and accepted, it is argued, and once our society comes to define the roles of stepparenthood more clearly, the problems of stepfamilies will diminish.

This may be a largely incorrect understanding of the situation. The reason why unrelated stepparents find their parenting roles more stressful and less satisfying than biological parents is probably due much less to social stigma and to the uncertainty of their obligations, as to the fact that they gain fewer intrinsic emotional rewards from carrying out those obligations. The parental relationship is unique in human affairs. In most social relationships, the reciprocity of benefits is carefully monitored and an imbalance is regarded as exploitative. But in the parental relationship, as evolutionary psychologists Martin Daly and Margo Wilson (1988) pointed out, "the flow of benefits is prolongedly, cumulatively, and ungrudgingly unbalanced" (p. 83). They continued: "Organisms have evolved to expend their very lives enhancing the fitness prospects of their descendants.... Parental investment is a precious resource, and selection must favor those parental psyches that do not squander it on nonrelatives" (p. 83). On the inherent emotional difficulties of parenting by nonrelatives, Daly and Wilson (1988) cited one study (Duberman, 1975) that found "only 53% of stepfathers and 25% of stepmothers could claim to have 'parental feeling' toward their stepchildren, and still fewer to 'love' them" (p. 84).

If, as the findings of evolutionary biology strongly suggest, there is a biological basis to parenting, we must question the view, widespread in the social sciences, that parenthood is merely a social role anyone can play if only they learn the part. Again, Daly and Wilson (1987) were forceful on this point:

> The prevalent conception of parenthood itself as a "role" (with stepparenthood being another role, partially overlapping that of natural parenthood) is profoundly misleading in its implication of arbitrary substitutability. A role is something that any competent actor who has studied the part can step into, but parental love cannot be established at will. Parents care profoundly—often selflessly—about their children, a fact with immense behavioral consequences about which the shallow metaphor of "parental roles" is mute (p. 117).

This is not to deny, of course, that strong feelings of parental love can be activated in substitute parents, including many and perhaps most stepparents and most adoptive parents. As Daly and Wilson (1988) noted, the psychology of parental love "can, after all, be activated with surprising intensity toward a nonhuman pet" (p. 84). One could even say, as Lynn White (1994) does, that in view of biological predispositions, "stepfamilies are amazingly successful." The only point is that, given their very special nature, parental feelings and parental love are inherently more difficult to develop among persons unrelated to a given child.

The difficulties of parenting by unrelated individuals can also be found in adoption situations, where a growing body of evidence suggests that adopted children fare somewhat worse than do children from intact families (Brodzinsky, Radice, Huffman, and Merkler, 1987; Deutsch, 1992; Lindholm and Touliatos, 1980). Bear in mind that parents of adopted children have noteworthy parenting advantages over stepparents in that they tend to have fewer conflicting relationships with biological parents and, having freely and deliberately decided to adopt, they may be more strongly motivated to the task of childrearing. Unlike most stepparents, their entry into the parenting relationship is not incidental to the establishment of the adult pair-bond. Also, because in most adoption situations neither parent is related to the child, from a sociobiological perspective there is "no exploitation of one partner's efforts for the other's fitness benefit" (Daly and Wilson, 1988, p. 84).

The biosocial perspective presented in this essay leads to the conclusion that we as a society should be doing much more to halt the growth of stepfamilies. It is important to give great respect to those stepfamilies that are doing their job well, and to provide both assistance and compassion for those that are experiencing difficulties. But such efforts should not overshadow the paramount importance of public policies designed to promote and preserve two-biological-parent families, and of endeavors to reverse the cultural drift toward radical individualism and the decline of marriage.

Only very limited suggestions can be provided within the confines of this essay as to what such public policies and cultural endeavors might entail. An overriding goal of public policy should be to increase the proportion of children who grow up with their two marred parents and decrease the proportion of children who do not. We should seek to promote family formation through marriage and discourage nonmarital pregnancies, to foster stable and enduring marriages, and to decrease the prevalence of divorce (National Commission on America's Urban Families, 1993). Appropriate measures include (a) the widespread promotion of premarital counseling and marital enrichment programs, (b) the reform of state laws on marriage and divorce so that the social importance of marriage is explicitly stated and meaningful waiting periods for divorce are adopted or extended in cases involving minor children, (c) promulgation of the view at all levels of society that nonmarital pregnancies are wrong and that fatherhood is a lifelong commitment, (d) redesign of the current welfare system so that marriage and the family are empowered rather than denigrated, and (e) revision of the federal tax code to provide more favorable treatment for married couples.

The power of public policy, however, pales in comparison with the general drift of our culture. Fortunately, there are some hopeful signs that a cultural turnaround is possible (Popenoe, 1994). As previously noted, a rapidly accelerated cultural trend from collectivist values that favor social bonds to individualist values that favor personal choice has been a prominent social fact of recent decades. But cultural change can be dialectical and cyclical as well as linear. Not all cultural values can simultaneously be maximized, and one generation comes to value, because they have less of it, what their parent's generation rejected. The 1950s was an era of strong social bonds. Taking these bonds largely for granted, the baby boom children of the 1950s shifted during the late 1960s and 1970s in the direction of what had been relatively lacking in their lives—personal choice/self-fulfillment.

In the 1990s (thirty years and one generation later), a cultural mini-shift back to social bonds may be underway. There appears to be a new realization that, as much as each individual desires personal choice, we also need—and society surely needs—strong social bonds. In the family sphere, some have called this cultural shift "the new familism" (Popenoe, 1992). With the very important exception that an enduring sense of family obligation and the desire to put children first are held as paramount values, the new familism does not represent a call to return to the modern (traditional) nuclear family. In place of the male domination and full-time housewife of the earlier family form, the new nuclear family ideal is a 50/50 division of power and decision-making between husband and wife, and a firm understanding that both women and men will share a common (though not necessarily identical) commitment to the work force over the course of their lives.

The new familism shift is led by the maturing baby boomers, now at the family stage of the lifecycle and family-oriented as never before. Spurred both by concerns for their own offspring and by growing evidence that recent family changes have hurt children, the huge cohort of middle-aged, childrearing baby boomers have already clearly shifted the media in a more profamily direction. As the baby boomers age and become even more aware of the importance of social bonds, the effect of this huge cohort on our cultural values could be enormous.

Another group potentially involved in the cultural shift is the "babyboom echo" children of the divorce revolution, now coming into adulthood with a troubled childhood to look back on and a new resolve to avoid the path their parents took. Their situation is ambivalent, however. They tend to favor marital permanence more than their own parents did, for example, perhaps because they do not take the family as much for granted as their parents did (Moore and Stief, 1989). But will their insecure childhoods prove damaging to their family hopes, as suggested by the evidence that children of divorce have a higher rate of divorce in their own marriages? We can only hope that this empirical finding will not stand the test of time.

Another source of cultural change is the economy. If affluence breeds radical individualism, then moderate economic decline may generate more family solidarity through promoting a "hunkering-down" attitude in which people look to their social ties for support, and married couples have fewer opportunities to break up. However, the unemployment and poverty an economic downturn inevitably fosters is no one's prescription for a happy marriage.

Finally, there is the social institution typically overlooked by social scientists: religion. If the accumulated sociological evidence is correct, religion has long played an important role in promoting marriage and family solidarity. There are some signs of a religious reawakening in the United States. Whether a new religiosity in fact develops, and what it may mean for marriage, remains to be seen. But one thing seems clear. Marriage, an institution with a profound social purpose, cannot long prevail in a culture based solely on personal expression and individual interest.

Notes

1.   The percentage of stepchildren would, of course, be higher if children over age eighteen were added, and if stepchildren living with unmarried patents were included. Data on the latter are unavailable. Children of unmarried stepparents are typically classified as living in mother-only families and a substantial number of stepchildren are probably so classified. In Great Britain, 9 percent of children under sixteen lived in 1985 with a natural mother and a stepfather, 7 percent in legally married and 2 percent in nonmarital cohabiting unions (Kiernan, 1992). It is also important to note that a higher percentage of children than indicated "live in a stepfamily"; they are the biological children of the parents, stepsiblings but not stepchildren. An estimated one third of all children living in stepfamilies fall into this category (Glick. 1989).

2.   This figure improved to almost 50 percent by the early eighteenth century (Rutman and Rutman, 1984). By the turn of the twentieth century, the parental death rate had declined dramatically, but was still high: about 75 percent of fifteen-year-olds had two living parents (Uhlenberg, 1983), as did 72 percent of eighteen-year-olds (Hernandez, 1993). By 1940, most of the modern decline in parental death rate had occurred: about 88 percent of children born at that time still had two living parents when they finished childhood.

3.   Estimated from U.S. Bureau of the Census (1992) and Hernandez (1993). Estimates for 1960 from personal communication with Hernandez (September 1993).

4.   Estimated from U.S. Bureau of the Census (1992) and Hernandez (1993). Estimates for 1960 from personal communication with Hernandez (September, 1993).

5.   Mott (1990), using 1979-1986 data from the National Longitudinal Survey of the Labor Market Experience of Youth, determined that about 60 percent of youth who did not have a resident biological father "had access to a male figure either in or out of the home who may potentially be considered a father or father substitute." He was unable to determine, however, how many of these men actually filled the various role obligations of a father.

6.   It is necessary, especially for a social science audience, for me to insert some caveats. (a) Biology does not necessarily determine behavior; it merely predisposes people to act in certain ways rather than others, or to feel more comfortable acting one way rather than another. (b) Our biological nature is not necessarily immutable; it is subject to much personal and cultural control. (c) What is biologically inherent in human nature is not necessarily "good" or "right." Good and right are cultural concepts, designed to guide human behavior in ways that benefit society as a whole.

7.   There is evidence that, still to this day, "we enjoy being in savannah vegetation, prefer to avoid both closed forests and open plains, will pay more for land giving us the impression of being on a savannah, mold recreational environments to be

8.   more like savannahs, and develop varieties of ornamental plants that converge on the shapes typical of tropical savannahs" (Orians, 1980, cited in Symons, 1985, p. 137).

8.   In only about 3 percent of all mammal species do males form a long-term relationship with females. Monogamy is most common among birds: 90 percent of bird species are monogamous. High rates of avian monogamy are found because nestling birds are so helpless, and avian mothers (who don't lactate) are commonly no better suited to parenting tasks than fathers (Mock and Fujioka 1990).

9.   For an intriguing perspective that the rise of complex, culturally based societies represents a "social cage" that has produced tensions with our primate biological legacy, see Maryanski and Turner (1993).

References

Barkow, J. H. (1989). *Darwin Sex and Status: Biological Approaches to Mind and Culture*. Toronto: University of Toronto Press.

Beer, W. R. (1989). *Strangers in the House: The World of Stepsiblings and Half-Siblings*. New Brunswick, NJ: Transaction Publishers.

Bellah, R. N., Madsen, R., Sullivan, W. M., Swidler, A., and Tipton. S. M. (1985). *Habits of the Heart: Individualism and Commitment in American Life*. Berkeley: University of California.

Betzig, L. (1986). *Despotism and Differential Reproduction: A Darwinian View of History*. New York: Aldine de Gruyter.

Betzig, L. (1989). "Causes of Conjugal Dissolution: A Cross-Cultural Study." *Current Anthropology* 30, 654–676.

Bray, J. H. (1988). "Children's Development during Early Remarriage." In E. M. Hetherington and I. D. Arasteh (eds.). *Impact of Divorce: Single Parenting and Stepparenting on Children* (pp. 279–298). Hillsdale, NJ: Lawrence Erlbaum Associates.

Bray, J. H., Berger, S. H., Boethel, C. L., Maymi, J. R., and Touch, G. (August 1992). "Longitudinal Changes in Stepfamilies: Impact on Children's Adjustment." Paper presented at the annual meeting of the American Psychological Association. Washington, DC.

Brodzinsky, D. M., Radice, C., Huffman, L., and Madder, K. (1987). "Prevalence of Clinically Significant Symptomatology in a Nonclinical Sample of Adopted and Nonadopted Children." *Journal of Clinical Child Psychology* 16 (4), 350–356.

Bumpass, L. L. (1990). "What's Happening to the Family: Interactions between Demographic and Institutional Change." *Demography* 27 (4), 483–498.

Bumpass, L. L. and Sweet, J. A. (1989). "Children's Experience in Single-Parent Families: Implications of Cohabitation and Marital Transitions." *Family Planning Perspectives* 6, 256–260.

Cherlin, A. (1978). "Remarriage as an Incomplete Institution." *American Journal of Sociology* 84, 634–650.

Cherlin, A. and Furstenberg, F. F., Jr. (1988). "The Changing European Family: Lessons for the American Reader." *Journal of Family Issues* 9 (3), 291–297.

Collins, S. (1991). "British Stepfamily Relationships, 1500-1800." *Journal of Family History* 16 (4), 331–344.

Daly, M. and Wilson, M. (1983). *Sex, Evolution, and Behavior* (2nd ed.). Belmont, CA: Wadsworth.

Daly, M. and Wilson, M. (1985). "Child Abuse and Other Risks of not Living with Both Parents." *Ethology and Sociobiology* 6, 197–210.

Daly, M. and Wilson, M. (1987). "The Darwinian Psychology of Discriminative Parental Solicitude." *Nebraska Symposium on Motivation.*

Daly, M. and Wilson, M. (1988). *Homicide.* New York: Aldine de Gruyter.

Davis, K. (1985). "The Meaning and Significance of Marriage in Contemporary Society." In K. Davis (ed.). *Contemporary Marriage* (pp. 1–21). New York: Russell Sage Foundation.

Dawson, D. A. (1991). "Family Structure and Children's Health and Well-Being: Data from the 1988 National Health Interview Survey on Child Health." *Journal of Marriage and the Family* 53 (3), 573–584.

Degler, C. N. (1980). *At Odds: Women and the Family in America from the Revolution to the Present.* New York: Oxford University Press.

Deutsch, C. K. (1992). "The Overrepresentation of Adoptees in Children with the Attention Deficit Disorder." *Behavioral Genetics* 12 (2), 231–238.

Dobash, R. P., Dobash, R. E., Wilson, M., and Daly, M. (1992). "The Myth of Sexual Symmetry in Marital Violence." *Social Problems* 39 (1), 71–87.

Draper, P. and Harpending, H. (1982). "Father Absence and Reproductive Strategy: An Evolutionary Perspective." *Journal of Anthropological Research* 38 (3), 255–273.

Draper, P. and Harpending, H. (1987). "Parent Investment and the Child's Environment." In J. B. Lancaster, J. Altmann, A. S. Rossi, and L. R. Sherrod (eds.). *Parenting across the Life Span: Biosocial Dimensions* (pp. 207–235). New York: Aldine de Gruyter.

Duberman, L. (1975). *The Reconstituted Family: A Study of Remarried Couples and Their Children.* Chicago, IL Nelson-Hall.

Espenshade, T. J. (1985). "The Recent Decline of American Marriage." In K. Davis (ed.). *Contemporary Marriage* (pp. 53–90). New York: Russell Sage Foundation.

Fisher, H. (1992). *Anatomy of Love: The Natural History of Monogamy, Adultery, and Divorce.* New York: Norton.

Flinn, M. V. (1992). "Paternal Care in a Caribbean Village." In B. S. Hewlett (ed.). *Father-Child Relations: Cultural and Biosocial Contexts* (pp. 57–84). New York: Aldine de Gruyter.

Frayser, S. (1985). *Varieties of Sexual Experience: An Anthropological Perspective on Human Sexuality.* New Haven, CT: HRAF Press.

Furstenberg, F. F., Jr. (1988). "Child Care after Divorce and Remarriage." In E. M. Hetherington and J. D. Arasteh (eds.). *Impact of Divorce, Single Parenting, and Stepparenting on Children* (pp. 245–261). Hillsdale, NJ: Lawrence Erlbaum Associates.

Furstenberg, F. P. Jr. (1990). "Divorce and the American Family." *Annual Review of Sociology* 16. 379–403.

Furstenberg, F. F. Jr. and Nord. C. W. (1985). "Parenting Apart: Patterns of Childbearing after Marital Disruption." *Journal of Marriage and the Family* 47 (4), 893–905.

Furstenberg, F. F. Jr., Nord, C. W., Peterson, J. L., and Zill, N. (1983). "The Life Course of Children of Divorce: Marital Disruption and Parental Contact." *American Sociological Review* 48 (2), 656–658.

Gaulin, S.J.C. and Schlegel. A. (1980). "Paternal Confidence and Paternal Investment: A Cross-Cultural Test of a Sociobiological Hypothesis." *Ethology and Sociobiology* 1, 301–309.

Giles-Sims, J. (1984). "The Stepparent Role: Expectations, Behavior and Sanctions." *Journal of Family Issues* 5, 116–130.

Giles-Sims, J. and Crosbie-Burnett, M. (1989). "Stepfamily Research: Implications for Policy, Clinical Interventions, and Further Research." *Family Relations* 38 (1), 19–23.

Glendon, M. A. (1989). *The Transformation of Family Law.* Chicago: University of Chicago Press.

Glick, P. C. (1989). "Remarried Families, Stepfamilies, and Stepchildren: A Brief Demographic Profile." *Family Relations* 38 (1), 24–27.

Goldsmith, T. H. (1991). *The Biological Roots of Human Nature*. New York: Oxford University Press.

Goode, W. J. (1970). *World Revolution and Family Patterns*. New York: The Free Press.

Goode, W. J. (1993). *World Changes in Divorce Patterns*. New Haven, CT: Yale University Press.

Gordon, M. (1989). "The Family Environment of Sexual Abuse: A Comparison of Natal and Stepfather Abuse." *Child Abuse and Neglect* 13, 121–130.

Hallpike, C. R. (1986). *The Principles of Social Evolution*. Oxford: Clarendon.

Hamilton, W. D. (1964). "The Genetic Evolution of Social Behavior I, II." *Journal of Theoretical Biology* 7, 7–52.

Hamilton, III, W. J. (1984). "Significance of Paternal Investment by Primates to the Evolution of Adult Male-Female Associations." In D. M. Taub (ed.). *Primate Paternalism* (pp. 309–335). New York: Van Nostrand.

Heaton, T. B. (1990). "Marital Stability Throughout the Child-Rearing Years." *Demography* 27 (1), 55–63.

Hetherington, E. M. (1987). "Family Relations Six Years after Divorce." In K. Pasley and M. Ihinger-Tollman (eds.). *Remarriage and Stepparenting Today: Current Research and Theory* (pp. 185–205). New York: Guilford.

Hetherington, E. M. and Jodl, K. M. (1994). "Stepfamilies as Settings for Child Development." In A. Booth and J. Dunn (eds.). *Stepfamilies: Who Benefits? Who Does Not?* (pp. 55-79). Hillsdale, NJ: Lawrence Erlbaum.

Hetherington, E. M., Stanley-Hagen, M., and Anderson, E. L (1989). "Marital Transitions: A Child's Perspective." *American Psychologist* 4 (2), 303–312.

Hernandez, D. J. (1993). *America's Children*. New York: Russell Sage Foundation.

Hewlett, S. A. (1991). *When the Bough Breaks: The Cost of Neglecting Our Children*. New York: Basic Books.

Hinde, R. A. (1987). *Individuals, Relationships and Culture: Links between Ethology and the Social Sciences*. New York: Cambridge University Press.

Ihinger-Tallman, M. (1988). "Research on Stepfamilies." *Annual Review of Sociology* 14, 25–48.

Jacob, H. (1988). *Silent Revolution: The Transformation of Divorce Law in the United States*. Chicago: University of Chicago Press.

Johansson, S. R. (1987). "Neglect, Abuse, and Avoidable Death: Parental Investment and the Mortality of Infants and Children in the European Tradition." In R. J. Gelles and J. B. Lancaster (eds.). *Child Abuse and Neglect: Biosocial Dimensions* (pp. 57–93). New York: Aldine de Gruyter.

Kertzer, D. I. (1991). "Household History and Sociological Theory." *Annual Review of Sociology* 17, 155–179.

Kiernan, K. E. (1992). "The Impact of Family Disruption in Childhood on Transitions Made in Young Adult Life." *Population Studies* 46, 213–234.

Lancaster, J. B. and Langer, C. S. (1987). "The Watershed: Change in Parental-Investment and Family Formation Strategies in the Course of Human Evolution." In J. B. Lancaster, J. Altmann, A. S. Rossi, and L. R. Sherrod (Eeds.). *Parenting Across the Life Span: Biosocial Dimensions* (pp. 187–205). New York: Aldine de Gruyter.

Larson, J. (1992, January). "Understanding Stepfamilies." *American Demographics*, 36-40.

Laslett, P. (1977). *Family Life and Illicit Love in Earlier Generations*. New York: Cambridge University Press.

Leakey, R. and Lewin, R. (1992). *Origins Reconsidered*. New York: Doubleday.

Lee, G. R. and Whitbeck, L. B. (1990). "Economic Systems and Rates of Polygyny." *Journal of Comparative Family Studies* 21 (1), 13–24.

Lenski, G., Lenski, J., and Nolan, P. (1991). *Human Societies* (6th ed.). New York: McGraw-Hill.

Lindholm, B. W. and Touliatos, J. (1980). "The Psychological Adjustment of Adopted and Nonadopted Children." *Psychological Reports* 46 (1), 307–310.

Louv, R. (1990). *Childhood's Future*. Boston, MA: Houghton Mifflin.

Lovejoy, C. O. (1981). "The Origin of Man." *Science* 211 (4480), 341–350.

Macfarlane, A. (1986). *Marriage and Love in England 1300–1840*. New York: Basil Blackwell.

Maryanski, A. and Turner, J. H. (1993). *The Social Cage: Human Nature and the Evolution of Society*. Stanford. CA: Stanford University Press.

Mintz, S. and Kellogg, S. (1988). *Domestic Revolutions: A Social History of American Family Life*. New York: The Free Press.

Mock, D. W. and Fujioka, M. (1990). "Monogamy and Long-Term Pair Bonding in Vertebrates." *Trends in Ecology and Evolution* 5 (2), 39–43.

Modell, J., Furstenberg, F. F. Jr. and Strong, D. (1978). "The Timing of Marriage in the Transition to Adulthood: Continuity and Change, 1860–1975." *American Journal of Sociology* 84, S120–S150.

Moore, K. A. and Stief, T. M. (1989). *Changes in Marriage and Fertility Behavior: Behavior versus Attitudes of Young Adults*. Washington, DC: Child Trends.

Morgan, S. P., Lye, D., and Condran, G. (1988). "Sons, Daughters, and the Risk of Marital Disruption." *American Journal of Sociology* 94 (1), 110–129.

Mott, F. L. (1990). "When is a Father Really Gone? Paternal-Child Contact in Father Absent Homes." *Demography* 27 (4), 499–517.

Moynihan, D. P. (1986). *Family and Nation*. San Diego, CA: Harcourt Brace.

National Commission on America's Urban Families (1993). *Families First*. Washington, DC: U.S. Government Printing Office.

Orians, G. H. (1980). "Habitat Selection: General Theory and Application to Human Behavior." In J. S. Lockard (ed.). *The Evolution of Human Social Behavior*. New York: Elsevier.

Peck, J. R. and Feldman, M. W. (1988). "Kin Selection and the Evolution of Monogamy." *Science* 240, 1672–1674.

Phillips, R. (1989). *Putting Asunder: A History of Divorce in Western Society*. Cambridge: Cambridge University Press.

Popenoe, D. (1992). "Fostering the New Familism: A Goal for America." *The Responsive Community* 2 (4), 31–39.

Popenoe, D. (1993). "American Family Decline, 1960–1990: A Review and Appraisal." *Journal of Marriage and the Family* 55 (3), 527–542.

Popenoe, D. (1994). "The Family Condition of America: Cultural Change and Public Policy." In H. Aaron, T. Mann, and T. Taylor (eds.). *Values and Public Policy* (pp. 81–112). Washington, DC: Brookings Institution.

Preston, S. (1984). "Children and the Elderly: Divergent Paths for America's Dependents." *Demography* 21, 435–457.

Roussel, L. (1989). *La Famille Incertaine*. Paris: Editions Odile Jacob.

Russell, D.E.H. (1983). "The Incidence and Prevalence of Intrafamilial and Extrafamilial Sexual Abuse of Female Children." *Child Abuse and Neglect* 7, 133–146.

Russell, D.E.H. (1984). "The Prevalence and Seriousness of Incestuous Abuse: Stepfathers vs. Biological Fathers." *Child Abuse and Neglect* 8, 15–22.

Rutman, D. B. and Rutman, A. H. (1984). *A Place in Time: Middlesex County, Virginia. 1650–1750*. New York: Norton.

Scott, J. P. (1989). *The Evolution of Social Systems*. New York: Gordon & Breach.

Seltzer, J. A. and Bianchi, S. M. (1988). "Children's Contact with Absent Parents." *Journal of Marriage and the Family* 50, 663–677.

"Shuttle Diplomacy." (1993, July/August). *Psychology Today*, p. 15.

Smith, M. S. (1988). "Research in Developmental Sociobiology: Parenting and Family Behavior." In K. B. MacDonald (ed.). *Sociobiological Perspectives on Human Development* (pp. 271–292). New York: Springer-Verlag.

Stone, L. (1977). *The Family, Sex and Marriage in England 1500–1800*. New York: Harper & Row.

Sugarman, S. D. and Kay, H. H. (eds.). (1990). *Divorce Reform at the Crossroads*. New Haven, CT: Yale University Press.

Symons, D. (1985). "Darwinism and Contemporary Marriage." In K. Davis (ed.). *Contemporary Marriage* (pp. 133–155). New York: Russell Sage Foundation.

Thomson, E., McLanahan, S. S., and Curtin, R. B. (1992). "Family Structure, Gender, and Parental Socialization." *Journal of Marriage and the Family* 54 (2), 368–378.

Thornton, A. (1989). "Changing Attitudes toward Family Issues in the United States." *Journal of Marriage and the Family* 51 (4), 873–893.

Tiger, L. and Fox, R. (1971). *The Imperial Animal*. New York: Holt, Rinehart & Winston.

Timms, D.W.G. (1991). *Family Structure in Childhood and Mental Health in Adolescence* (Project Metropolitan Research Report No. 32). Stockholm, Sweden: University of Stockholm.

Trivers, R. L. (1972). "Parental Investment and Sexual Selection." In B. Campbell (ed). *Sexual Selection and the Descent of Man* (pp. 136–179). Chicago: Aldine Atherton.

Uhlenberg, P. (1983). "Death and the Family." In M. Gordon (ed.). *The American Family in Historical Perspective* (pp. 169-178). New York: St. Martin's Press.

U.S. Bureau of the Census (1992). "Marriage, Divorce and Remarriage in the 1990s." In *Current Population Reports* (pp. 23-180). Washington, DC: U.S. Government Printing Office.

van den Berghe, P. L. (1988). "The Family and the Biological Base of Human Sociality." In E. E. Filsinger (ed.). *Biosocial Perspectives on the Family* (pp. 39-60). Newbury Park, CA: Sage.

van den Berghe, P. L. (1990). *Human Family Systems: An Evolutionary View*. Prospect Heights, OH: Waveland Press.

Waite, L. and Lillard, L. A. (1991). "Children and Marital Disruption." *American Journal of Sociology* 96 (4), 930–953.

Watkins, S. C., Menken, J. A., and Bongaarts, J. (1987). "Demographic Foundations of Family Change." *American Sociological Review* 52 (3), 346–358.

White, L. (1994). "Stepfamilies Over the Life Course: Social Support." In A. Booth and J. Dunn (eds.). *Stepfamilies: Who Benefits? Who Does Not?* (pp. 109–137). Hillsdale, NJ: Lawrence Erlbaum.

White, L. K. and Booth, A. (1985). "The Quality and Stability of Remarriages: The Role of Stepchildren." *American Sociological Review* 50 (5), 689–698.

Whyte, M. K. (1978). *The Status of Women in Preindustrial Societies*. Princeton, NJ: Princeton University Press.

Wilson, M. I., Daly, M., and Weghorst, S. J. (1980). "Household Composition and the Risk of Child Abuse and Neglect." *Biosocial Science* 12, 333–340.

Wilson, M. I. and Daly, M. (1987). "Risk of Maltreatment of Children Living with Stepparents." In R. L. Gelles and J. B. Lancaster (eds.). *Child Abuse and Neglect: Biosocial Dimensions* (pp. 215-232). New York: Aldine de Gruyter.

Yankelovich, D. (1994). "How Changes in the Economy are Reshaping American Values." In H. J. Aaron, T. Mann, and T. Taylor (eds.). *Values and Public Policy* (pp. 16–53). Washington, DC: Brookings Institution.

Zill, N. (1988). "Behavior, Achievement, and Health Problems among Children in Stepfamilies: Findings from a National Survey of Child Health." In E. M. Hetherington and J. D. Arasteh (eds.). *Impact of Divorce, Single Parenting, and Stepparenting on Children* (pp. 325–368). Hillsdale, NJ: Lawrence Erlbaum.

Zill, N. and Schoenborn, C. A. (1990, November). *Developmental, Learning, and Emotional Problems: Health of Our Nation's Children. United States. 1988 Advance Data* (Report N. 120). Washington, DC: National Center for Health Statistics.

6

A World Without Fathers

The decline of fatherhood is one of the most basic, unexpected, and extraordinary social trends of our time. Its dimensions can be captured in a single statistic: in just three decades, between 1960 and 1990, the percentage of children living apart from their biological fathers more than doubled, from 17 percent to 36 percent. By the turn of the century, nearly 50 percent of American children may be going to sleep each evening without being able to say goodnight to their dads.

No one predicted this trend, few researchers or government agencies have monitored it, and it is not widely discussed, even today. But the decline of fatherhood is a major force behind many of the most disturbing problems that plague American society: crime and delinquency; premature sexuality and out-of-wedlock births to teenagers; deteriorating educational achievement; depression, substance abuse, and alienation among adolescents; and the growing number of women and children in poverty.

The current generation of children and youth may be the first in our nation's history to be less well off—psychologically, socially, economically, and morally—than their parents were at the same age. The United States, observes Senator Daniel Patrick Moynihan (D-NY), "may be the first society in history in which children are distinctly worse off than adults."

Even as this calamity unfolds, our cultural view of fatherhood itself is changing. Few people doubt the fundamental importance of mothers. But fathers? More and more, the question of whether fathers are really necessary is being raised. Many would answer no, or maybe not. And to the degree that fathers are still thought necessary, fatherhood is said by many to be merely a social role that others can play: mothers, partners, stepfathers, uncles and aunts, grandparents. Perhaps the script can even be rewritten and the role changed—or dropped.

There was a time in the past when fatherlessness was far more common than it is today, but death was to blame, not divorce, desertion, and out-of-wedlock births. In early seventeenth-century Virginia, only an estimated 31 percent of white children reached age eighteen with both parents still alive. That percentage climbed to 50 percent by the early eighteenth century, to 72 percent by the turn of the twentieth century, and close to its current level by 1940. Today, well over 90 percent of America's youngsters reach eighteen with two living parents. Almost all of today's fatherless children have fathers who are alive, well, and perfectly capable of shouldering the responsibilities of fatherhood. Who would ever have thought that so many men would choose to relinquish them?

Not so long ago, the change in the cause of fatherlessness was dismissed as irrelevant in many quarters, including among social scientists. Children, it was said, are merely losing their parents in a different way than they used to. You don't hear that very much anymore. A surprising finding of recent social science research is that it is decidedly worse for a child to lose a father in the modern, voluntary way than through death. The children of divorced and never-married mothers are less successful in life by almost every measure than the children of widowed mothers. The replacement of death by divorce as the prime cause of fatherlessness, then, is a monumental setback in the history of childhood.

Until the 1960s, the falling death rate and the rising divorce rate neutralized each other. In 1900, the percentage of all American children living in single-parent families was 8.5 percent. By 1960, it had increased to just 9.1 percent. Virtually no one during those years was writing or thinking about family breakdown, disintegration, or decline.

Indeed, what is most significant about the changing family demography of the first six decades of the twentieth century is this: because the death rate was dropping faster than the divorce rate was rising, by 1960 more children were living with both of their natural parents than at any other time in world history. The figure was close to 80 percent for the generation born in the late 1940s and early 1950s.

But then the decline in the death rate slowed, and the divorce rate skyrocketed. "The scale of marital breakdowns in the West since 1960 has no historical precedent that I know of, and seems unique," says Lawrence Stone, the noted Princeton University family historian. "There has been nothing like it for the last 2,000 years, and probably longer."

Consider what has happened to children. Most estimates are that only about 50 percent of the children born during the 1970-84 "baby bust" period will still live with their natural parents by age seventeen—a staggering drop from nearly 80 percent.

One estimate paints the current scene in even starker terms and also points up the enormous difference that exists between whites and blacks. By age seventeen, white children born between 1950 and 1954 had spent 8 percent of their lives with only one parent; black children had spent 22 percent. But among those born in 1980, by one estimate, white children will spend 31 percent of their childhood years with one parent and black children 59 percent.

In theory, divorce need not mean disconnection. In reality, it often does. One large survey in the late 1980s found that about one in five divorced fathers had not seen his children in the past year, and less than half of divorced fathers saw their children more than several times a year. A 1981 survey of adolescents who were living apart from their fathers found that 52 percent had not seen them at all in more than a year; only 16 percent saw their fathers as often as once a week. Moreover, the survey showed fathers' contact with their children dropping off sharply with the passage of time after the marital breakup.

The picture grows worse. Just as divorce has overtaken death as the leading cause of fatherlessness, out-of-wedlock births are expected to surpass divorce later in the 1990s. They accounted for 30 percent of all births by 1991; by the turn of the century they may account for 40 percent of the total (and 80 percent of minority births). And there is substantial evidence that having an unmarried father is even worse for a child than having a divorced father.

Across time and cultures, fathers have always been considered essential—and not just for their sperm. Indeed, until today, no known society ever thought of fathers as potentially unnecessary. Marriage and the nuclear family—mother, father, and children—are the most universal social institutions in existence. In no society has the birth of children out of wedlock been the cultural norm. To the contrary, a concern for the legitimacy of children is nearly universal.

At the same time, being a father is universally problematic for men. While mothers the world over bear and nurture their young with an intrinsic acknowledgment and, most commonly, acceptance of their role, the process of taking on the role of father is often filled with conflict and doubt. The source of this sex-role difference can be plainly stated. Men are not biologically as attuned to being committed fathers as women are to being committed mothers. The evolutionary logic is clear. Women, who can bear only a limited number of children, have a great incentive to invest their energy in rearing children, while men, who can father many offspring, do not. Left culturally unregulated, men's sexual behavior can be promiscuous, their paternity casual, their commitment to families weak. This is not to say that the role of father is foreign to male nature. Far from it. Evolutionary scientists tell us that the development of the fathering capacity and high paternal investments in offspring—features not common among our primate relatives—have been sources of enormous evolutionary advantage for human beings.

In recognition of the fatherhood problem, human cultures have used sanctions to bind men to their children, and of course the institution of marriage has been culture's chief vehicle. Marriage is society's way of signaling that the community approves and encourages sexual intercourse and the birth of children, and that the long-term relationship of the parents is socially important. Margaret Mead once said, with the fatherhood problem very much in mind, that there is no society in the world where men will stay married for very long unless culturally required to do so. Our experience in late twentieth-century

America shows how right she was. The results for children have been devastating.

In my many years as a sociologist, I have found few other bodies of evidence that lean so much in one direction as this one: on the whole, two parents—a father and a mother—are better for a child than one parent. There are, to be sure, many factors that complicate this simple proposition. We all know of a two-parent family that is truly dysfunctional—the proverbial family from hell. A child can certainly be raised to a fulfilling adulthood by one loving parent who is wholly devoted to the child's well being. But such exceptions do not invalidate the rule any more than the fact that some three-pack-a-day smokers live to a ripe old age casts doubt on the dangers of cigarettes.

The collapse of children's well being in the United States has reached breathtaking proportions. Juvenile violent crime has increased six-fold, from 16,000 arrests in 1960 to 96,000 in 1992, a period in which the total number of young people in the population remained relatively stable. Reports of child neglect and abuse have quintupled since 1976, when data were first collected. Eating disorders and rates of depression have soared among adolescent girls. Teen suicide has tripled. Alcohol and drug abuse among teenagers, although it has leveled off in recent years, continues at a very high rate. Scholastic Aptitude Test scores have declined nearly 80 points, and most of the decline cannot be accounted for by the increased academic diversity of students taking the test. Poverty has shifted from the elderly to the young. Of all the nation's poor today, 38 percent are children.

One can think of many explanations for these unhappy developments: the growth of commercialism and consumerism, the influence of television and the mass media, the decline of religion, the widespread availability of guns and addictive drugs, and the decay of social order and neighborhood relationships. None of these causes should be dismissed. But the evidence is now strong that the absence of fathers from the lives of children is one of the most important causes.

The most tangible and immediate consequence of fatherlessness for children is the loss of economic resources. By the best recent estimates, the income of the household in which a child remains after a divorce instantly declines by about 21 percent per capita on average, while expenses tend to go up. Over time, the economic situation for the child often deteriorates further. The mother usually earns considerably less than the father, and children cannot rely on their fathers to pay much in the way of child support. About half of previously married mothers receive no child support, and for those who do receive it, both the reliability and the amount of the payment drop over time.

Child poverty, once endemic in America, reached a historic low point of 14 percent in 1969 and remained relatively stable through the 1970s. Since then, it has been inching back up. Today more than 20 percent of the nation's children (and 25 percent of infants and toddlers) are growing up in poverty.

The loss of fathers' income is the most important cause of this alarming change. By one estimate, 51 percent of the increase in child poverty observed during the 1980s (65 percent for blacks) can be attributed to changes in family structure. Indeed, much of the income differential between whites and blacks today, perhaps as much as two-thirds, can be attributed to the differences in family structure. Not for nothing is it said that marriage is the best antipoverty program of all. The proliferation of mother-headed families now constitutes something of a national economic emergency. About a quarter of all family groups with children—more than half of all black family groups—are headed by mothers, which is almost double the 11.5 percent figure in 1970. No other group is so poor, and none stays poor longer. Poverty afflicts nearly one out of every two of these families, but fewer than one in ten married-couple families. Mother-headed families account for 94 percent of the current caseload for Aid to Families with Dependent Children (AFDC).

Things are likely to get worse before they get better. Poverty is much more severe among unmarried mothers—the fastest-growing segment of the poverty population—than among divorced mothers.

Economic difficulties—which translate into poorer schooling and other handicaps—ultimately account for a considerable share of the disadvantages found among fatherless children. By the best recent estimates, however, economic status accounts for no more than half of these disadvantages. The latest and most authoritative review of this research is *Growing Up with a Single Parent* (1994), by sociologists Sara McLanahan of Princeton University and Gary Sandefur of the University of Wisconsin. Reviewing five large-scale social surveys and other evidence (and after adjusting for many income-related factors), they concluded: "Children who grow up with only one of their biological parents (nearly always the mother)...are twice as likely to drop out of high school, 2.5 times as likely to become teen mothers, and 1.4 times as likely to be idle—out of school and out of work—as children who grow up with both parents."

Such conclusions will no longer come as a surprise to many Americans. Yet it was not so long ago that the divorce revolution was given a strangely positive cast in American popular culture. If breaking up is better for parents, it was thought, it cannot be all that bad for children. What keeps parents happy should also keep children happy.

In part, this was a convenient, guilt-retarding rationalization for parents who were breaking up. But it was supported by many social scientists as well. In the 1970s, at the height of the divorce revolution, many social scientists were remarkably sanguine about the effects of fatherlessness. Typical was the work of Elizabeth Herzog and Cecelia Sudia. In a 1973 report written for the U.S. Children's Bureau entitled "Children in Fatherless Families," they concluded from a review of existing studies that the "evidence concerning [juvenile delinquency, school achievement, and masculine identity] is neither clear enough nor firm enough to demonstrate beyond doubt whether fatherless boys are or are not overrepresented" in problem groups.

Herzog and Sudia went so far as to discount any negative effects of divorce and fatherlessness. They claimed that discord and conflict in the home prior to a divorce are more detrimental than a father's absence after the divorce and concluded that, therefore, "one is forced to prefer a 'good' one-parent [read: fatherless] home for a child." From this sort of lesser-of-two-evils conclusion, it was but a short step in the minds of some social scientists to the view that divorce is for the best for parents and children alike.

What do fathers do? Much of what they contribute to the growth of their children, of course, is simply the result of being a second adult in the home. Bringing up children is demanding, stressful, and often exhausting. Two adults can not only support and spell each other; they can offset each other's deficiencies and build on each other's strengths.

Beyond being merely a second adult or third party, fathers—men—bring an array of unique and irreplaceable qualities that women do not ordinarily bring. Some of these are familiar, if sometimes overlooked or taken for granted. The father as protector, for example, has by no means outlived his usefulness. His importance as a role model has become a familiar idea. Teenage boys without fathers are notoriously prone to trouble. The pathway to adulthood for daughters is somewhat easier, but they still must learn from their fathers, as they cannot from their mothers, how to relate to men. They learn from their fathers about heterosexual trust, intimacy, and difference. They learn to appreciate their own femininity from the one male who is most special in their lives (assuming that they love and respect their fathers). Most important, through loving and being loved by their fathers, they learn that they are love-worthy.

Recent research has given us much deeper—and more surprising—insights into the father's role in childrearing. It shows that in almost all of their interactions with children, fathers do things a little differently from mothers. What fathers do—their special parenting style—is not only highly complementary to what mothers do but is by all indications important in its own right for optimum childrearing.

For example, an often-overlooked dimension of fathering is play. From their children's birth through adolescence, fathers tend to emphasize play more than caretaking. This may be troubling to egalitarian feminists, and it would indeed be wise for most fathers to spend more time in caretaking. Yet the father's style of play seems to have unusual significance. It is likely to be both physically stimulating and exciting. With older children it involves more physical games and teamwork requiring the competitive testing of physical and mental skills. It frequently resembles an apprenticeship or teaching relationship: come on, let me show you how.

Mothers tend to spend more time playing with their children, but theirs is a different kind of play. Mothers' play tends to take place more at the child's level. Mothers provide the child with the opportunity to direct the play, to be in charge, to proceed at the child's own pace. Kids, at least in the early years, seem to prefer to play with daddy. In one study of two-and-a-half-year-olds who were given a choice, more than two-thirds chose to play with their father.

The way fathers play has effects on everything from the management of emotions to intelligence and academic achievement. It is particularly important in promoting the essential virtue of self-control. According to one expert, "children who rough house with their fathers...usually quickly learn that biting, kicking, and other forms of physical violence are not acceptable." They learn when enough is enough and when to "shut it down."

A committee assembled by the Board on Children and Families of the National Research Council concluded that children "learn critical lessons about how to recognize and deal with highly charged emotions in the context of playing with their fathers. Fathers, in effect, give children practice in regulating their own emotions and recognizing others' emotional clues." The findings of a study of convicted murderers in Texas are probably not the product of coincidence: 90 percent of them either did not play as children or played abnormally.

At play and in other realms, fathers tend to stress competition, challenge, initiative, risk taking, and independence. Mothers, as caretakers, stress emotional security and personal safety. On the playground, fathers will try to get the child to swing ever higher, higher than the person on the next swing, while mothers will be cautious, worrying about an accident. It's sometimes said that fathers express more concern for the child's longer-term development, while mothers focus on the child's immediate well being (which, of course, in its own way has everything to do with a child's long-term well being). What is clear is that children have dual needs that must be met. Becoming a mature and competent adult involves the integration of two often-contradictory human desires: for communion, or the feeling of being included, connected, and related, and for agency, which entails independence, individuality, and self-fulfillment. One without the other is a denuded and impaired humanity, an incomplete realization of human potential.

For many couples, to be sure, these functions are not rigidly divided along standard female-male lines. There may even be a role reversal in some cases, with men largely assuming the female style and women the male style. But these are exceptions that prove the rule. Gender-differentiated parenting is of such importance that in childrearing by homosexual couples, either gay or lesbian, one partner commonly fills the male-instrumental role while the other fills the female-expressive role.

It is ironic, however, that in our public discussion of fathering, it is seldom acknowledged that fathers have a distinctive role to play. Indeed, it's far more often said that fathers should be more like mothers (and that men generally should be more like women—less aggressive, less competitive). While such things may be said with the best of intentions, the effects are perverse. After all, if fathering is no different from mothering, males can easily be replaced in the home by women. It might even seem better to do so. Already viewed as a burden and obstacle to self-fulfillment, fatherhood thus comes to seem superfluous and unnecessary as well.

We know, however, that fathers—and fatherlessness—have surprising impacts on children. Fathers' involvement seems to be linked to improved quantitative and verbal skills, improved problem-solving ability, and higher academic achievement. Several studies have found that the presence of the father is one of the determinants of girls' proficiency in mathematics. And one pioneering study found that the amount of time fathers spent reading was a strong predictor of their daughters' verbal ability.

For sons, who can more directly follow their fathers' example, the results have been even more striking. A number of studies have uncovered a strong relationship between father involvement and the quantitative and mathematical abilities of their sons. Other studies have found a relationship between paternal nurturing and boys' verbal intelligence.

How fathers produce these intellectual benefits is not yet clear. No doubt it is partly a matter of the time and money a man brings to his family. But it is probably also related to the unique mental and behavioral qualities of men: the male sense of play, reasoning, challenge, and problem solving, and the traditional male association with achievement and occupational advancement.

Men also have a vital role to play in promoting cooperation and other "soft" virtues. We don't often think of fathers in connection with the teaching of empathy, but involved fathers, it turns out, may be of special importance for the development of this important character trait, essential to an ordered society of law-abiding, cooperative, and compassionate adults. Examining the results of a twenty-six-year longitudinal study, a trio of researchers reached a "quite astonishing" conclusion: the most important childhood factor of all in developing empathy is paternal involvement in childcare. Fathers who spent time alone with their children more than twice a week, giving meals, baths, and other basic care, reared the most compassionate adults.

Again, it is not yet clear why fathers are so important in instilling this quality. Perhaps merely by being with their children they provide a model for compassion. Perhaps it has to do with their style of play or mode of reasoning. Perhaps it is somehow related to the fact that fathers typically are the family's main arbiter with the outside world. Or perhaps it is because mothers who receive help from their mates have more time and energy to cultivate the soft virtues. Whatever the reason, it is hard to think of a more important contribution that fathers can make to their children.

Fatherlessness is directly implicated in many of our most grievous social ills. Of all the negative consequences, juvenile delinquency and violence probably loom largest in the public mind. Reported violent crime has soared

550 percent since 1960, and juveniles have the fastest-growing crime rate. Arrests of juveniles for murder, for example, rose 128 percent between 1983 and 1992.

Many people intuitively believe that fatherlessness is related to delinquency and violence, and the weight of research evidence supports this belief. Having a father at home is no guarantee that a youngster won't commit a crime, but it appears to be an excellent form of prevention. Sixty percent of America's rapists, 72 percent of its adolescent murderers, and 70 percent of its long-term prison inmates come from fatherless homes. Fathers are important to their sons as role models. They are important for maintaining authority and discipline. And they are important in helping their sons to develop both self-control and feelings of empathy toward others.

Unfortunately, the die for the near future has already been cast. The teenage population is expected to grow in the next decade by as much as 20 percent—even more for minority teenagers—as the children of the baby boomers grow up. Many of these restless youngsters will come of age without fathers. Criminologist James Fox warns of "a tremendous crime wave…in the next 10 years" fueled by what he calls "the young and the ruthless." In 1993, for example, there were 3,647 teenage killers; by 2005, Fox expects there will be 6,000.

The twin to the nightmare specter of too many little boys with guns is too many little girls with babies. Fatherlessness is again a major contributing factor.

During the past three decades, there has been a dramatic increase in the percentage of teenagers engaging in sexual activity. In the mid-1950s, only 27 percent of girls had sexual intercourse by age eighteen; in 1988, 56 percent of such girls—including fully a quarter of fifteen-year-olds—had become sexually active.

About one million teen pregnancies occur in the United States each year, giving this nation the highest teen pregnancy rate in the industrialized world. Twelve percent of all women aged fifteen to nineteen (21 percent of those who have had sexual intercourse) become pregnant each year. Fifty percent of these pregnancies end in births, 35 percent end in abortions, and about 14 percent end in miscarriages. Of all children born out of wedlock, most will grow up fatherless in single-parent households.

Again, there are many factors involved in this trend, including everything from the earlier age at which girls now reach sexual maturity to the weakening of cultural norms. Yet as important as any of these, if not more so, is fatherlessness. The research lends strong support to the common-sense proposition that fathers play a key role in the development of their daughters' sexual behavior. Analyzing data from the National Child Development Study, a major British longitudinal study that followed the lives of thousands of children born in 1958, researcher Kathleen Kiernan found that young women with divorced or separated parents are more likely to form unions in their teens, to have a child at an early age, and to bear children outside marriage. Kiernan highlighted one important characteristic that opens the door to other problems: girls from single-parent families are more likely to leave home at an earlier age than other girls.

The presence of a surrogate father does not help. Indeed, one of the best-established findings concerning stepfamilies is that the children—particularly girls—leave such households at an earlier age than do kids in single-parent households or in two-parent households.

On the face of it, there would seem to be at least one potentially positive side to fatherlessness: without a man around the house, the incidence of child abuse might be expected to drop. Unfortunately, quite the opposite has happened.

According to recent surveys, some 20 percent of adult women and 5 to 10 percent of adult men have experienced sexual abuse at some time during their childhood. Physical abuse of children is more common still, being about twice as prevalent as sexual abuse. Most evidence points to a real increase in both major forms of child abuse in recent decades.

One of the greatest risk factors in child abuse, found by virtually every investigation that has ever been conducted, is family disruption, especially living in a female-headed, single-parent household. In 1981, 43 percent of children who were reported to have been abused were living in such households.

Sexual abuse is one form of child abuse. Most of the victims (80 percent of the cases reported to child protection authorities) are girls, and most of the perpetrators are men. But less than half of the offenders are family members and close relatives, and only 10 to 30 percent are strangers. The remainder are acquaintances of various kinds, including neighbors, peers, and mothers' boyfriends.

Why does living in a fatherless household pose such hazards for children? Two explanations are usually given: the children receive less supervision and protection and they are also more emotionally deprived, which leaves them vulnerable to sexual abusers, who commonly entrap children by offering affection, attention, and friendship. Fatherlessness is closely involved in both of these explanations. Even a diligent absent father can't supervise or protect his children the way a live-in father can. Nor is he likely to have the kind of relationship with his daughter that is usually needed to give her a foundation of emotional security and a model for nonsexual relationships with men.

A special problem for children living with single mothers is that these mothers rely heavily on childcare providers who are not relatives. The danger is greatest, of course, when the childcare provider is male. One study of sexual abuse in Iowa found that male sitters were responsible for almost five times as much sexual abuse as female sitters, even though they provided only a very small overall proportion of childcare.

By all accounts, mothers' boyfriends are another serious problem, although we lack hard data to prove it. Certainly, such predatory men are much in the news. One often hears, for example, of men who take up with a woman solely because they desire the possibility of sexual access to her daughter, and of women who urge their boyfriends to play daddy with their children, thus providing the boyfriend with an ease of access that can lead to inappropriate behavior.

Among sexual abusers who are blood relatives, only a small fraction are fathers. The great majority are uncles, grandfathers, brothers and stepbrothers, and male cousins. When a father is the perpetrator, he is typically not the natural father but a surrogate father. In a study conducted in San Francisco of 930 adult women, for example, it was found that daughters are at least seven times more likely to be abused by their stepfathers than by their biological fathers. Approximately one out of every six women who had a stepfather as a principal figure in her childhood years was sexually abused by him, compared to only one out of every forty women who had a biological father.

Some biological fathers certainly are sexually abusive toward their daughters, however, and their numbers may be increasing. Paradoxically, this too may be related to growing fatherlessness, or at least to the circumstances that surround family breakup.

Compared to abusing stepfathers, for example, biological fathers gone bad are more likely to live hardscrabble lives, with very bad marriages, alcohol and drug problems, and poverty. Abuse is also more common in single-parent families in which the father is the single parent, and such families are growing more numerous. Third, fathers who are not in the home much and are less involved in nurturing activities are more likely to abuse their children. Strong attachment and bonding between father and daughter in infancy may be a critical ingredient in preventing later child abuse, but with so many children born out of wedlock, early bonding is something that fewer natural fathers will experience.

Still, it remains something of a puzzle why a natural father would break the universal incest taboo. There is evidence from preindustrial societies that the less confident a father is that a daughter is really his offspring, the more likely he is to have an incestuous relationship with her. Societies in which fathers have low "paternity confidence," a term used by evolutionary psychologists, tend also to be societies with a higher incidence of incestuous relationships. ("Maternity is a fact," observed the Roman jurist Baius, "paternity is a matter of opinion.") Alas, we don't need a statistical test to believe that paternity confidence must be dropping in America in the wake of the sexual revolution.

One important difference between physical abuse of children and sexual abuse is somewhat surprising: women are often the abusers. Yet fatherlessness is still an important factor. A mother is much more likely to be abusive and to allow others to mistreat her child when she does not have the support of an actively involved father. Indeed, the majority of preadolescent victims of physical abuse (and especially of more severe forms of abuse) are boys, who are generally harder to control.

Probably the most serious threat to children in single-parent families is the mother's boyfriend. In a study of physical abuse in single-mother households, education expert Leslie Margolin found that 64 percent of the nonparental abuse was committed by such men. (Nonrelatives such as daycare providers and adolescent babysitters were a distant second, with 15 percent, followed by relatives.)

Why this tremendous overrepresentation of boyfriends? One explanation is drawn from evolutionary biology. These men are unrelated to the child, notes Margolin, and a caregiver's level of protection and solicitude toward a child is directly proportional to shared genetic heritage. And, as this theory predicts, other male nonrelatives were significantly more abusive than male relatives.

The domestic threat posed by unrelated adult males reappears tragically in stepparent households, one of America's fastest growing family forms. Many studies have found that a child is far more likely to be physically abused by a stepfather than by a natural father. One investigation, by evolutionary psychologists Margo Wilson and Martin Daly, found that preschoolers in the Canadian city of Hamilton living with one natural parent and one stepparent in 1993 were forty times more likely to become child-abuse statistics than children living with two natural parents.

Another group that has suffered in the new age of fatherlessness is, perhaps unexpectedly, women. In this new era, Gloria Steinem's oft-quoted quip that a woman without a man is like a fish without a bicycle no longer seems quite so funny. There is no doubt that many women get along very well without men in their lives and that having the wrong men in their lives can be disastrous. But just as it increases assaults on children, fatherlessness appears to generate more violence against women.

Such violence, especially family or domestic violence committed by intimates, has been common throughout history. Now that women enjoy more legal protections and are less likely to marry, one might suppose that such crimes would diminish. Instead, they have increased.

Partly this is a matter of arithmetic. More than two-thirds of violence (assault, robbery, and rape) against women is committed by unrelated acquaintances or strangers. As the number of unattached males in the population goes up, so does the incidence of violence toward women.

Or consider the fact that, of the violence towards women that is committed by intimates and other relatives, only 29 percent involves a current spouse, whereas 42 percent involves a close friend or partner and another 12 percent an ex-spouse. As current spouses are replaced by nonspouses and exes, violence towards women increases.

In fact, marriage appears to be a strong safety factor for women. A satisfactory marriage between sexually faithful partners, especially when they are raising their own biological children, engenders fewer risks for violence than probably any other circumstance in which a woman could find herself. Recent surveys of violent-crime victimization have found that only 12.6 of every 1,000 married women fall victim to violence, compared with 43.9 of every 1,000 never-married women and 66.5 of every 1,000 divorced or separated women.

Men, too, suffer grievously from the growth of fatherlessness. The world over, young and unattached males have always been a cause for social concern. They can be a danger to themselves and to society. Young unattached men tend to be more aggressive, violent, promiscuous, and prone to substance abuse; they are also more likely to die prematurely through disease, accidents, or self-neglect. They make up the majority of deviants, delinquents, criminals, killers, drug users, vice lords, and miscreants of every kind. Senator Moynihan put it succinctly when he warned that a society full of unattached males "asks for and gets chaos."

Family life—marriage and childrearing—is an extremely important civilizing force for men. It encourages them to develop those habits of character, including prudence, cooperativeness, honesty, trust, and self-sacrifice, that can lead to achievement as an economic provider. Marriage also focuses male sexual energy. Having children typically impresses on men the importance of setting a good example. Who hasn't heard at least one man personally testify that he gave up certain deviant or socially irresponsible patterns of life only when he married and had children?

The civilizing effect of being a father is highlighted by a path-breaking social improvement endeavor in Cleveland. In the inner-city Hough neighborhood, social worker Charles Ballard has been turning around the lives of young black men through his Institute for Responsible Fatherhood and Family Revitalization. Since 1982, using an intensive social-work approach that includes home visits, parenting programs, and group therapy sessions, he has reunited more than 2,000 absent, unwed fathers with their children.

The standard theory is that if you want inner-city men like these to be responsible fathers, you first must find them a job. But Ballard has stood this theory on its head. His approach is that you first must convince the young men of the importance of being a good father, and then they will be motivated to finish school and find work.

An independent evaluation of his approach showed that it really works. Only 12 percent of the young men had full-time work when they entered his program, but 62 percent later found such work, and another 12 percent found part-time jobs. Ninety-seven percent of the men he dealt with began providing financial support for their children, and 71 percent had no additional children out of wedlock.

Marriage by itself, even without the presence of children, is also a major civilizing force for men. No other institution save religion (and perhaps the military) places such moral demands on men. To be sure, there is a selection factor in marriage. Those men whom women would care to marry already have some of the civilized virtues. And those men who are morally beyond the pale have difficulty finding mates. Yet epidemiological studies and social surveys have shown that marriage has a civilizing effect independent of the selection factor. Marriage actually promotes health, competence, virtue, and personal well being. With the continued growth of fatherlessness, we can expect to see a nation of men who are at worst morally out of control and at best unhappy, unhealthy, and unfulfilled.

Just as cultural forms can be discarded, dismantled, and declared obsolete, so can they be reinvented. In order to restore marriage and reinstate fathers in the lives of their children, we are somehow going to have to undo the cultural shift of the last few decades towards radical individualism. We are going to have to re-embrace some cultural propositions or understandings that throughout history have been universally accepted but which today are unpopular, if not rejected outright.

Marriage must be reestablished as a strong social institution. The father's role must also be redefined in a way that neglects neither historical models nor the unique attributes of modern societies, the new roles for women, and the special qualities that men bring to childrearing.

Such changes are by no means impossible. Witness the transformations wrought by the civil rights, women's, and environmental movements, and even the campaigns to reduce smoking and drunk driving. What is necessary is for large numbers of adults, and especially our cultural and intellectual leaders, to agree on the importance of change.

There are many practical steps that can be taken. Employers, for example, can reduce the practice of uprooting and relocating married couples with children, provide generous parental leave, and experiment with more flexible forms of work. Religious leaders can reclaim moral ground from the culture of divorce and nonmarriage, resisting the temptation to equate things such as "committed relationships" with marriage. Marriage counselors, family therapists, and family-life educators can begin with a bias in favor of marriage, stressing the needs of the marriage at least as much as the needs of the client. As for the entertainment industry, pressure already is being brought to bear to curtail the glamorization of unwed motherhood, marital infidelity, alternative lifestyles, and sexual promiscuity.

What about divorce? Current laws send the message that marriage is not a socially important relationship that involves a legally binding commitment. We should consider a two-tier system of divorce law: marriages without minor children would be relatively easy to dissolve, but marriages with such children would be dissolvable only by mutual agreement or on grounds that clearly involve a wrong by one party against the other, such as desertion or physical abuse. Longer waiting periods for divorcing couples with children might also be called for, combined with some form of mandatory marriage counseling or marital education.

Because the causes of the decline of marriage and fatherhood lie mainly in the moral, behavioral, and even spiritual realms, the decline is mostly resistant to public policy and government cures. All of the western industrialized societies, regardless of governmental system and political persuasion, have been beset by the decline of family. The decline of marriage is almost as great in Sweden, with the West's most ambitious welfare state, as it is in the United States, the most laissez-faire of the industrialized nations.

Nevertheless, government policies do have some impact. While the statistical relationship of economic cycles to marriage and divorce is not particularly strong, for example, low wages, unemployment, and poverty have never been friendly to marriage. Government can do something about that. It can also remedy the decline in the value of the income tax exemption for dependent children and erase the tax code's "marriage penalty." As a society, moreover, we have decided, through a variety of government programs, to socialize much of the cost of growing old, but less of the cost of raising children. At the very least, we should strive for generational equity. But more than anything else, parents need time to be with their children, the kind of time that would be afforded by a more generous family leave policy.

We also should consider providing educational credits or vouchers to parents who leave the paid labor force to raise their young children. These parents are performing an important social service at the risk of damaging their long-run career prospects. Education subsidies, like those in the GI Bill of Rights, would reward parents by helping them resume their careers.

Government policies should be designed to favor married, childrearing couples. Some critics argue that the federal government should not involve itself in sensitive moral issues or risk stigmatizing alternative lifestyles. But recognizing such alternatives does not require treating them as equivalent to marriage. The government, moreover, regularly takes moral positions on a whole range of issues, such as the rights of women, income equality, and race relations. A position on the need for children to have two committed parents, a father and a mother, during their formative years is hardly a radical departure.

Today in America the social order is fraying badly. We seem, despite notable accomplishments in some areas, to be on a path of decline. The past three decades have seen steeply rising rates of crime, declining political and interpersonal trust, growing personal and corporate greed, deteriorating communities, and increasing confusion over moral issues. For most Americans, life has become more anxious, unsettled, and insecure.

In large part, this represents a failure of social values. People can no longer be counted on to conduct themselves according to the virtues of honesty, self-sacrifice, and personal responsibility. In our ever-growing pursuit of the self—self-expression, self-development, self-actualization, and self-fulfillment—we seem to have slipped off many of our larger social obligations.

At the heart of our discontent lies an erosion of personal relationships. People no longer trust others as they once did; they no longer feel the same sense of commitment and obligation to others. In part, this may be an unavoidable product of the modern condition. But it has gone much deeper than that. Some children across America now go to bed each night worrying about whether their father will be there the next morning. Some wonder whatever happened to their father. And some wonder who he is. What are these children learning at this most basic of all levels about honesty, self-sacrifice, personal responsibility, and trust?

What the decline of fatherhood and marriage in America really means, then, is that slowly, insidiously, and relentlessly our society has been moving in an ominous direction. If we are to make progress toward a more just and humane society, we must reverse the tide that is pulling fathers apart from their families. Nothing is more important for our children or for our future as a nation.

Part 3

Rebuilding the Nest

7

Fostering the New Familism:
A Goal for America

In the past thirty years the American family has been buffeted by a series of what many observers refer to as social revolutions. Sex has become separated from procreation through the contraceptive revolution, and from marriage through the sexual revolution, and marriage has become separated from parenthood through the divorce revolution. The American public is alarmed, and most Americans now believe that something is seriously amiss with our nation's family system.

Is there really anything to be alarmed about? After all, Americans have worried about "family decline" for the past 100 years or more. For example, many turn-of-the-century progressives, deeply concerned about "free love," lower fertility, and several decades of steep divorce increases, deplored what President Theodore Roosevelt called "race suicide." Later, in the 1920s and 1930s, came the famous studies of *Middletown* (Muncie, Indiana) in which Robert and Helen Lynd uncovered strong signs over a thirty to forty year period of growing marital discord, increasing generational conflict, reduced parental authority, and declining dominance of the home. And in 1939, the famous black sociologist E. Franklin Frazier documented with alarm the great damage done to black families in the move to cities. It appears that only in the 1950s was American society relatively sanguine about its family trends (which is one reason why so many conservatives today long for that era's return), and the basis for today's public alarm is that the family as an institution has progressively weakened since the fifties.

A host of statistics supports this fact, the same statistics that have generated the term "revolution." These statistics, now well known, document the unprecedented increases in such phenomena as divorce, single-parent families, and nonmarital teenage pregnancies. Indeed, the family's decline since the 1950s has been particularly dramatic because that era was an especially familistic period, a time of very high marriage and birth rates and relatively low divorce rates.

If recent family trends were merely a continuation of long-term shifts, we could perhaps rest more comfortably. In many ways the family has been weakening since the beginning of recorded time: first, through a "loss of functions" to other institutions, such as schools, religious organizations, and governments, and second, through a weakening of the extended kin network in which most families traditionally have been imbedded. These trends have led in the Western world to the modern "isolated nuclear family." It is the case, however, that in the past thirty years a new dimension of family decline has been added: the voluntary breakup of the isolated nuclear family on a vast scale. Over thousands of years the institution of the family has stripped down to its bare nucleus, and now that nucleus appears to be splitting apart.

Children at Stake

Despite this disturbing new development, many things in our society have markedly improved over the past thirty years. Women now have an equality and an independence that they never had before. Men, too, now have more freedom and are less subject to the strain of being the family's only breadwinner. More people than ever before may be enjoying a good sex life. And, in general, life today is more fair, a much wider range of individual lifestyles is tolerated, cultural diversity is celebrated rather than despised, and people who simply get a bad draw in life are less stigmatized. For most people, life provides more opportunities than ever. So why should recent family change be a cause for alarm?

In one word, children. Unfortunately, the kind of society that maximizes opportunities for adult expressive individualism (and many of the benefits I just mentioned are of that nature) is not a society that enhances healthy child development. It is a fact that much of the voluntary family breakup occurring recently has had a negative impact on children. Certainly, I have never met the child who did not want to be raised, if possible, by both biological parents who stayed together and cooperated in childrearing at least until the child's maturity (and hopefully for life). Yet the chances of that occurring today are rapidly diminishing, currently standing at about 50/50. I have also never heard of a successful childrearing approach that did not involve a tremendous amount of contact time between adults and children—for good childrearing there is absolutely no substitute for positive adult-child relationships. Yet the amount of time parents and other adults spend with children is rapidly diminishing. However one looks at the issue, maintaining strong families and successfully rearing children conflict to some degree with the pursuit by adults of opportunistic individualism.

The consequences for children of recent family change can be seen all around us, and the picture is not a pretty one. There are record-high, and in many cases increasing, rates among juveniles and adolescents of delinquency, suicide, depression, obesity/anorexia, drug abuse, and nonmarital pregnancies. In studies of these problems, the social factor that invariably emerges as a prime cause is the disintegrating condition of the family. Intact nuclear families can clearly be dysfunctional, but the weight of the evidence strongly points to the generally lower quality of postnuclear families, especially single-parent families and stepfamilies.

This mounting evidence is in keeping with the popular view of the situation. In my Marriage and the Family classes at Rutgers, for example, there is seldom a student who comes from a divorced home who does not dearly wish that the divorce could have been avoided, and who does not simultaneously pledge to do everything possible to prevent divorce from happening in his or her own future family. A female student raised by her biological mother and the mother's boyfriend, and whose father was divorced and remarried three times and now lives with his girlfriend, had this to say: "I will be very careful when selecting a husband because I intend for my marriage to last forever. I *never* want to get divorced. I am really looking forward to starting a 'traditional' nuclear family of my own because I think that will add an aspect of peace and stability to my life." A male student from a broken home who is estranged from both parents and was raised by his grandfather said: "I would like to have two children and give them the family setting that I didn't have…the family means everything…I will do my best to obtain the precious family experiences."

Some Positive Changes

In spite of the abundant negative evidence that has accumulated, many among the nation's scholarly and intellectual elite have shown tremendous resistance to the notion that the family revolution of our time should be cast in a negative light. The most commonly heard bottom-line phrase of this resistance is that "the family is not declining it is just changing," the implication being that it may even be changing for the better. Many scholars have worked overtime to demonstrate that everyone has benefited from recent family changes, even including children; at least, they argue, children have not been seriously hurt. Why has such a resistance developed?

First, many recent family changes *have* been for the good. With easy divorce available, a married woman who is seriously abused by her husband can now get out of the relationship, which she previously might have been stuck in for life. Thanks to increased tolerance, adults and children who through no fault of their own end up in "non-traditional" families are not marked for life by social stigma. Based on a companionship of equals, many marriages today are more emotionally satisfying than ever before.

The major resistance, of course, has come from women. For 150 years, during the reign of what we now call the traditional nuclear family, women were relegated for most of their adult lives to the "separate sphere" of the home as mothers and wives. Especially with declining fertility and the changing nature of work, this role came to be confining for many women. The whole point of the modern women's movement has been to change the role of women as prescribed by this traditional family type so as to secure a more equal place for women in work and public life. This movement has been highly successful, and for most women it represents progress, not decline. It is no wonder that many women are frightened at the mere thought that society could shift back and undo all of their hard-won gains.

Fundamentally, the family problem today is one of cultural overreaction. The good life is always a delicate balance of conflicting values and forces, and it is not difficult for societies to lose their footing. In the family realm, our society's overreaction has grown increasingly serious. The pendulum has swung too far. In seeking to rid ourselves of the traditional form of the nuclear family, something only a few now wish to recover, we have come close to rejecting the very ideal of the nuclear family itself—a classic case of throwing out the baby with the bath water.

Yes, we can probably get along without the traditional form of the nuclear family. But it is hard to discern a real alternative to the nuclear family—a mother and a father living together and sharing responsibility for their children, and for each other—as the best structure for child development and the smooth continuity of generations. Although the case can be made that it is better still, at least for children, to have some larger structure like an extended family as society's basic childrearing unit, such larger structures today seem entirely out of the question. If we find it difficult to live with just one spouse, how could we ever think of going back to living with grandparents, aunts, and uncles? Other alternatives have been tried, including communes, group marriages, and collective houses, but all have been found seriously wanting (where are they today?). Some single-parent families and stepfamilies are very effective, but the overall success rate of these family types is grim.

It is becoming increasingly clear that if we want successful childrearing, strong local communities, and a smooth continuity among the generations, most children will have to be raised by nuclear families. There are no viable substitutes for families that simultaneously are able to combine—as nuclear families do—emotional intimacy, sexuality of the parents, and the nurturing of children. The nuclear family is not just a social ideal; it is a social essential.

But in view of all that has happened in recent decades, how can we as a society begin to reconstruct the nuclear family as our basic unit? How can we uphold the virtues of the nuclear family without returning to the lifestyles of the 1950s, and thereby compromise the movement of women toward full participation in the economy and in public life, and stigmatize those who are not fortunate enough to have strong nuclear families? That is the task that lies before us, the task, using the title of a recent book, of "rebuilding the nest."

The New Familism

Fortunately, our task is made easier by what appears to be the beginning of an important cultural shift toward what can be called "the new familism." In recent years the issue of "family values" has been the ideological captive of right-wing groups like the Moral Majority, whose very championship of the cause has polarized the nation's intellectual elite on family matters, causing the left both to react defensively and to defer to other issues. The left-wing rejection of the "family values" issue was strongly encouraged by the fact that the right-wing version of this issue meant not just support for the nuclear family but specifically for the traditional nuclear family, something the left could not abide. The left was pulled further away from this issue by radical feminist, gay, and lesbian groups, who naturally were promoting their own family, or nonfamily, agendas. Roughly at the time of the Moral Majority's demise, however, a new constellation of ideological forces was seen to be emerging. Today, in a very exciting cultural development, pro-family values are again being openly espoused by the nation's traditionally left-leaning elite.

What is the source of this immanent cultural shift? The simple answer is that there has been a generational change. In 1990 more babies were born in America than in any year since 1964, the birthrate having returned almost to the replacement level, and there is nothing like having children to shift one's ideology in a pro-family direction. Many of the nation's intellectual elite were among those giving birth. Thus, while the dominant-elite ideologies of the past few decades have been generated by the huge cohort of baby boomers who delayed marriage and enjoyed a singles lifestyle as no generation had before it, this cohort has now moved into the thirty-something parental years: the peak of the baby boom was 1957; persons born that year are now thirty-five years old!

The evidence is growing that the new familism of young adults is also being promoted by the children of the baby boomers, that is, the children born to the early cohorts of baby boomers in the heavily divorce-prone 1970s who are now in their teens and coming into adulthood. A solid case can be made that the baby-boom generation, coming from the strong families of the 1950s, took the family for granted. To this generation, self-expression and self-fulfillment were the pressing values of the age—at least in their years of prolonged youth. To their children, however, often battle-scarred from family turmoil, the world looks quite different. As many national studies—as well as the sentiments of my students—have indicated, the children of divorce, although their statistical chances of a successful marriage may not be so great, are outspokenly supportive of the importance of marital permanence and strong, divorce-free families.

Each of these indicators bespeaks a certain dialectical quality to cultural change. Many scholars have noted that key cultural values tend to shift in importance over approximately thirty-year cycles, or the length of one generation. It may be no coincidence, therefore, that we are seeing the rise of a new familism just thirty years after the momentous cultural changes of the 1960s. Other contributors to the new familism should also be noted, however: AIDS and the quieting of the sexual revolution, the decline of radical feminism, and growing evidence—now widely dispersed in the media—that recent family changes *have* hurt children.

How to Foster the New Familism

Whatever its sources, the new spirit of familism could become a powerful bulwark of the national task of rebuilding the nest. I see this task in primarily cultural, rather than political or economic, terms. Government family policies are important, and some economic redistribution is necessary, but ultimately the nest cannot be rebuilt unless a new culture of familism overtakes the out-of-balance absorption with self that now dominates American society. Such a cultural transformation cannot easily be manipulated, but when the time is right it is amazing how swiftly attitudes and values can change. Witness the enormous changes over the past thirty years in deep-seated cultural attitudes toward blacks, women, the natural environment and, let's add, smoking.

The time is precisely right, in my opinion, for the development of a new culture of familism in America. Here are a few steps that could foster it:

1. Scholarly analysis and expert inquiry should bring the issue more to public attention. Professor Jean Bethke Elshtain and I co-chair the Council on Families in America, sponsored by the Institute for American Values and made up of leading scholars and family experts, designed to do just that. Combining new research on family values among a cross-section of American families with the expert opinion of scholars, we hope to influence the national debate and establish a national family agenda.

2. The national family debate should be reshaped. We must break away from the polarized debate (mostly among the elite) that has pitted right against left, the stern moral traditionalists against the freewheeling advocates of new lifestyles. The overwhelming majority of Americans, whose lives are governed more by personal experience than by ideology, fall between these two poles. They seek a reasonable adaptation to social change, but not one that means giving up the basic family and child-centered values that maintain social order and continuity. They value the nuclear family as society's fundamental institution, but they don't wish to be straightjacketed by rigid moralists.

3. One elite group should be singled out for special attention—the "family life experts." Belying their professional title, many of these ex-

perts have been especially vulnerable to the persuasions of those who would undercut the nuclear family. Their textbooks and advice literature are filled with the call not just for more sensitivity to, but actually open advocacy of, "family diversity." Again, I have yet to meet the child—or even the single mother or stepparent—who desires "family diversity" nearly as much as these experts.

4. Finally, a mass movement among parents should be promoted. If a Green Movement can reshape America's environmental attitudes, why can't a New Familism Movement reshape America's family attitudes? Concerned parents across the nation, together with their allies, must find more effective ways to band together at the grassroots level: In a society that increasingly isolates them, not only do parents need new social networks, but a more collective voice on their part could become a powerful force for cultural change.

In the national task of rebuilding the nest, there is one goal that the new familism movement should *not* pursue—the goal of trying to reconstruct the traditional family of the 1950s. That family had two characteristics a growing number of younger Americans today—both men and women—are no longer willing to accept: the lingering male dominance, a legacy of centuries; and the lifelong removal of women from the labor force, a legacy of the past 150 years. The goal should be to foster a new form of the nuclear family in which there is a 50/50 division of power and decision-making between wife and husband, and a firm understanding that both women and men will share a common (though not necessarily identical) commitment to the workforce over the course of their lives.

Two key characteristics of the traditional nuclear family should be restored or preserved at all costs, however: an enduring sense of family obligation, and the desire to put children first. Without these two qualities, the nuclear family becomes a hollow shell. They must be a *sine qua non* of the new familism.

I will conclude by returning to the voice of my students. In discussing their future family plans, here is a fairly typical passage: "I firmly believe in the small nuclear family as the best way to raise children. I do not believe that the husband has to be the breadwinner. Nor do I believe that the wife has to give up everything in order to have a baby. A happy marriage with a lifetime commitment with no divorce is the most important thing." That's the new familism— as stated by one of my male students.

Here's the new familism—as stated by one of my female students: "My marriage will ideally consist of the modern version of traditional roles. I want to work before I have kids, and after, I hope to be able to stay home and raise them. However, my husband will also help me in all aspects of home life... Childcare will be a joint responsibility... All decisions regarding everything will also be made jointly... And although I only have a 50/50 chance, I believe that my marriage will last forever."

8

The Roots of Declining Social Virtue: Family, Community, and the Need for a "Natural Communities Policy"

To succeed, every society must have a very large percentage of adults who act as good citizens and uphold high moral standards. Yet, with a declining sense of civic obligation and rising social disorder, America today appears in this respect to be in a social recession. Especially over the past thirty years, we have seen a substantial weakening of social virtue. Trust in social institutions and support for public endeavors has withered. More dramatically, we have seen remarkable increases in the most repellent forms of antisocial behavior, especially violent crime. The social environment that has emerged seems to be generating alarming rates of such personal pathologies as suicide, substance abuse, eating disorders, psychological stress, anxiety, and unipolar depression.

According to a universally held and, I believe, correct understanding of the situation, high moral standards and prosocial behavior are largely learned in childhood. To find out what has gone wrong in America, therefore, we must look to the situation of children and the changing conditions of childhood. Unfortunately, what we find is cause for much apprehension. Historians have noted that the socialization of children has undergone more radical changes since 1960 than at any time in the past 150 years.[1] The result? A number of observers and national commissions have said that America may have the first generation of children in its history who are worse off in important behavioral and psychological respects than their parents were at the same stage of life.[2]

How can this social deterioration have happened? After all, there are fewer children in each family today and therefore more adults theoretically available to care for them; fewer children are born to teenagers and fewer are unwanted; children in some respects are healthier, materially better off, and they spend more years in school. In addition, there is more national concern for children's rights, for child abuse, and for psychologically sound childrearing practices.

The broad answer to what has gone wrong is that children are creatures of their environment, and the environment for childrearing in America has taken a marked turn for the worse. Much of the attention has focused on the institution of the family, which certainly has declined in major respects.[3] The breakup rate of families has skyrocketed, for example, as has the rate of births to unwed mothers. Adults—especially men—are less connected to family life than ever before. Parents are spending less time with their children. Is it any wonder that a weakened family is less able to produce children who have the character traits on which social virtue is based, children who are kind and considerate, trusting and trustworthy, responsible and hardworking, honest and cooperative, and respectful of rules and authority?

A family focus is undoubtedly correct, as far as it goes. If parents fail, society fails. The social science evidence concerning what parents must do to raise socially responsible children will be reviewed below. But parents cannot do the job all by themselves. Just as the child is dependent on the family, the family is dependent on the surrounding community. Childrearing is a highly demanding, anxiety-producing, and difficult endeavor, one that throughout world history has never been left solely to parents (let alone a single parent) to the degree that it is in our society today. Parents normally have functioned in highly supportive communities, where the entire community is geared to the task. In the words of a commonly heard proverb, "It takes a whole village to raise a child."[4]

Parents need three types of social support in childrearing: emotional support in the form of love and acceptance from other adults, instrumental support such as the provision of information and advice and help with routine tasks, and the reinforcement of social expectations about what is and is not appropriate behavior.[5] For the moral development of children, no aspect of community support is more important than the community's ability to reinforce the social expectations of parents; that is, to express a *consensus of shared values.* Young people need to hear a consistent message about what is right and wrong from all the important adults in their lives; they need not only a social community but a *moral* community. As psychologist William Damon has noted, "The acid test of whether there is a community at all is the extent to which moral guidance for the young is shared among all who come in contact with them."[6]

Therein lies a childrearing problem of enormous magnitude in America today. How many communities do we have left that provide a consensus of shared values and in which the moral guidance of the young is shared by all? Pitifully few. Indeed, it is hard to think of communities that are more poorly designed for children than those of the United States. How we deal with this problem in the future will largely determine our nation's ability to persevere as a society with a measure of civic virtue. It is time for a radical shift in how we think about our communities and how we build them.

Raising a Moral Child

Let us begin with a review of the conditions of successful childrearing, looking at parent-child interaction, family structure, and the characteristics of family-supportive communities. A great deal is now known about the childrearing conditions that give rise to socially responsible children and adults who have competence, character, and social virtue.[7] The irony is that the more we learn about the optimum conditions of childrearing, the more we see these conditions being eroded before our very eyes.

Overestimating the effects on adults of the social environment within which they grew up is easy. Children can be very adaptable, and some successful adults come from the worst of social situations. Also, genetic endowment no doubt plays a much larger role in human behavior than most social scientists are willing to admit. Recent studies of identical twins reared in very different social environments[8] and siblings reared in the same social environment[9] should give all social scientists pause for reflection. They report a strong hereditability of most psychological traits, ranging from 50 percent to 70 percent, and there is certainly enough evidence for "constitutional factors" to provide an out for parents whose children do not turn out well and to recommend humility for parents whose children do. (The old saying is that parents tend to be cultural determinists—until their second child is born.) A useful formulation of the nature-nurture combination is that individual development is the result of individual organismic factors acting in relation to aspects of the environment which can facilitate or impede that development.[10] In any event, there is no evidence to suggest that genetic or biological changes explain why the present generation of children is worse off than their parents were at the same age. What has changed is the social environment in which children are being raised.

Parent-Child Interaction

The social science research of recent decades has pointed up three key dimensions of the parental socialization process as having particular importance for the development of socially responsible children: emotional attachment, prosocial behavior, and conformity to rules with respect for authority. First, many studies have concluded that, beyond the basic needs for physical protection and nutrition, a critical need of children growing up is to have warm, intimate "attachment" relationships with their parent or parents. As social psychologist Willard W. Hartup has concluded, "A child's effectiveness in dealing with the social world emerges largely from experience in close relationships."[11] The overriding importance of close relationships in childhood is contained in a series of propositions presented to UNESCO by Urie Bronfenbrenner, summarizing what he refers to as "the main findings of the scientific revolution that has occurred in the study of human development":

1.   In order to develop—intellectually, emotionally, socially, and morally—a child requires participation in progressively more complex reciprocal activity, on a regular basis over an extended period in the child's life, with one or more persons with whom the child develops a strong, mutual, irrational, emotional attachment and who is committed to the child's well being and development, preferably for life.

2.   The establishment of patterns of progressive interpersonal interaction under conditions of strong mutual attachment enhances the young child's responsiveness to other features of the immediate physical, social, and—in due course—symbolic environment that invite exploration, manipulation, elaboration, and imagination. Such activities, in turn, also accelerate the child's psychological growth.[12]

These findings were anticipated, of course, by such classic figures as Sigmund Freud and Charles Cooley and are heavily influenced by the pioneering work of the late John Bowlby and his followers, who have conducted the empirical research on "attachment theory."[13]

There is growing evidence that early attachment experiences shape not only child development but also attitudes and behavior throughout one's life. People growing up without satisfactory attachment experiences are at higher risk of becoming anxious, insecure, or avoidant in social relationships, both as children and later as adults.[14] For example, a recent longitudinal study that followed people over a thirty-six-year period found that the dimension of childhood correlating most closely with being socially accomplished as an adult (i.e., "having a long, happy marriage, children, and relationships with close friends at midlife") was having had "a warm and affectionate father or mother."[15] This factor was far more important than having grown up in a family with "parental harmony" or with a childhood that was "not difficult." Early attachment experiences are also important for developing a trusting view of others. Through attachment experiences people learn to desire the approval of others and to have the belief that—given certain conditions—they can count on such approval. This is an important basis of social trust.

Humans almost certainly have a genetic predisposition to engage in close relationships, but it is a predisposition that can be facilitated or impeded by the environment. A childrearing environment that generates strong attachments no doubt can be created by the mother—or by some other adult caregiver—alone. "Survivors" or "resilient children," the children from deeply deprived socioeconomic backgrounds who are successful as adults, typically have the common denominator of at least one adult who was devoted to their welfare.[16] But it is much more likely that strong attachments can be created when more than one adult is involved, as noted by Bronfenbrenner's third proposition:

3.   The establishment and maintenance of patterns of progressively more complex interaction and emotional attachment between caregiver

and child depend in substantial degree on the availability and involvement of another adult, a third party who assists, encourages, spells off, gives status to, and expresses admiration and affection for the person caring for and engaging in joint activity with the child.[17]

Although this proposition is written with the nonspecific "third party," it provides the justification—if any were needed—for the traditional role of the father in assisting the mother, which virtually every society has institutionalized through marriage. The most successful embodiment of this proposition in modern societies is the two-biological parent family where the father takes a strong interest in his children's and their mother's welfare.

It is the lack of a "third party," presumably, that is a major reason why single-parent families are less successful in child outcomes than their two-parent counterparts. Much has been written in recent years about the advantages, or lack thereof, of two-parent families. A 1992 front-page article in the *Washington Post* referred to "a searching reevaluation by social scientists," concluding that "the conventional two-parent household may be far less critical to the healthy development of children than previously believed." Some social scientists refer to "the misguided belief that children will receive better parenting in intact families." My reading of the research is that the relative success of the two-parent family can be considered a confirmed empirical generalization, indeed, about as confirmed a generalization as one can draw from the social sciences.[18] A review of research on the relationship between family structure and school achievement, for example, concluded, "I believe the consistency of the finding that living in a two-parent household is a benefit to achievement is evident; while not all differences reach significance, virtually none are found in the opposite direction."[19] Another research review concluded, "research on anti-social behavior consistently illustrates that adolescents in mother-only households...are more prone to commit delinquent acts."[20] A third states, "What is clear is that the multiple economic, social, and psychological life stresses of being a single or a visiting or a remarried parent...weaken the family in its child-rearing and child-protective functions."[21] Finally, a recent nationwide study of teenagers, based on the 1988 National Health Interview Survey of Child Health, concluded that "young people from single-parent or step families were two to three times more likely to have had emotional or behavioral problems than those who had both of their biological parents present in the home."[22]

Beyond attachment, and the emotional security and ability to maintain close relationships that it brings, lies the second of the key dimensions of the parental socialization process: the need for children to develop "prosocial" patterns of behavior, that is, voluntary, altruistic behavior intended to benefit others, such as helping, sharing, and comforting. It is this behavior upon which the success of any society depends. As with attachment, there is evidence to suggest that humans are genetically predisposed to engage in prosocial behavior and that the seeds of prosocial behavior are manifest very early in a child's life, contrary to the classic notion that young children are born purely self-interested and amoral.[23] But again, the social environment can either facilitate or impede this inborn impulse.

Warm, supportive parenting of the type involved in attachment experiences provides a foundation for the development of prosocial behavior. In the words of several prominent psychologists, "Individual failures in moral development...begin with poor attachment bonds between an infant and its caretakers." But good attachment is not sufficient. Prosocial behavior and moral values must be purposefully taught and reinforced by caregivers. This is especially true in individualistic and competitive societies such as the United States where, compared to traditional societies, everyday life is not so marked by cooperation and helping among kin and neighbors.[25]

Social science research on prosocial behavior is of fairly recent vintage, most earlier work having focused on negative behaviors such as aggression and violence. The main conclusions of this research, few of which are counterintuitive, are as follows:[26] Children often learn by imitation or modeling, and the more consistently caring and altruistic the parent is, the more the child will be. Prosocial behavior can also be taught verbally, and children continually should be receiving such instruction. But instruction works much better when word and deed are allied; the words of parents who preach altruism but do not practice it themselves may have little lasting effect. It is also important to encourage (but not force) prosocial behavior in various ways so that children have the chance actually to practice it, especially in relationships among siblings. Prosocial and moral issues are encountered daily by children through their relationships with others and these relationships can provide valuable learning experiences when guided and reinforced by adults.[27]

A most significant research finding is that prosocial behavior is heavily dependent on developing strong feelings of sympathy and empathy in children, on teaching them to take the perspective of the other.[28] Sympathy and empathy can be promoted in many ways, but one of the most important is through positive forms of discipline. Certain disciplinary techniques are more effective than others. By far the most effective in promoting sympathy, empathy, and thereby prosocial behavior involves the use of reasoning or "inductions," specifically pointing out the consequences of the child's behavior for other people ("Look at the way you hurt her; now she feels bad."). Such an approach takes time but is far preferable to "power-assertive" forms of discipline that involve physical punishment or the deprivation of privileges. Indeed, such punitive discipline, especially if used to excess, is actually detrimental for a child's prosocial development. Rather than an outward-looking empathy, it generates an inward-looking concern for the self and self-preservation.

The third key dimension of parental socialization is instilling in children a respect for authority and a sense of obligation to comply with social rules. A healthy family has its own set of rules, such as prohibitions against dishonesty, theft, and violence, that parallel those of the healthy society. In this respect the family is a miniature social system, with parents as the chief promoters and enforcers of social order. Some believe that children who have strong allegiance to family rules and social order will have difficulty developing an allegiance to the rules of larger social systems, but this is not the case. It is through relations with parents (and later other adults) that children learn about social rules in general and thereby develop a respect for society and its legitimate authority. Using other terms, this can be expressed as the development of conscience—an internalized constraint against certain actions, the violation of which generates anxiety.

The parents' task is to communicate and demonstrate to their children the purpose of social rules and, when necessary, enforce the rules by applying various sanctions, both positive and negative. In families where children are firmly attached and prosocial behavior has been promoted, negative sanctions are minimal. The close relationship that parents have with their children is normally enough to insure cooperation.

The outcome of this socialization process within the family is critically important for the larger society, which in the final analysis is based on regulation and hierarchy and the shared willingness of citizens to conform to social norms. "The child's respect for parental authority," notes William Damon, "sets the direction for civilized participation in the social order when the child later begins assuming the rights and responsibilities of full citizenship." Indeed, in Damon's view, "the child's respect for this authority is the single most important moral legacy that comes out of the child's relationship with the parent."[29]

The Strong Family

What kinds of families are best able to generate in their children emotional attachment, prosocial behavior, and respect for rules and authority? Analogous to the fashion in psychological research that has emphasized antisocial over prosocial behavior, there has been a great deal of sociological research on dysfunctional families but surprisingly little on strong, successful families. Recently, however, a number of family researchers have identified the characteristics of such families to be: "Enduring, cohesive, affectionate, and mutually-appreciative, and in which family members communicate with one another frequently and fruitfully."[30] Strong families are seldom "trouble free." Many have experienced health, financial, and other problems, but they are adaptable and able to deal with crises in a constructive manner.

This set of characteristics holds few surprises; it is one that any grandmother would probably present. One of the qualities most frequently mentioned by researchers is effective communication. In strong families, communication is clear, open, and frequent. "Family members talk to each other often, and when they do, they are honest and open with each other."[31] Another very important, underlying characteristic is commitment. In strong families there is a commitment to the family as a unit and a sense of the family as constituting a team with special identity and meaning. Members are willing to take action and sacrifice, if necessary, to preserve family well being.[32] This same quality is found in strong, enduring marriages. Not only does each spouse consider the other a best friend, but each is committed to staying with the other for life.

Strong families also tend to have an "authoritative" disciplinary style.[33] Scholars agree that a child's moral capacities are best developed under an approach "in which firm demands are made of the child while at the same time there is clear communication between adult and child about the nature and justification of these demands."[34] Disciplinary styles can be arrayed on a continuum ranging from restrictive to permissive. When combined with a continuum of parent-child relationships ranging from "warm" to "cold," the authoritative style is sometimes referred to as "warm-restrictive" or "loving discipline." This disciplinary style encourages children to value adult approval, readily internalize rules, and abide by those rules.

The other major disciplinary styles have different child outcomes. An oversimplified summary of each follows: Warm-permissive parents tend to generate children who will be self-confident and socially outgoing, but who will frequently ignore or bend the rules ("affable but spoiled"); cold-restrictive parents tend to generate children who are anxious and sullen, but compliant; cold-permissive parents (probably the worst combination) produce children who are hostile and rule defying, with a high probability for delinquency. There is reason to believe that both the warm-permissive and cold-permissive approaches are on the increase, especially with the rapid growth of single-parent families in which one person has the sole responsibility for childrearing.

Compared to the others, the preferred warm-restrictive disciplinary style takes by far the most time. Parents must be able to make time for their children and be with them to provide both love and discipline. Indeed, the ability and willingness to spend time together are powerful factors underlying almost all aspects of the strong family. It takes a great deal of time to have the kind of warm, repetitive interactions on which successful family life is based, interactions which include many routines and family traditions and lead to the development of a rich family subculture that has lasting meaning for its members. This is why the "time famine" that currently faces so many American families is a national calamity.

Supportive Communities

Probably everyone in America would agree that strong family ties raise the probability of producing virtuous offspring. The chances of becoming a successful and socially responsible adult are increased substantially if one is raised in a loving, structured, supportive family environment. Much less well understood, however, is the fact that to be strong, a family requires a supportive environment of its own.[35] Strong families tend to be well connected to the local community. They have external resources in the form of friends, family, and neighbors, and they participate actively in community organizations; they are not as socially isolated as less successful families. Strong families that are fortresses in an alien community obviously can be found but these are exceptions. One of the most important distinguishing characteristics of families that abuse their children, for example, is social isolation.[36] Indeed, the recent increase in child abuse could well stem in part from the growing social isolation of families.

What kinds of communities promote strong families? The list of characteristics of strong families noted above can just as well be applied to communities: "enduring, cohesive, and mutually-appreciative, and in which community members communicate with one another frequently and fruitfully." In short, communities that are stable, have a strong consensus of values, and in which people frequently interact with respect to those values, are supportive communities.[37]

Turning to childrearing, the importance of the local community is summarized by Bronfenbrenner's fourth proposition about human development:

4.   The effective functioning of child-rearing processes in the family and other child settings requires establishing ongoing patterns of exchange of information, two-way communication, mutual accommodation, and mutual trust between the principal settings in which children and their parents live their lives. In contemporary societies, these settings are the home, child-care programs, the school, and the parents' place of work.[38]

The central significance of the community for moral development is this: moral development in children takes place in part through repetition and reinforcement, and through adapting fundamental moral values to a variety of social circumstances beyond the family. As the child moves into the outside world, the moral lessons taught by the parents must be sustained by others. In an intensive ten-year study of ten communities across America, Francis Ianni found the existence of a local consensus of values to be the key predictor of adolescent adjustment, a far stronger predictor than such variables as affluence or ethnicity. In his words:

Congeniality among their values and clarity and consistency in their guidance are essential to the adolescent, who is engaged in a *search for structure*, a set of believable and attainable expectations and standards from the community to guide the movement from child to adult status. If the values expressed by different community sectors are at odds...the teenager cannot be expected to accept their good will or trust their judgment.[39]

Yet all across America, community value dissensus is in the ascendancy. Much attention has focused on public schools and their failure to provide value reinforcement. Another important area of value conflict is between families and the world of work, which typically operates as if workers had no families. One of the most significant examples of value conflict in America today, of course, is between the values families try to teach their children and those commonly expressed through the mass media.

American parents today believe that they are a beleaguered lot, living in an increasingly hostile community environment where value consensus is more and more problematic. Their neighborhoods have become anonymous, their neighbors are disinterested, and crime and personal security are constant problems. They feel isolated and unappreciated and view their task as a lonely and risky one. Popular culture has become an enemy, not a friend. To make matters worse, their own parents now live at a distance, and they have fewer and fewer relatives on whom to rely for personal support.

Human Evolution and the American Experience

For a fuller understanding of the importance of the community for family functioning, it is useful to provide a brief excursus into human evolution. Human beings are tribal animals; our attitudes, instincts, and behaviors have been shaped by tribal experiences.[40] For most of our existence on earth, human personalities have been locked into close-knit and orderly social groupings, whether nomadic bands, small villages, or extended families. With the family as their basic building block, these groupings were glued together socially by strong loyalties and commitments based on family relatedness, a shared geographic area, a common religion, and a single ethnic group—forms of social connectedness that today we call "traditional."[41] Survival apart from such groupings was rare and individualism was unknown; the personal and the social were one.

From an evolutionary perspective, it is reasonable to say that we are biologically adapted in large measure to living an intense social life among our own kind, and we suffer when we do not have these strong, primordial ties. Put another way, our natural inclination is to want to have close personal ties and to be included in strong groups that have clear values and a stable social structure, a social situation that can provide us with a sense of identity and belonging. When we do not have close ties and strong groups we feel alienated, lonely, depressed, spiritually empty, and often worse—wretched, useless, and self-destructive.[42] The strength of social ties—what anthropologist Raoul Naroll refers to as a moralnet—varies from culture to culture around the world. Studies of these cultures have shown that the stronger the social ties, the fewer the social and personal problems.[43]

In the last few centuries, first in the West and later in other parts of the world, the culture of modernity—noted for its extreme individualism—has been transplanted onto our tribal human nature and our tribal social groupings. Modernity has brought enormous rewards. The creative impulses of individualism generated the growth of science and technology, and human beings have materially prospered as never before. The new focus on the individual brought political democracy, with considerable increases in individual dignity, personal liberty, interpersonal equality, and human justice. And the weakening of group ties has probably been instrumental in reducing inter-tribal warfare. Such warfare was elevated on the world scale to become the scourge of the twentieth century. Indeed, human advances under the culture of modernity have been so impressive that it is thought today that civilizational progress and individual differentiation from the group go hand in hand; that individualism is the natural and progressive successor to tribalism and cultural collectivism.[44] And certainly, very few people today wish to return to the past.

Because of the tremendous successes of modernity, it is tempting to think that further progress rests on removing whatever tribalism remains, on getting rid for all time of "localism" and "parochialism" and enabling us all to pledge allegiance to but a single, universal human tribe. We must be very cautious about this strategy, however. The need for close ties and strong groups is an indelible part of human nature; it cannot be stamped out. As Michael Walzer recently has said:

> Tribalism names the commitment of individuals and groups to their own history, culture, and identity, and this commitment…is a permanent feature of human social life. The parochialism that it breeds is similarly permanent. It can't be overcome; it has to be accommodated, and therefore the crucial universal principle is that it must always be accommodated: not only my parochialism but yours as well, and his and hers in their turn…our common humanity will never make us members of a single universal tribe. The crucial commonality of the human race is particularism.[45]

This broad issue could be addressed from many perspectives. The most important one is that modernity not only has rewards, as noted above, but also social costs: personal pathology and community disorder. These have become as much the hallmarks of modernity as material and technological growth and democracy. The negative impact has been greatest on children, who are the most sensitive expression of social conditions. At the personal level, radical individualism has an uneasy fit with our biologically evolved human nature, and it is not at all certain that a further loosening of social ties in favor of individual choice will generate more human happiness and well being. Indeed, we may not be as happy today as in times past. The generation of new personal "psychological" pathologies can be seen all around us. At the social level, while we may be making progress toward an international social order, our internal "tribal social order" has fallen on hard times. The gradual weakening of family and community ties, in short, of the traditional forms of social connectedness, has generated an alarming increase in community disorder.

The social costs (and perhaps also the rewards) of modernity are greater in the United States than anywhere else. This may not be the view of immigrants to this country from the Third World, who have not yet shared many of modernity's benefits, but it is the growing opinion of close observers of American society who have done careful, comparative examinations of recent social trends. Especially since the 1960s, a time when American society underwent a massive attempt to rid itself of "tribal mentalities" and traditional social relationships, the social costs have grown. (So, of course, have some important rewards, such as greater equality for women and minorities.)

The United States has become possibly the most multi-tribal society of all time. In the sense of trying fully to blend together multiple ethnic, racial, and religious groupings, our diversity and cultural pluralism are legendary. This is both our strength and our weakness.[46] It is a strength because diversity can be stimulating, generating creativity and achievement. It is a weakness because diversity can be psychologically and morally overwhelming, generating moral relativism, hyper-individualism, and, ultimately, community and social decline. As fellow sociologist Peter Berger recently has commented, "Pluralism creates a condition of permanent uncertainty as to what one should believe and how one should live; but the human mind abhors uncertainty."[47]

Tolerance of the strange and the diverse in America today has become a social essential.[48] Indeed, tolerance and "intergroup relations" have become consuming goals of our nation (some might say all-consuming because—as necessary as they are—they increasingly distract us from other important concerns and issues). Often implicit in these goals is the weakening of group identities and group ties, the idea being that people with weaker ties will be more tolerant. But the emergence of a society in which all semblance of tribalism is gone poses a serious threat to social order and further human development because it mismatches with human nature. In the words of political philosopher Michael J. Sandel, "Intolerance flourishes most where forms of life are dislocated, roots unsettled, traditions undone."[49] Along similar lines, ethicist Andrew Oldenquist has written, "Our social problems are not due nearly as much to the competition of loyalties as to their absence...they are due to alienation, loss of belonging, to not having affiliations about which one deeply cares."[50]

A major task of our age, therefore, is this: While seeking to maximize individual development and respond to the exigencies of an ever-diversifying social environment, we must at the same time maintain some semblance of tribalism—which boils down to protecting and cultivating the primordial institutions of family and community.[51] This may sound like a tall if not improbable order, but it is the only reasonable choice we have.

American Communities and Family Life

American communities are strikingly unfit for children. If the building of American communities had been left to the wise planner in the sky, and if the needs and interests of children had been the primary goal, our residential communities would be very different from what now exists. The major drawbacks for children, considering the optimum conditions of childrearing discussed earlier, are as follows:

First, children need and want social stability and a stable social structure. They want to feel psychologically and socially secure in a place where they can "belong" and feel at home and where common values are shared by those with whom they come into contact. Yet American communities are transient, anonymous, diverse, and increasingly unfriendly and even hostile to children.

Second, children need and want a community where they feel physically secure, a place where they can freely play in the neighborhood without fear of bodily harm. Yet American neighborhoods are the most crime ridden of any industrialized society.

Third, children need and want a community that is accessible to them. Yet most American metropolitan environments are built at a scale that depends on the use of the automobile, a mode of transportation that is available to children only through adults.

Fourth, children need and want a community where their parents and other adults will be with them a great deal of the time. Yet most American communities are arranged in such a way that parents have to commute long distances to work, further extending their already long work hours. The typical American neighborhood is now filled during the day with empty homes.

Fifth, children need and want a rich local community life, with many community activities and events that draw families together to share good times. Yet community events across America, such as parades and community fairs, are in decline. The typical "community event" for most children has become a trip to the mall or movie complex or a few friends getting together to rent a video.

Sixth, children need and want free time, with a certain sense of carefreeness in which they can follow the path of their own imaginations. Yet the community lives of many American children have become increasingly regimented and scheduled through daycare, school sports and other organized recreation, part-time jobs for teenagers, and many other activities that typically take place far from home (and often involve elaborate carpool efforts).

The list could go on. Some of these drawbacks apply especially to the inner-city ghetto. But many apply to the type of community in which the average American now lives, the low-density suburb of a medium-sized metropolitan area. If not for children, we might ask, then for what or whom were such suburbs built? They were built primarily for economic efficiency; most residents would gladly leave such areas if they could find employment and services in smaller, more friendly places. They were built for the adult who has maximum use of the automobile, disregarding the situation not only of children but also the elderly, the poor, and the infirm and disabled. They were built by and for men, who are generally more mobile and whose lives, more than women's, are enriched by places of work (which have become the principle community for many). Women as well as children do not thrive in such areas. And they were built with the goal of privatizing family life, the opposite of what children want. The building of most American low-density suburbs involved simply constructing spacious houses on whatever land was vacant, with little thought given to the very real social needs of the majority of residents.

What can be done? How can we foster communities that are more oriented to the needs of children, communities—if you will—that have more of the qualities of a tribal village? There are two broad approaches to fostering community life in America. One focuses on residential areas or locality groups, people who live together in a common neighborhood or local area. The other focuses on nonresidential "interest" communities, or groups of people who live apart from one another but who constitute a network of social interaction and who share common interests and values. This second approach is the one being gradually played out in America, partly by default.

Historically, most residential areas have also been "functional communities" where people have networks of social interaction and share common values and interests. But physical proximity of residence is no longer the principal basis for social relationships among most adults. Increasingly unfulfilled by the locality group, people's strong desire for community largely has taken on a non-geographic dimension, what sociologists refer to as "dispersal of social ties." This reliance on nonresidential communities is not a wholly satisfactory solution to the problem, however, and it in some ways exacerbates it.

Nonresidential Communities

As residential areas in America have become increasingly diverse and amorphous, the strategy of Americans has been to give up on these as social communities and create "communities without propinquity" or far-flung social networks—communities of interest made up of like-minded people who live in many different residential areas. This has been the characteristic strategy of urban dwellers. As cities grow and become more diverse, neighborhoods weaken and urbanites develop citywide social networks. Many cities still have remnants of a prior urban form, the mostly working-class "urban villages," but these are rapidly disappearing.

The best example of nonresidential communities in America today are those formed through religious institutions. More Americans belong to religious groups than to any other type of voluntary association. One reason is that, of all the social institutions, religious institutions are the only ones that are involved with the entire family during each stage of its lifecycle. Typically, a strong local church will draw its parishioners from a great distance, and much of the social life of the members takes place through the church. When schools are added to the mix, the religious community becomes even more insulated from the locality; neighborhood schools in the residential community are given up in favor of private, religiously oriented schools, a phenomenon that has grown like wildfire in recent years. The strength of such religious communities in America today, fewer and fewer of which are organized along parish lines, is something that sets us apart from almost all other advanced, industrial societies. Especially outside of cities, fundamentalist Christian groups have become one of our strongest and most rapidly growing community types. They have also been quite successful, not incidentally, in maintaining social order and high moral standards among their members.

The important role of nonresidential communities in contemporary American life has been raised forcefully by the work of James S. Coleman and Thomas Hoffer in their comparison of public and private high schools.[52] They make the point that the comparative success of Catholic schools is due in large part to the fact that these schools are connected to functional communities made up of parents who share similar values about education and who interact to promote their children's educational achievement. They note that such functional communities greatly augment the resources available to parents in their interactions with the school and in their supervision of their children's schoolwork and their children's associations with others. It is important to point out that to be a fully functioning community, both sharing values ("value communities") and social interaction are essential. Many private schools constitute value communities but the community effect is weakened because parents do not interact much with one another. Public schools, in contrast, are typically attached to neighborhoods, which lack both the value consensus and social network components.[53]

To promote academic achievement and moral behavior in children, it is undoubtedly important for schools to share the same values as the families who send them students. This proposition has long provided the impetus for those favoring "neighborhood schools." And, as neighborhoods themselves weaken as functioning communities, it has provided the impetus behind today's concern for "school choice" through use of vouchers. As Nathan Glazer recently has suggested, school choice permits "those who can create stronger communities to choose the schools in which the norms they respect and want to see realized can be enforced and will be generally accepted."[54] A major issue with school choice, however, is the potential negative consequences for those pupils who are left behind in the old neighborhood schools.

Other nonresidential sources of community are less encompassing of the full range of life activities. Examples are voluntary associations, such as adult service organizations and organizations based on ethnic heritage, and especially places of work. Much has been written about how the workplace in America has become a community for many people, especially those without families. In Japan, the workplace is much more community-providing than in the United States, although there the family is also strong. Much more can and needs to be done in America to make the workplace family-friendly. But the problem with the workplace as a source of community is the inherent instability of employment. Once a person is laid off—an all too familiar event in America today—that is the end of the community relationship.

A case can be made for fostering each of these nonresidential community forms. Without them, with what are people left? The problem is, however, that as each becomes stronger, the residential area grows weaker as a functioning community—toward a state of obsolescence in which each family and even each individual family member has its own set of personalized and non-overlapping nonresidential communities. A clear example is the shift to private schools and its inevitable consequences for neighborhood schools.

Residential Areas as Communities

Is it really such a good idea to largely give up on the residential community and shift to a wide range of nonresidential interest communities? I think not. We, as a nation, should be doing everything possible to bring neighborhoods and towns back to their historical, natural form—as functioning communities.

First, let us review why residential areas have declined as functioning communities:

1.   Most residents no longer work in them.
2.   The distance between home and work has increased.
3.   They have become culturally diverse.
4.   They have a high turnover of population.
5.   Mothers are no longer at home during the day.
6.   The automobile has reduced pedestrian interaction.
7.   Security problems have grown, leading to increased privatization.
8.   Households have shrunk; with fewer people at home, the household becomes less attached to the locality.

An additional problem for childrearing families is that these families have become a distinct minority in most American localities; they now make up less than a third of all households nationwide, compared to more than 75 percent of all households in the last century.

These trends manifestly constitute a major structural change in society. Many of them cannot be undone; others could be modified, but we may not want to do that for other reasons. Such structural change constitutes a major obstacle to attempts to restore residential areas as important functioning communities in the lives of families.

With the deck so stacked, why is it nevertheless important to give serious consideration to such a restoration? Consider the social costs of the shift from residential to nonresidential communities. First, it is fundamentally unfair to our less privileged citizens. The more privileged in life tend to have more voluntary social relationships and connections outside of local areas, whereas the poor, the infirm, the handicapped, the elderly, and especially children—with their limited means and accessibility—are left behind to fend for themselves locally. For these segments of the population, the local residential area is still their main community, and there is little they can do about that fact. While for a well-heeled (especially male) adult there might be only a minimal negative impact from a home environment marked by unfriendliness, anonymity, and worse, for children and childrearing families the impact can be great. This form of inequality lies behind the recent "civic liberalism" proposals of Mickey Kaus. Rather than being so concerned with income inequalities and income redistribution, he argues, liberals should concentrate their efforts on building a public sphere in which all Americans can share and be respected as equals.[55]

Second, the shift to nonresidential communities generates neighborhood disorder, delinquency, and crime through a breakdown of informal social control.[56] One of the community changes today's parents most often note from the time they were growing up is neighborhood insecurity. For security reasons, children and teenagers are not able to wander freely about the neighborhood as they once were. Parents have deep concerns for their safety, and their whereabouts must now be known at all times. Juvenile delinquency has increased, and many teenage peer groups have become virulent. The social control of teenagers clearly depends not only on what is happening within the household but also on what is happening within the community.[57]

The amount of disorder in residential areas is strongly related to neighborhood upkeep and to the informal social control activities of residents, such as neighborhood watch and bystander intervention (e.g., being on the lookout for unruly behavior in public places and taking responsibility for reporting it, when necessary, to the police). It is very important in this regard for neighborhoods to be stable and cohesive, with citizens groups, block associations, and other neighborhood organizations and activities. Yet the shift by local residents to nonresidential sources of community severely weakens their neighborhood attachment. Neighborhood disorder, in turn, helps to generate neighborhood decline and makes the neighborhood a more likely target for outside criminals.[58] In the face of growing neighborhood decline and crime, residents tend to withdraw still further from the local community into their own private communities and private lives, setting off a spiral of neighborhood decay that can be seen today all across America.

Third, going beyond the immediate needs of children and other local residents, the weakening of residential communities exacerbates in some ways the problems of diversity in American life. As neighborhoods decline, caused either by market or government forces, those who are financially and temperamentally able move away, often leaving the old neighborhoods and local areas to the needy, the weak, and the disturbed. Not just neighborhoods but entire towns and cities are affected. The widespread geographic separation of rich and poor occurs, quite apart from considerations of common moral values. And America becomes differentiated into massive, isolated, lifestyle enclaves based mainly on wealth and privilege. Natural villages and towns of the past, by comparison, contained a broad mix of income groups, not within each neighborhood but within the local area. For better or worse, the citizens of these areas had to struggle—face to face—to create a common life.

Developing a Natural Communities Policy

To improve the conditions for childrearing in America today, nothing may be more important than trying to protect and cultivate those natural, tribal- or village-like communities that still remain—communities which have families as their basic building blocks and in which a mix of people through free association and sets of relational networks maintain a common life. This could be called a "natural communities" policy. It is a policy that, at minimum, enjoins both the market and the state from doing further damage to civil society. The wishes and concerns of local cultural groupings should be deeply respected, and functioning local communities should in some cases be protected from the intrusion of outsiders. Natural communities, like natural environments, should never be taken for granted. Social environments should be thought of as every bit as fragile and as worth preserving as natural environments, with a similarly intricate and easily damaged ecological network. Just as we now require environmental and family impact statements for some pending national legislation, perhaps we should also be thinking in similar terms about the impact of public policies on functioning social communities.

Unmistakably, the development of a natural communities policy faces a legal and social minefield. Unfortunately, the issues can barely be introduced here. There are the obvious concerns about racial and ethnic discrimination and about constitutionally guaranteed human rights. Many existing communities in America are far from "natural," including those at the top that function more to preserve property values than to promote a common life and those at the bottom, the urban and rural ghettos of the poor. This raises the serious issue of which existing communities, in fact, should be protected under a natural communities policy. Moreover, we must be concerned about community-supporting impulses running awry, as sometimes happened in the "community action" programs of the 1960s when a handful of self-selected community leaders benefited far more than community residents.[59]

Most importantly, the stability of American society rests precariously on a balance between local autonomy and national solidarity. From one perspective, the rise of strong, new "tribal" groupings along racial and ethnic lines seems already to be pulling America apart at the seams. Utmost care is necessary, therefore, to avoid the furtherance of a "moral exclusiveness" in local communities. Especially as children grow older, for example, they must be taught the necessity of nested and overlapping group loyalties that extend well beyond their local groupings.[60]

Also, a natural communities policy would have to be counterbalanced by a national solidarity policy that fosters those common values and traditions that have held the nation together. This should involve national and local service—the bringing together of people from different backgrounds and requiring them to work together to help build the nation as well as foster mutual respect and tolerance, a policy strongly promoted by the Communitarian movement.[61] And it should involve a strong, uniform national curriculum to be incorporated into our primary and secondary schools, along the lines suggested by Chester Finn, which includes not only fundamental subjects such as math, science, and writing but also our national and Western history and traditions.[62] Similarly, institutions of higher education should do more to promote national solidarity through stressing our common Western values.

A natural communities policy would foster a certain kind of "multiculturalism" in American life. I am not referring here to the multiculturalism sometimes espoused on the nation's college campuses, which centers around an "ideology of oppression" and involves a mostly individualistic power struggle to overturn the dominant society.[63] I am referring instead to the multiculturalism espoused by respectable and respected community leaders, persons whose goal in life is to raise their own families in a decent and orderly society. These are people who are working hard to achieve the American dream but who at the same time cherish their own cultures and cultural identity.[64]

The following are some specific goals that a comprehensive natural communities policy might include:[65]

1. *Foster residential stability.* Many studies have shown that the length of time spent in a community is the best predictor of community attachments: the longer one lives in a community, the more publicly attached to it one becomes.[66] People usually move for two reasons: jobs and housing. Obviously, it is important for this reason to maintain high levels of employment. Less obviously, much needless mobility is created by large areas that are homogeneous in housing type. Simply to find more appropriate space—for example, when children are added to a family or when one retires—it is necessary to leave the community entirely. Every local area, therefore, should be encouraged to provide a broad mix of housing types.

2. *Enforce community moral standards.* As a nation, we have become utterly preoccupied with individual rights. To be strong, local residential communities must necessarily be moral communities, and the

assumptions that all rights rest with the individual and that local government should be morally neutral are antithetical to the continued existence of such communities. We do not need a new agenda of group rights, but we do need, as legal scholar Mary Ann Glendon has pointed out, "a fuller concept of human personhood and a more ecological way of thinking about social policy."[67] Without violating the Bill of Rights, local communities should have more autonomy in establishing and enforcing their own values and moral standards.

3.   *Provide more public facilities.* The best communities are those with a rich measure of facilities and services available to all. This includes schools, hospitals, libraries, parks and playgrounds, youth centers, museums, and public transportation. The community with few public facilities and services need not wonder for long why its citizens are living in a myriad of diverse outside worlds, why they have scant local interest, and why they are quietly moving away.

4.   *Favor the development of smaller cities and towns.* Studies have found that "the larger the community a person lives in, the less likely he or she is to say that it is 'a good place to live'...and to be fully satisfied with their immediate neighborhood."[68] Most people say they would prefer to live in a place smaller than that in which they currently live, provided they had reasonable access to jobs and public services; it is the search for community that drives their preference. Small cities and towns, because they are closer to the "human scale," have measurable community-giving advantages over large urban agglomerations.

5.   *Support local political and social autonomy.* To the extent possible, political decision-making should be decentralized so local communities have more autonomy. Political autonomy and social autonomy are linked; one enhances the other. The subsidiarity principle should be followed: No political function or social task should be assigned to a unit that is larger than necessary to do the job.

6.   *Promote functional balance.* Metropolitan conditions have fostered a tremendous specialization of local areas, with people living in one place, working at another, shopping at a third, and recreating at a fourth. There are obvious social advantages to bringing these functions into closer proximity with one another.

7.   *Protect homogeneous neighborhoods.* I am not thinking here necessarily of racial and ethnic enclaves but of family-focused enclaves of people who share similar values and have a similar lifestyle.[69] American liberals have long looked askance at homogeneous neighborhoods (with the exception of those in which they live) as undemocratic. But people strongly prefer to live next door to others with whom they feel comfortable and can form close friendships,[70] and there is no reason they should not be allowed to—especially families with children. Provided they are functioning communities, homogeneous neighborhoods, possibly up to the size necessary to support neighborhood schools, should be protected and encouraged.

What should not be protected or encouraged are artificially homogeneous towns and cities. Most towns of the past in this country were quite heterogeneous, at least in terms of social class. Their children grew up among their own kind in their own neighborhoods, under a network of local social control, but as they grew older and extended their activities beyond the neighborhood, they came into contact with unlike people. Thus, as children matured, increasing diversity was introduced to them, especially at the high school and college levels. Because these towns contained a range of income groups and sometimes ethnic groups as well, the conflicting political interests arising from this diversity were dealt with largely at the local level.

All things considered, the best possible American residential community would be a moderately sized, functionally balanced, public-facilities rich, and politically bounded town that represented a microcosm of our society with a mixture of income, ethnic, racial, and religious groups. Within the town, each group would tend to live in its own separate neighborhoods, but all the groups would intermix in the public and political spheres. Unfortunately, we are drifting ever further from this community ideal.

Conclusion

The seedbed of social virtue is childhood. Social virtue is in decline in the United States for two main reasons—a decline in family functioning and a decline in community functioning. The two are closely linked. To help them have the knowledge, ability, time, and will to raise socially responsible children, parents must be attached to strong moral communities. Yet such communities, under a withering assault from state, market, and cultural influences, have fallen on hard times. When moral communities fail, families fail.

There is no evidence that realistic social alternatives exist for the traditional "tribal" structures of family and community. Whatever their condition, these primordial social structures remain powerful determinants of people's lives. To help restore social virtue, we as a nation should seek to protect and cultivate natural communities, preferably along residential lines. As individuals, we should seek to stay married, stay accessible to our children, stay active in our local communities, and stay put.

Notes

1.   Steven Mintz, "The Family as Educator: Historical Trends in Socialization and the Transmission of Content Within the Home," in William J. Weston, ed., *Education and the American Family: A Research Synthesis* (New York: New York University Press, 1989), p. 110.

2.   National Commission on Children, *Beyond Rhetoric: A New American Agenda for Children and Families* (Washington, DC: U.S. Government Printing Office, 1991); The National Commission on the Role of the School and Community in Improving Adolescent Health, *Code Blue: Uniting for Healthier Youth* (Alexandria, VA: National Association of State Boards of Education, 1990).

3.   See David Popenoe, "American Family Decline, 1960–1990: A Review and Appraisal," *Journal of Marriage and the Family* 55 (No. 3, 1993), pp. 527–42.
4.   Cited in *The Responsive Community* 2 (No. 3, 1992), p. 93.
5.   Jay Belsky, "The Determinants of Parenting: A Process Model," *Child Development* 55 (1984), pp. 83–96.
6.   William Damon, "Common Sense on Morality and Today's Youth," *The Responsive Community* 2 (No. 4, 1992), p. 87.
7.   James Q. Wilson, *The Moral Sense* (New York: Free Press, 1993).
8.   Thomas J. Bouchard Jr. and Matthew McGue, "Genetic and Rearing Environmental Influences on Adult Personality: An Analysis of Adopted Twins Reared Apart," *Journal of Personality* 58 (No. 1, 1990), pp. 263–92; Thomas J. Bouchard Jr., David T. Lykken, Matthew McGue, Nancy L. Segal, and Auke Tellegen, "Sources of Human Psychological Differences: The Minnesota Study of Twins Reared Apart," *Science* 25 (October 1990), pp. 223–28.
9.   Robert Plomin, "Environment and Genes: Determinants of Behavior," *American Psychologist* 44 (No. 2, 1989), pp. 105–11; Judy Dunn and Robert Plomin, *Separate Lives: Why Siblings Are So Different* (New York: Basic Books, 1990).
10.   F. D. Horowitz, *Exploring Developmental Theories: Toward a Structural/Behavioral Model of Development* (Hillsdale, NJ: Erlbaum, 1987).
11.   Willard W. Hartup, "Social Relationships and Their Developmental Significance," *American Psychologist* 44 (No. 2, 1989), pp. 120–26.
12.   Urie Bronfenbrenner, "Discovering What Families Do," in David Blankenhorn, S. Bayme, and J. B. Elshtain, eds., *Rebuilding the Nest: A New Commitment to the American Family* (Milwaukee, WI: Family Service America, 1990), pp. 27–38.
13.   John Bowlby, *A Secure Base: Parent-Child Attachment and Healthy Human Development* (New York: Basic Books, 1988).
14.   The need for close relationships continues in adulthood and may be the most important factor in adult health and well being. See James S. House, Karl R. Landis, and Debra Umberson, "Social Relationships and Health," *Science* 241 (1989), pp. 540–45.
15.   Carol E. Franz, David C. McClelland, and Joel Weinberger, "Childhood Antecedents of Conventional Social Accomplishment in Midlife Adults: A 36-Year Prospective Study," *Journal of Personality and Social Psychology* 60 (No. 4, 1991), p. 586.
16.   Emmy E. Werner and Ruth S. Smith, *Overcoming the Odds: High Risk Children from Birth to Adulthood* (Ithaca, NY: Cornell University Press, 1992).
17.   Bronfenbrenner, "What Families Do," p. 33.
18.   David Popenoe, "The Controversial Truth: Two-Parent Families are Better," *New York Times*, December 26, 1992; David Popenoe, "Scholars Should Worry About the Disintegration of the American Family," *Chronicle of Higher Education*, April 14, 1993, p. A48. See also Barbara Dafoe Whitehead, "Dan Quayle Was Right," *Atlantic Monthly* 271 (No. 4, April 1993), pp. 47–84.
19.   Ann M. Milne, "Family Structure and the Achievement of Children," in William J. Weston, ed., *Education and the American Family: A Research Synthesis* (New York: New York University Press, 1989), p. 57.
20.   David H. Demo and Alan C. Acock, "The Impact of Divorce on Children," *Journal of Marriage and the Family* 50 (No. 3, 1988), p. 639.
21.   Judith S. Wallerstein, "The Long-Term Effects of Divorce on Children: A Review," *Journal of the American Academy of Child and Adolescent Psychiatry* 30 (No. 3, May 1991), p. 359.
22.   Nicholas Zill and Charlotte A. Schoenborn, "Developmental, Learning, and Emotional Problems: Health of Our Nation's Children, United States, 1988," Advance

Data: 120 (Washington, DC: National Center for Health Statistics, 1990). For another report on this survey, with similar findings, see Deborah A. Dawson, "Family Structure and Children's Health and Well-Being: Data from the 1988 National Health Interview Survey on Child Health," *Journal of Marriage and the Family* 53 (No. 3, 1991), pp. 573-84.

23.   R. L. Trivers, *Social Evolution* (Menlo Park, CA: Benjamin /Cummings, 1985); Christopher Badcock, *Evolution and Individual Behavior* (Cambridge, MA: Basil Blackwell, 1991); Judith Dunn, *The Beginnings of Social Understanding* (Cambridge, MA: Harvard University Press, 1988); Robert A. Hinde, *Individuals, Relationships, and Culture* (New York: Cambridge University Press, 1987).

24.   Robert Hogan, John A. Johnson, and Nicholas P. Emler, "A Socioanalytic Theory of Moral Development," in William Damon, ed., *Moral Development: New Directions for Child Development*, vol. 2 (San Francisco: Jossey Bass, 1978), p. 15.

25.   Beatrice B. Whiting and Carolyn P. Edwards, *Children of Different Worlds: The Formation of Social Behavior* (Cambridge, MA: Harvard University Press, 1988); J.W.M. Whiting and Beatrice B. Whiting, *Children of Six Cultures: A Psychocultural Analysis* (Cambridge, MA: Harvard University Press, 1975).

26.   Nancy Eisenberg, *The Caring Child* (Cambridge, MA: Harvard University Press, 1992); Nancy Eisenberg and Paul H. Mussen, *The Roots of Prosocial Behavior in Children* (New York: Cambridge University Press, 1989).

27.   William Damon, *The Moral Child: Nurturing Children's Natural Moral Growth* (New York: The Free Press, 1988).

28.   The direct evidence linking criminality with lack of empathy for others is very strong. See James Q. Wilson and Richard I. Herrnstein, *Crime and Human Nature* (New York: Simon and Schuster, 1985), chapter 7.

29.   Damon, *The Moral Child*, p. 52.

30.   Maria Krysan, Kristin A. Moore, and Nicholas Zill, *Research on Successful Families* (Washington, DC: Child Trends, 1990), p. 2; see also Maria Krysan, Kristin A. Moore, and Nicholas Zill, *Identifying Successful Families: An Overview of Constructs and Selected Measures* (Washington, DC: Child Trends, 1990).

31.   Krysan, Moore and Zill, *Research on Successful Families*, pp. 4–5.

32.   Nick Stinnett and John DeFrain, *Secrets of Strong Families* (Boston, MA: Little Brown, 1985).

33.   On this style, see Diana Baumrind, "Rearing Competent Children," in William Damon, ed., *Child Development Today and Tomorrow* (San Francisco: Jossey-Bass, 1989).

34.   Damon, *The Moral Child*, p. 117.

35.   Urie Bronfenbrenner, Phyllis Moen, and James Garbarino, "Child, Family, and Community," in Ross D. Parke, ed., *Review of Child Development Research*, vol. 7 (Chicago: University of Chicago Press, 1983).

36.   Robert T. Ammerman, in Robert T. Ammerman and Michel Hersen, eds., *Children at Risk: An Evaluation of Factors Contributing to Child Abuse and Neglect* (New York: Plenum Press, 1990); Gay Young and Tamra Gately, "Neighborhood Impoverishment and Child Maltreatment," *Journal of Family Issues* 9 (No. 2, 1988), pp. 240–254; James Garbarino and Deborah Sherman, "High Risk Neighborhoods and High Risk Families: The Human Ecology of Child Maltreatment," *Child Development* 51 (1980), pp. 188–98.

37.   Several studies have found that community instability, as measured by the social mobility of residents, is the best predictor of high aggregate divorce rates. See Lynn K. White, "Determinants of Divorce: A Review of Research in the Eighties," *Journal of Marriage and the Family* 52 (No. 4, 1990), pp. 904–12.

38.   Bronfenbrenner, "What Families Do," p. 36.
39.   Francis A. I. Ianni, *The Search For Structure: A Report on American Youth Today* (New York: Free Press, 1989), p. 262.
40.   See, for example, David Maybury-Lewis, *Millenium: Tribal Wisdom and the Modern World* (New York: Penguin Books, 1992).
41.   This is not to say that all preliterate societies are or were "harmonious, peaceful, benign and content." See Robert B. Edgerton, *Sick Societies: Challenging the Myth of Primitive Harmony* (New York: Free Press, 1992).
42.   See Andrew Oldenquist, *The Non-Suicidal Society* (Bloomington, IN: University of Indiana Press, 1986).
43.   Raoul Naroll, *The Moral Order: An Introduction to the Human Situation* (Beverly Hills, CA: Sage, 1983).
44.   Christopher Lasch, *The True and Only Heaven: Progress and Its Critics* (New York: W. W. Norton, 1991).
45.   Michael Walzer, "The New Tribalism," *Dissent* (Spring 1992), p. 171.
46.   See, for example, the collection of articles entitled "On the Importance of Being Tribal and the Prospects for Creating Multicultural Community," *Utne Reader* (July/August 1992), pp. 67–95.
47.   Peter Berger, *A Far Glory: The Quest for Faith in an Age of Credulity* (New York: Free Press, 1992), p. 45.
48.   For a recent statement of this issue, see "American Values: Life, Liberty and Try Pursuing a Bit of Tolerance Too," *The Economist* 5 (September 1992).
49.   Michael J. Sandal, "Morality and the Liberal Ideal," *New Republic* 190 (May 7, 1984), p. 17.
50.   Oldenquist, *The Non-Suicidal Society*, p. 127.
51.   This is closely related to the ideas of protecting "social capital" advanced by James Coleman; protecting "mediating institutions" advanced by Peter Berger and Richard Neuhaus; and protecting "civil society" advanced by Alan Wolfe. See James S. Coleman, *Foundations of Social Theory* (Cambridge, MA: Belknap Press, Harvard, 1990); Peter L. Berger and Richard John Neuhaus, *To Empower People: The Role of Mediating Structures in Public Policy* (Washington, DC: American Enterprise Institute, 1977); Alan Wolfe, *Whose Keeper? Social Science and Moral Obligation* (Berkeley, CA: University of California, 1989).
52.   James A. Coleman and Thomas Hoffer, *Public and Private High Schools: The Impact of Communities* (New York: Basic Books, 1987).
53.   Laurence Steinberg, "Communities of Families and Education," in William I. Weston, ed., *Education and the American Family: A Research Synthesis* (New York: New York University Press, 1989).
54.   Nathan Glazer, "The Real World of Urban Education," *The Public Interest* 106 (1992), p. 75.
55.   Mickey Kaus, *The End of Equality* (New York: Basic Books, 1992).
56.   See Allan V. Horwitz, *The Logic of Social Control* (NY: Plenum Press, 1990).
57.   One major empirical study concluded: "Communities characterized by sparse friendship networks, unsupervised teenage peer groups, and low organizational participation had disproportionately high rates of crime and delinquency." Robert I. Sampson and W. Byron Groves, "Community Structure and Crime: Testing Social Disorganization Theory," *American Journal of Sociology* 94 (No. 4, 1989), p. 799.
58.   Wesley J. Skogan, *Disorder and Decline: Crime and the Spiral of Decay in American Neighborhoods* (New York: Free Press, 1990).
59.   Nathan Glazer, *The Limits of Social Policy* (Cambridge, MA: Harvard University Press, 1988).

60. See Oldenquist, *The Non-Suicidal Society*, chapter 10.
61. See "The Responsive Communitarian Platform: Rights and Responsibilities," 1991/
     92, *The Responsive Community* 2 (No. 1, 1991/92), pp. 4–20; and Amitai Etzioni,
     The Spirit of Community: Rights, Responsibilities, and the Communitarian Agenda
     (New York: Crown Publishers, 1993).
62. Chester Finn, *We Must Take Charge: Our Schools and Our Future* (New York:
     Free Press, 1991).
63. See Arthur M. Schlesinger, Jr., *The Disuniting of America: Reflections on a
     Multicultural Society* (New York: W. W. Norton, 1992).
64. This is similar to the important distinction between "pluralistic" and "particularis-
     tic" multiculturalism made by Diane Ravitch in "Multiculturalism: E Pluribus
     Plures," *The American Scholar* (Summer 1990).
65. Several of these are further developed in David Popenoe, *Private Pleasure, Public
     Plight: American Metropolitan Community Life in Comparative Perspective* (New
     Brunswick, NJ: Transaction Publishers, 1989), chapter 10.
66. John Kasarda and M. Janowitz, "Community Attachment in Mass Society," *Ameri-
     can Sociological Review* 39 (1974), pp. 328–39; Robert I. Sampson, "Local Friend-
     ship Ties and Community Attachment in Mass Society: A Multilevel Systemic
     Model," *American Sociological Review* 53 (No. 5, 1988), pp. 766–79.
67. Mary Ann Glendon, *Rights Talk: The Impoverishment of Political Discourse*
     (New York: Free Press, 1991), p. 137.
68. Angus Campbell, *The Sense of Well-Being in America* (New York: McGraw Hill,
     1981), p. 150.
69. See Oscar Newman, *Community of Interest* (Garden City, N.Y.: Anchor Press/
     Doubleday, 1980).
70. William A. V. Clark, "Residential Preferences and Residential Choices in a
     Multiethnic Context," *Demography* 29 (No. 3, 1992), pp. 451–66.

9

Modern Marriage:
Revising the Cultural Script

Of all the parts in the cultural scripts of modern societies, few have become more vague and uncertain than those concerning marriage and marital gender roles. Should we even bother to marry? And if and when we do marry and have children, who should do what—within the home and outside of it? Throughout history the answers to both of these questions have been relatively clear. Marriage is one of the few universal social institutions, found in every known culture. And in most historical cultures the scripts for marital gender roles have been unambiguously formulated; indeed, in the world's remaining premodern societies the prescription of marital gender roles is a principal cultural focal point.

In the industrialized nations today, marriage is becoming deinstitutionalized. Growing numbers of people are cohabiting outside of marriage. The assigned roles for husband and wife are endlessly negotiated, especially with regard to the allocation of work and childcare responsibilities. You work now, I'll work later—no, let's both work. I'll take care of the kids while you work—no, let's both take care of the kids. One may call it the growth of personal freedom and self-fulfillment, and for many women it has been just that. But such endless negotiation is no way to run a family—or a culture. The whole point of a cultural script, or in sociological terms an institutionalized set of social norms, is to provide people in common situations with social expectations for behavior that are geared to maintaining long-term societal well being and promoting generational continuity.

Is there not some way out of this predicament? With full realization that I am climbing out on a long limb, I believe that a new set of role expectations for marriage and marital gender roles can be established that is adapted to the new conditions of modern life and that, in a balanced and fair manner, maximizes the life experiences of men, women, and children, helps to maintain social order, and represents a "best fit" with biosocial reality. The purpose of this chapter is to review the sociocultural and biological bases for a new set of marital norms and to put forth for discussion some tenets toward establishing these norms.

An Assumption and Some Alternatives

If the family trends of recent decades are extended into the future, the result will be not only growing uncertainty within marriage, but the gradual elimination of marriage in favor of casual liaisons oriented to adult expressiveness and self-fulfillment. The problem with this scenario is that children will be harmed, adults will probably be no happier, and the social order could collapse. For this chapter, therefore, I hold the assumption that marriage is a good and socially necessary institution worthy of being preserved in some form, and that the alternative of "letting things go on as they are" should be rejected.

In considering what marriage path modern societies should take instead, several broad alternatives have been widely discussed. We could try to restore the traditional nuclear family of breadwinning husband and full-time housewife that flourished in the 1950s (a time when marriage rates were at an all-time high). This alternative, I suggest, is neither possible nor desirable. We could encourage married women to shift to the traditional marital role of men, centered on a full-time career and involving a high level of detachment from the home, leaving the children to be raised by someone else. This would mean, however, that large numbers of children would face the highly undesirable prospect of being raised in institutional daycare. Or we could encourage married men to shift to the so-called "new man" role in which, based on the ideal of social androgyny, men and women in marriage fully share both outside work and childcare on an exactly fifty-fifty basis. There are a variety of problems with this solution, which I will discuss.

In place of these alternatives, what is needed is a marriage pattern and set of marital gender-role expectations that will feel "comfortable" yet be reasonably fair and equitable to both men and women, that stands the best chance of generating an enduring marriage, and that will benefit children. (Of these factors, the generation of a lasting marriage is often overlooked, yet it is wisely said that the very best thing parents can give their children is a strong marriage.) Obviously, this is a tall order, and there are some basically conflicting needs that must be reconciled—those of men, of women, of children, and of society as a whole.

Setting the Scene: Today's Confusion Over Marital Roles

For about 150 years, from the early eighteenth century to the 1960s, what we now call the traditional nuclear family was the prevailing family ideal in American culture. The main distinguishing characteristics of this family form were a legally and culturally dominant breadwinning husband and an economically dependent full-time housewife; both parents were devoted to raising their children, but the wife played the role of primary nurturer and teacher.[1] Marital gender role expectations were unequivocally clear.

At least in its distribution across the American population, this family form had its apogee in the 1950s. More adults were able to live up to these family expectations in "the fifties" than at any other period of our history. Part of the reason is demographic. For women born between the periods of 1830 to 1920, maternal and child mortality rates steadily declined and marriage rates increased.[2] A high point was reached in America by the mid-twentieth century in the percentage of women who married, bore children who survived, and had husbands who lived jointly with them until at least the age of fifty.[3] This was a time when death rates had dropped sharply, leaving many fewer widows, and divorce rates had not reached their current high levels. Another reason is economic. The 1950s in America was an era of unparalleled affluence and economic growth, enabling many families to live comfortably on the income of a single wage earner.

Then, with the coming of age of the baby boom generation in the 1960s, traditional family expectations began to falter. Associated with this faltering was what many today see as "family decline," not just a shift to some different family form but a manifest weakening of the family as an institution—especially as regards the care of children.[4] Today, even though many Americans would probably still claim the traditional nuclear family as their family ideal, a sizable segment of the younger generation—especially the college educated—has largely rejected it.

Much confusion over family expectations and marital gender roles now exists. To the degree that they think about such things, young people coming into adulthood today are highly uncertain about the kind of marital gender roles they want, although almost everyone plans to marry eventually and nearly 90 percent are likely to do so if current age-specific rates continue.[5] Many men still tend to prefer the traditional family form, yet a growing number would also like their wives to work in order to bring in a second income. At the same time, most men believe that childrearing is fundamentally a woman's responsibility. Many women plan to work after they are married and have children, often believing that they will have to in order to make ends meet. And many college-educated women desire to have full-blown work careers combined with marriage. Among women, both ordinary workers and careerists are uncertain about how they will mesh work goals with family responsibilities and childcare.

Some women (and a few men), especially those influenced by left-feminist thinking, hold to a new ideal of coequal and fully shared breadwinning and parenting, what can be called social androgyny. Believing that primary authority for childcare should rest with women, however, this is an arrangement that few men seem prepared to accept. Some women and men intend to rely heavily on daycare to raise children, thus lessening the direct childcare responsibilities of both parents (for single parents, of course, this is sometimes a necessity). In general, women expect their husbands to play a larger role than earlier generations of fathers did in the home and with children. And, although resistance among men is seemingly widespread, the evidence points to a growing, albeit still modest, equalization of gender roles in this respect.[6]

Before children arrive, marital gender roles across all segments of society now tend to be relatively similar to one another, or "egalitarian." Typically, both partners work outside the home, and both share in the domestic responsibilities. Cooking, for example, can be done by either sex. Moreover, with ever-increasing median ages at first marriage and at the birth of the first child, such marital-role similarity takes up an ever-longer portion of each person's life, especially if one includes the stage of premarital cohabitation that precedes more than half of all formal marriages today. Indeed, males and females living together with similar roles and no children has become a formative period of young adulthood, a far cry from the days when women (especially) lived with their parents until they married, and then had children soon thereafter.

If people today never moved beyond this stage of life, the present chapter would not have to be written. With the coming of children, however, the situation of marital-role similarity suddenly changes. Far from bringing joy to the new parents, an abundance of scholarly studies has shown that the least happy time in the life course of recently married couples is when they have young children.[7] A major reason is that the division of labor within the household abruptly shifts, and gender-role expectations become uncertain; it is no longer clear who should do what. Marital gender-role expectations not only become ambiguous, but they typically revert to their traditional family form—with wife at home taking care of the children and husband becoming the sole breadwinner—to a degree far beyond anything anticipated by either party.

The marital-role stresses that arise from this sudden change can be enormous, especially after the couple has settled in with their new infant. Frequently, the wife becomes resentful and the husband becomes angry. The wife becomes resentful because she has had to leave her job while her husband is still occupationally progressing and because her husband doesn't help out enough. Often, in addition, she herself has had little preparation for the trials and tribulations that come with infant care. Also, she suddenly finds herself economically dependent (and perhaps guilty about not contributing financially), vulnerable, and stuck at home doing a job that has low status in our society. The husband, meanwhile, is angry because of his sudden new responsibilities and loss of freedom and because he has diminished sexual access to his wife and no longer receives as much of her attention. The baby has become the important figure in the home and the new focus of the wife's affections. While having young children (especially sons) slightly retards the chances of divorce, the animosities set up during this period are often long lasting and can lead to eventual breakup.[8] The animosities negatively impact not only the marriage, of course, but also the children.

Probably the most common piece of advice now offered to young people at this stage of life is that "every situation is different," and they will simply have to work things out for themselves—find what is best for them. But this is not "cultural advice"; it is an unthoughtful reaction in an over-optioned society. It does forcefully raise the question, however: If not the marital roles of the traditional nuclear family, then what? The traditional roles were at least clear-cut: the wife's job in life was childrearing, and the husband's was to provide economically for the mother-child unit.

The Traditional Nuclear Family: Why We Cannot Return

While some are tempted to think that a return to the era of the traditional nuclear family would provide a solution to this set of problems, there are powerful reasons why this is neither desirable nor possible. To understand these reasons, we must consider why the traditional nuclear family fell into decline in the first place. Although most readers are probably well aware of the causes for this decline, they are worth a moment's reflection.

Social change of the past few centuries has affected women's roles much more than men's. Throughout history, the role of married men has principally been that of provider and protector of the mother-child unit. And, in virtually every known human society, the main role of married women has been that of child nurturer. Unlike today, however, married women almost never undertook the childrearing task all by themselves. Many others were around to help, especially older children, parents, and other close relatives. Most mothers were involved as well in what was the equivalent in preindustrial times of today's paid labor force where "productive work" took place, the typical work being home-generated agricultural production.

It was not until economic conditions permitted, mainly after the industrial revolution, that women left the labor force and became full-time mothers.[9] Although most American women in the last century were in the labor market sometime during their lives, the pattern was typically this: They finished school at fourteen or fifteen and only worked until they got married in their early twenties. They then soon had children, and for the rest of their lives (shorter than today) they played the role of mother of at-home children. At the turn of the twentieth century, less than 10 percent of married women were gainfully employed, and the chances were that a woman would die before her last child left home.[10]

But by the late 1940s, the Bureau of Labor Statistics listed nearly half of all American women as "essentially idle." They did not have children under eighteen, did not work in the labor force, and were not aged or infirm, a combination leading to the proverbial "bored housewife."[11] In what represents a major historical shift, only about one-third of the adult life of the average married women today will be spent as the mother of at-home children. This is because of later ages at first marriage and birth of the first child, average family sizes of less than two children, and a much longer lifespan. Thus, even if one were to assume that a woman's main purpose in life is to be a mother, that role today clearly would no longer take up more than a fraction of her adult years. Moreover, because of the high divorce rate, a woman may well spend one-half to two-thirds of her adulthood not only without children but also without a husband to care for and to rely on economically, forcing her to rely on her own resources.

With such a steep reduction in the portion of women's lives that is taken up by marriage and childrearing, is it any wonder that women have been looking more to their own careers as separate individuals, and attaching less importance to their domestic roles? Under the new social circumstances, the demographers Kingsley Davis and Pietronella van den Oever have noted, "for best results [women] must choose an occupation early in order to get the necessary training, and they must enter employment while young and remain employed consistently in order to build up experience, seniority, reputation, and whatever other cumulative benefit comes from occupational commitment."[12]

The Downside

"Once under way," Davis and van den Oever continue,

the system of change exhibits a dynamic of its own. Insofar as demographic trends lead women to downgrade marriage and stress employment, they also lead them to reduce not only their dependence on their husbands but also their service to them. Men, in turn, are induced to reconsider the costs and benefits of marriage. They sense that, at older ages, men are increasingly scarce compared with women, that they do not have to marry to enjoy female company, and that if they do marry, their role as father and family head has somehow been eroded. Not surprisingly, the divorce rate rises to unprecedented levels, making marriage less secure and therefore less valuable for both sexes. Marriage undergoes attrition in two ways: it is postponed or not undertaken at all, and when it is undertaken, it is increasingly brittle.[13]

The available evidence suggests that, for durable demographic and economic reasons, this scenario of "family decline" has largely come to pass and it has been accompanied by some devastating personal and social consequences.[14] First, more families have broken up, fatherlessness has rapidly increased, and parents have had less time to spend with their children. Such family instability has undoubtedly been an important factor in the decline of child well being in recent years, as indicated by numerous statistics.[15] Second, women have not entirely been well served. There is substantial evidence that almost all women deeply want not just a job or a career or financial independence, but also to be a mother and to have a strong and hopefully lasting relationship with a man.[16] And while women's financial independence has improved, their family relationships have deteriorated.[17] Third, and least widely discussed, there have been important negative repercussions for men. Despite the great importance for cultures to direct men into family roles (men gain tremendously in health and happiness from marriage and fatherhood, and single men are a universal social problem), any "new men" have probably been more than offset by men who have largely abandoned family life.

In all, society has suffered. Such trends are surely a major component in the view of most adult Americans today that, in many ways, "things are not as good as they were when I was growing up."

The Nuclear Family: Elements to Be Maintained

If the era of the traditional nuclear family must be recognized as a thing of the past, and if we should not continue in the direction we are headed, then what? Rather than the alternatives of institutional daycare or androgynous gender roles in marriage, a strong case can be made for the maintenance of relatively traditional marital gender roles—*but only at the stage of marriage when children are young.* This case is based on the requirements of optimal child development, on the biological differences between men and women, and on what is ultimately personally fulfilling for men and women and what they "really want" out of marriage.

Childrearing Requirements

No one has spoken more eloquently about the requirements for optimum child development than Urie Bronfenbrenner. He recently summarized the main findings of the "scientific revolution" that has occurred in the study of human development. Two of his findings bear special attention:[18]

1. In order to develop—intellectually, emotionally, socially, and morally—a child requires participation in progressively more complex reciprocal activity, on a regular basis over an extended period in the child's life, with one or more persons with whom the child develops a strong, mutual, irrational attachment and who is committed to the child's well-being and development, preferably for life.
2. The establishment and maintenance of patterns of progressively more complex interaction and emotional attachment between caregiver and child depend in substantial degree on the availability and involvement of another adult, a third party, who assists, encourages, spells off, gives status to, and expresses admiration and affection for the person caring for and engaging in joint activity with the child.

Here we have not just the "main findings of the scientific revolution," but a statement of a relatively traditional division of labor in marriages between husbands and wives. Note that as they stand the statements are gender neutral, but we shall turn to that issue below.

The key element in proposition number one is the "irrational attachment" of the child with at least one caretaker. Empirical support for this proposition has grown enormously in recent years, mostly stemming from the many psychological studies that have upheld "attachment theory"—the theory that infants have a biosocial necessity to have a strong, enduring socioemotional attachment to a caretaker, especially during the first year of life. This is what pioneering attachment theorist John Bowlby has called starting life with "a secure base."[19] Empirical studies have shown that failure to become attached, to have a secure base, can have devastating consequences for the child, and that patterns of attachment developed in infancy and childhood largely stay with the individual in adulthood, affecting one's relationships and sense of well being.[20]

The work on attachment theory has been paralleled by research showing some negative effects of placing infants in group care. While still controversial, a widely discussed finding is that extensive (more than twenty hours per week) nonparental care initiated during the first year of life is likely to cause attachment problems (insecurity, aggression, and noncompliance) in children.[21] Some recent evidence suggests that negative consequences may also occur from nonparental care during the second year of life.[22] None of this research is conclusive; social science research seldom is. But it certainly supports what almost every grandmother would have told us from the outset—that there is considerable risk during the first few years of life in the reduction of infant-parent contacts and in nonparental childrearing.

After the child reaches age three, on the other hand, there is little or no evidence that limited, high quality daycare has any ill effects on children.[23] Indeed, American children have long gone to "nursery school" at ages three and four, and group care at these ages is common in most other industrialized nations, including Japan.[24]

Why is close contact with a parent so important in the first few years of life? Because parents are typically motivated, like no one else, to provide warm and supportive care for their children. The task of parenting could be, and occasionally is, successfully accomplished by a nonrelated caretaker, such as a full-time nanny. But attachment is much less likely in group settings, where there is normally a high caretaker-child ratio and also a very high turnover of staff members.

But why should the primary parent of young children ordinarily be a mother and not a father? There is now a substantial body of evidence that fathers can do the job "if they are well-trained and strongly motivated."[25] Some scholars have turned this research into the message that "daddies make good mommies, too," holding that the two roles might really be interchangeable.[26] Yet it is much harder to train and motivate men than women for childcare. Most dads do not want to be moms, and they do not feel comfortable being moms. And, in my opinion, neither children nor society in general benefits from such androgyny. To understand why the sexes are not interchangeable with one another in childcare, it is necessary to review the biological differences between them.

Biological Differences Between the Sexes

No society in the world has ever been known to exist in which men were the primary caretakers of young children, and the reason for this certainly has much to do with the biological nature of males and females. Unfortunately, any discussion of biologically influenced sex differences has in recent years been fraught with peril. As historian Carl Degler has noted, the idea of a biological rootedness to human nature was almost universally accepted at the turn of the twentieth century, only to all but vanish from social thought as the century wore on, mainly due to the vigorous (and reasonably successful) battle against sexism (and racism).[27] Understandably, this knowledge blackout on the discussion of sex differences was associated with the need to challenge centuries-old stereotypes about the capacities of women, and to overcome strong resistances to a more forceful and equal role for women in economic and public life. The result was, however, that about the only sex differences that everyone within the academic community has been willing to accept over the past few decades are that women menstruate and are capable of becoming pregnant, giving birth, and lactating and that men are on average taller and muscularly stronger. But, when they have been discussed at all, the behavioral implications of even these differences are left vague.

Today, the full recognition of biological influences on human behavior is returning, albeit very slowly. Although the idea is still foreign, even inimical, to most social scientists, in probably no other area has the idea of biological roots to human nature become more widely discussed than in the field of sex and gender. A cover story in *Time* on "Sizing Up the Sexes" began, "Scientists are discovering that gender differences have as much to do with the biology of the brain as with the way we are raised."[28]

Having been trained as a sociologist, I have long been partial to sociocultural explanations. But I must say, quite apart from the scientific evidence, that after a lifetime of experiences that consisted, in part, of growing up in a family of four boys and fathering a family of two girls, I would be utterly amazed if someone were to prove that biology is unimportant in gender differences. The "natural and comfortable" way that most males think, feel, and act seems to me fundamentally different from the way most women think, feel, and act, and I have encountered these differences across the world's societies. (I probably need add that I don't believe one way is better than the other; indeed, I find the symmetry and complementarity remarkable, even astonishing.)

It is not that biology is "determinant" of human behavior; that is a poorly chosen word. All human behavior represents a combination of biological and sociocultural forces, and it makes little sense, as sociologist Alice Rossi has stressed, to view them "as separate domains contesting for election as primary causes."[29] Also, the case can certainly be made, in the promotion of female equality, for a culture's not accentuating the biological differences that do exist. (Cultures differ radically in this respect; consider the difference in gender roles between Arab cultures and Nordic cultures.) Yet in my judgment a stronger case should be presented at this time, one of declining family stability and personal well being, for a more frank acknowledgement of the very real differences between men and women. More acknowledgement by both sexes of the differences between them in sexual motives, cognitive styles, and communication patterns, for example, would probably make for stronger marriages,[30] and recognition that the roles of father and mother are not interchangeable would probably make for better parenting.

Differences between men and women have universally been found with respect to four behavioral/psychological traits: aggression and general activity level, cognitive skills, sensory sensitivity, and sexual and reproductive behavior.[31] That differences are universally found does not unequivocally mean they are heavily influenced by biology, but it seems to me that the implication is stronger than for most other scientific findings about human affairs. Moreover, a large body of evidence points to the fact that many universally found differences are rooted in a distinct "wiring" of male and female brains, and in a pronounced hormonal variation between the sexes.[32]

What some call the greatest behavioral difference is in aggression. From birth onward, boys tend to be more aggressive and, in general, to have a higher physical activity level than girls. To a large degree, this accounts for the male dominance that universally has been prevalent in human societies.[33] Differences in male and female cognitive skills are less well known and perhaps not as large as aggressive behavior, but they are now widely confirmed by empirical studies. From early adolescence onward, males tend to have greater visual-spatial and mathematical ability than females, and females tend to have greater verbal ability than males. (Spatial ability refers to being able to mentally picture physical objects in terms of their shape, position, geography, and proportion.) Also, there is a female superiority in being more sensitive to all sensory stimuli. Females typically receive a wider array of sensory information, are able to communicate it better, and place a primacy on personal relationships within which such information is communicated.

In brief, while male strengths rest with "things and theorems," female strengths rest with personal relationships. Even shortly after birth, girls are more interested than boys in people and faces, whereas boys "just seem as happy with an object dangled in front of them."[34] That these differences become accentuated at adolescence strongly suggests the role of hormones, specifically testosterone in men and estrogen in women. The role of hormones gains further support from the fact that the behavioral differences decline at older age levels, when hormonal levels are dropping. It is also worth noting that males are the best and the worst with respect to several of these traits. Males, for example, disproportionately make up math geniuses, but also math dysfunctionals.

Not all of these behavioral differences, however, could be expected to have a direct effect on family behavior. Most important for family behavior are differences that stem from the dissimilar role of males and females in sexual activity and the reproductive process. The differential "sexual strategies" of men and women have long been commented on; in popular terminology, they roughly boil down to the fact that women give sex to get love, and men give love to get sex. The world over, sex is something that women have that men want, rather than vice versa, while relationships and intimacy are the special province of women.

Probably the most compelling explanation for male-female differences in sexuality and sexual strategies comes from the field of evolutionary psychology. It goes something like this:[35] In evolutionary terms, the goal of each individual's life is to perpetuate one's genes through reproduction and maximize the survival of all those with the same genes. In the mammalian world, the primary reproductive function is for males to inseminate and for females to harbor the growing fetus. Since sperm is common and eggs are rare (both being the prime genetic carriers), a different sexual or reproductive strategy is most adaptive for males and females, with males having more incentive to spread their sperm more widely among many females, and females having a strong incentive to bind males to themselves for the long-term care of their offspring.

Thus males universally are the more sexually driven and promiscuous while females are universally the more relationship oriented, setting up a continuing tension between the sexes. One psychologist found, for example, that the strongest predictor of sexual dissatisfaction for American males was "sexual withholding by the wife," and for females was "sexual aggressiveness by the husband."[36] And, according to the plausible explanation of evolutionary psychologists, men tend to be far more upset by their mate's sexual infidelity than vice versa because a man can never be certain that a child born by his mate is really his, while women tend to be much more upset by the loss of their mate's emotional fidelity, which threatens long-term commitment and support.

Male promiscuity à la the tom cat is not characteristic of humankind, however.[37] Wide variation in male sexual strategies can be found, ranging from the relatively promiscuous and low-paternal investment "cad" approach, in which sperm is widely distributed with the hope that more offspring will survive to reproduce, to the "dad" approach, in which a high paternal investment is made in a limited number of offspring.[38] But in every society the biological fathers of children are identified if possible, and required to hold some responsibility for their children's upbringing. In fact, compared to other species, human beings are noted for a relatively high paternal investment because human children have a long period of dependency and require extensive cultural training to survive, and because the character of human female sexuality (loss of estrus) encourages men to stay around.

Culture, of course, has a major say in which sexual strategies are institutionalized, and in all industrialized societies a very high paternal-investment strategy is the culturally expected one for males. Monogamy is strongly encouraged in these societies (although "serial monogamy" has become the norm in many nations, especially the United States), polygamy is outlawed, and male promiscuity is somewhat contained. Because it promotes high paternal investment, monogamy is well suited to modern social conditions.

Whatever the sexual strategies, our underlying biological nature dictates that every society faces the problem of how to keep men in the reproductive pair-bond. Especially for males, sex is rather ill designed for lasting marriages. Margaret Mead is once purported to have said that there is no society in the world where men will stay married for very long unless culturally required to do so. This is not to suggest that marriage isn't "good" for men, only that their inherited biological propensities push them in another direction.

Biologically, male attachment to the mother-child pair is said to be largely through the sexual relationship with the mother.[39] Many anthropologists have noted that motherhood is a biological necessity while fatherhood is mainly a cultural invention. Because it is not so biologically based as the mother's, a father's attachment to the children must be culturally fostered. Cross-cultural comparisons have shown that men are most likely to take active care of their children "if they are sure they are the fathers, if they are not needed as warriors and hunters, if mothers contribute to food resources, and if male parenting is encouraged by women."[40] Fortunately, these conditions largely prevail in modern societies. But bear in mind that it is not male care of infants that is at issue here. Universally, men have almost never been highly involved in childcare at the early stages of life.[41]

Sex Differences and Modern Family Behavior

What is the relevance for modern marriage and family behavior of all this biological and anthropological information? There is much evidence suggesting that men make a significant contribution to child development, especially in the case of sons, and that the absence of a male presence typically poses a handicap for the child.[42] Indeed, men's assistance to women in childrearing may be more important now than ever before because mothers have become so isolated from their traditional support systems. Even more than in the past, it is crucial to maintain cultural measures that induce men to take an active interest in their families.[43] It should be recognized, however, that the parenting of young infants is not a "natural" activity for males, and to perform well they require much training and experience plus encouragement from their wives.

All this said, there appear to be some dangers in moving too far in the direction of androgynous marital gender roles. Especially in American circumstances one hates to say anything that could possibly be used to feed stereotypes and to deter men from providing more help at home, yet it is important to point out that fully androgynous roles in marriage may not be best for child development, and they may not be the kind of personal relationships that men and women really want.

Regarding child development, a large body of evidence suggests that, while females may not have a "maternal instinct," hormonal changes occur after childbirth that strongly motivate women (but not men) to care for their newborn children.[44] These hormonal changes are linked, in part, to the woman's capacity to breastfeed. Also, a number of the female sex differences noted above are directly related to this stage of the reproductive process. "In caring for a nonverbal, fragile infant," it has been noted, "women have a head start in reading an infant's facial expressions, smoothness of body motions, ease in handling a tiny creature with tactile gentleness, and soothing through a high, soft, rhythmic use of the voice."[45] Such evidence provides a strong case for women, rather than men, being the primary caretakers of infants.

Men seem better able to perform the parental role after children reach the age of eighteen months, by which age children are more verbal and men don't have to rely so much on a wide range of senses.[46] Yet even at that age many studies have shown that men interact with children in a different way than women, suggesting that the father's mode of parenting is not interchangeable with that of the mother's; for example, men emphasize "play" more than "caretaking," and their play is more likely to involve a "rough-and-tumble" approach.[47] Moreover, there is evidence, to support the value of reasonably sex-typed parenting in which mothers are "responsive" and fathers are "firm"; one research review determined that "children of sex-typed parents are somewhat more competent than children of androgynous parents."[48] As social psychologist Willard W. Hartup has concluded, "The importance of fathers, then, may be in the degree to which their interactions with their children do not duplicate the mother's and in the degree to which they support maternal caregiving rather than replicate it."[49]

Less widely discussed, but probably no less important, is the effect of androgyny on the marriage relationship. The most common idea cited in this connection is that many men, being of a more independent spirit, will simply avoid marrying and having children if they are going to be asked to give up their independence and over-engage in "unnatural" nurturing and caretaking roles. And it is not as if they have few alternatives. Under the old system the marital exchange of sex for love was largely operative: if a man wanted regular sex (other than with prostitutes) he had to marry. Today, with permissive sexual standards and the availability of a huge pool of single and divorced women (to say nothing of married women), men obviously have abundant opportunities for sex outside of permanent attachments, much less those attachments that involve extensive childcare responsibilities.[50] Such a sociocultural reality may help to explain men's current delay of marriage, and the growing complaint of women that "men will not commit."

Nevertheless, most men eventually do marry and have children, and when they do they receive enormous personal benefits. My real concern, therefore, is not with men's delay of marriage (it is largely to the good) but rather with what happens to the marriage after it takes place. If it is the case that the best thing parents can do for their children is to stay together and have a good marriage, one serious problem with the "new man" alternative, in which dad tries to become mom, is that there is some evidence that marriages that follow this alternative are not very happy and have a high likelihood of divorce, especially those marriages in which a "role-reversal" has taken place.[51] This is a most significant consequence that is seldom discussed by "new man" proponents.

Why should marriages in which the husband is doing "just what he thought his wife always wanted" have a high breakup rate? The answer concerns the fundamental nature of modern marriages. Marriages today are based on two basic principles: companionship, by which husbands and wives are expected to be each other's close friends, and romantic love based on sexual attraction, by which husbands and wives are expected to be each other's exclusive sexual partners.[52] The joining of these two different principles is not without problems. For a good companion, you want someone who is as much like yourself as possible. But for a sexual partner, people tend to be attracted to the differences in the other. Therein lies a continuing tension that must be resolved if the modern marriages are to endure—the partners must be similar enough to remain best friends, but different enough so that sexual attraction is maintained.

The basis of sexual and emotional attraction between men and women is based not on sameness but on differences.[53] If we closely examine the marital roles of childrearing couples who have been able to stay together and remain interested in each other for a long period of time (an important area for new research), I doubt that we will find such couples relentlessly pursuing the ideal of social androgyny.

Seven Tenets for Establishing New Marital Norms

What I propose as a remedy for society's confusion over marital gender-role expectations, in conclusion, is a pattern of late marriage followed, in the early childrearing years, by what one could call a "modified traditional nuclear family." The main elements of this pattern can be summarized as follows. (I recognize, of course, that this pattern—being a set of normative expectations—is not something to which everyone can or should conform.)

1. Girls, as well as boys, should be trained according to their abilities for a socially useful paid job or career. It is important for women to be able to achieve the economic, social, and psychic rewards of the workplace that have long been reserved for men. It is important for society that everyone be well educated, and that they make an important work contribution over the course of their lives.

2. Young people should grow up with the expectation that they will marry, only once and for a lifetime, and that they will have children. Reproduction is a fundamental purpose of life, and marriage is instrumental to its success. Today, close to 90 percent of Americans actually marry and about the same percentage of American women have children; although these figures have been dropping, the social expectation in these respects is currently quite well realized. Lifetime monogamy is not so well realized, however, with the divorce rate now standing at over 50 percent.

3. Young adults should be encouraged to marry later in life than is common now, with an average age at time of marriage in the late twenties or early thirties (the average ages currently are twenty-six for men and twenty-four for women). Even later might be better for men, but at older ages than this for women who want children the "biological clock" becomes a growing problem.[54]

   From society's viewpoint, the most important reasons why people should be encouraged to marry relatively late in life are that they are more mature, they know better what they want in a mate, they are more established in their jobs or careers, and the men have begun to "settle down" sexually (partly due to a biological diminution of their sex drive). Age at marriage has proven to be the single most important predictor of eventual divorce, with the highest divorce rates found among those who marry in their teenage years.[55] But we must also recognize that both women and men want to have time, when they are young, to enjoy the many opportunities for personal expression and fulfillment that modern, affluent societies are able to provide.

   We should anticipate that many of these years of young adulthood will be spent in nonmarital cohabitation, an arrangement that often makes more sense than the alternatives to it, especially living alone or continuing to live with one's family of origin. I am not implying, much less advocating, sexual promiscuity here, but rather serious, caring relationships that may involve cohabitation.

4. From the perspective of promoting eventual family life, however, the downside to late age of marriage is that people live for about a decade or more in a non-family, "singles" environment that reinforces their personal drive for expressive individualism and conceivably reduces their impulse toward carrying out eventual family obligations, thus making the transition to marriage and childrearing more difficult.[56] To help overcome the anti-family impact of these years, young unmarried adults should be encouraged to save a substantial portion of their income for a "family fund"

with an eye toward offsetting the temporary loss of the wife's income after marriage and childbirth.

5.   Once children are born, wives should be encouraged to leave the labor market and become substantially full-time mothers for a period of at least a year to eighteen months per child. The reason for this is that mother-reared infants appear to have distinct advantages over those reared apart from their mothers. It is desirable for children to have full-time parenting up to at least age three, but after eighteen months—partly because children by then are more verbal—it is appropriate for fathers to become the primary caretakers, and some men may wish to avail themselves of the opportunity. At age three, there is no evidence that children in quality group care suffer any disadvantages (in fact, for most children there are significant advantages). Once children reach that age, therefore, the average mother could resume working part-time until the children are at least of school age, and preferably in their early to middle teen years, at which point she could resume work full-time. Alternatively, when the children reach the age of three the father could stay home part-time, and the mother could resume work full-time.

For women, this proposal is essentially the strategy known as "sequencing."[57] The main difficulty with it, as sociologist Phyllis Moen has noted, "is that child-nurturing years are also the career-nurturing years. What is lost in either case cannot be 'made up' at a later time."[58] Yet I would argue that it is possible to "make up" for career loss, but impossible to make up for child-nurturing loss. To make it economically more possible for a family with young children to live on a single income, we should institute (in addition to the "family fund") what virtually every other industrialized society already has in place: parental leave and child allowance programs. And, to help compensate women for any job or career setbacks due to their time out of the labor force, we should consider the development of "veterans benefits"-type programs that provide mothers with financial subsidies and job priorities when they return to the paid work force. In general, women must be made to feel that caring for young children is important work, respected by the working community.

6.   According to this proposal, the mother and not the father ordinarily would be the primary caretaker of infants. This is because of fundamental biological differences between the sexes that assume great importance in childrearing, as discussed above. The father should be an active supporter of the mother-child bond during this period, however, as well as auxiliary homemaker and care provider. Fathers should expect to spend far more time in domestic pursuits than their own fathers did. Their work should include not only the male's traditional care of the house as a physical structure and of the yard and car, but in many cases cooking, cleaning, and childcare, the exact distribution of such activities depending on the individual skills and talents of the partners. And, as noted above, after children reach age eighteen

months it may be desirable for the father and not the mother to become the primary caretaker. This means that places of employment must make allowances for substantial flextime and part-time job absence for fathers as well as for mothers.

7. It should be noted that there is some balancing out of domestic and paid-work roles between men and women over the course of life. Under current socioeconomic conditions husbands, being older, retire sooner than their wives. Also, in later life some role switching occurs, presumably caused in part by hormonal changes, in which women become more work-oriented and men become more domestic.[59] Given current male-female differences in longevity, of course, the average woman can expect to spend an estimated seven years of her later life as a widow.

Concluding Remarks

Later marriage, together with smaller families, earlier retirement, and a longer life in a society of affluence, provide both men and women in modern societies an historically unprecedented degree of freedom to pursue personal endeavors. Yet what David Gutmann has called the "parental imperative"[60] is also a necessary and important part of life, and during the parental years expressive freedom for adults must be curtailed in the interest of social values, especially the welfare of children.

Male breadwinning and female childrearing have been the pattern of social life throughout history, albeit not always in quite so extreme a form as found in modern societies over the past century and a half. Except perhaps for adult pair-bonds in which no young children are involved, where much social experimentation is possible, it is foolhardy to think that the nuclear family can or should be entirely scrapped. When children become a part of the equation, fundamental biological and social constraints come into play—such as the importance of mothers to young children—and central elements of the nuclear family are dismissed at society's peril. Rather than strive for androgyny and become continuously frustrated and unsettled by our lack of achievement of it, we would do much better to more readily acknowledge, accommodate, and appreciate the very different needs, sexual interests, values, and goals of each sex. And rather than the unisex pursuit of "freedom with a male bias," we should be doing more to foster a culture in which the traditional female values of relationship and caring are given a higher priority and respect.

In a much modified form, then, traditional marital gender-roles are necessary if the good of society—and of individuals—are to be advanced. But the period of time in which these gender roles still apply has become a relatively short phase of life, and not adult life in its entirety as once was the case. This leaves individuals abundant time for the pursuit of self-fulfillment through social roles of their own choosing.

Notes

1. Steven Mintz and Susan Kellogg, *Domestic Revolutions: A Social History of American Family Life* (New York: The Free Press, 1988); Carl N. Degler, *At Odds: Women and the Family in America from the Revolution to the Present* (New York: Oxford University Press, 1980).
2. Paul C. Glick, "The Family Life Cycle and Social Change," *Family Relations* 38 (No. 2, 1989), pp. 123–29.
3. Sandra L. Hofferth, "Updating Children's Life Course," *Journal of Marriage and the Family* 47 (No. 1, 1925), pp. 93–115.
4. David Popenoe, "American Family Decline: 1960–1990; A Review and Appraisal," *Journal of Marriage and the Family* 55 (No. 3, 1993), pp. 527–55.
5. Larry L Bumpass, "What's Happening to the Family? Interactions Between Demographic and Institutional Change," *Demography* 27 (No. 4, 1990), pp. 483–98.
6. Phyllis Bronstein and Carolyn Pape Cowan, *Fatherhood Today: Men's Changing Role in the Family* (New York: John Wiley, 1988).
7. Carolyn Pape Cowan and Philip A. Cowan, *When Partners Become Parents: The Big Life Change for Couples* (New York: Basic Books, 1992).
8. There has been a steep decline in the degree to which children retard divorce. See Linda Waite and Lee A. Lillard, "Children and Marital Disruption," *American Journal of Sociology* 96 (No. 4, 1991), pp. 930–53; Tim B. Heaton, "Marital Stability Throughout the Child-Rearing Years," *Demography* 27 (No. 1, 1990), pp. 55–63.
9. Louise A. Tilly and Joan W. Scott, *Women, Work and Family* (New York: Holt, Rinehart and Winston, 1978).
10. Kingsley Davis and Pietronella van den Oever, "Demographic Foundations of New Sex Roles," *Population and Development Review* 8 (No. 3, 1982), pp. 495–511.
11. Reported in "American Woman's Dilemma," *Life* 22 (No. 24, June 16, 1947), pp. 101–16.
12. Davis and van den Clever, "Demographic Foundation," p. 508.
13. Ibid.
14. David Popenoe, *Disturbing the Nest: Family Change and Decline in Modern Societies* (New York: Aldine de Gruyter, 1988).
15. Deborah A. Dawson, "Family Structure and Children's Health and Well-Being: Data from the 1988 National Health Interview Survey on Child Health," *Journal of Marriage and the Family* 53 (August 1991), pp. 573–84.
16. Sylvia Ann Hewlett, *A Lesser Life: The Myth of Women's Liberation in America* (New York: William Morrow, 1985).
17. Norval D. Glenn, "The Recent Trend in Marital Success in the United States," *Journal of Marriage and the Family* 53 (May 1991), pp. 261–70.
18. Urie Bronfenbrenner, "Discovering What Families Do," in David Blankenhorn, Steven Bayme, and Jean Bethke Elshtain, eds., *Rebuilding the Nest* (Milwaukee: Family Service America, 1990), pp. 27–38.
19. John Bowlby, *Attachment and Loss*, 3 vols. (New York: Basic Books, 1969–77).
20. Cindy Hazan and Philip B. Shaver "Love and Work: An Attachment-Theoretical Perspective," *Journal of Personality and Social Psychology* 59 (No. 2, 1990), pp. 270-80; Mary D. Salter Ainsworth, "Attachments Beyond Infancy," *American Psychologist* (April 1989), pp. 709–16; Robert S. Weiss, "The Attachment Bond in Childhood and Adulthood," in Colin Murray Parkes, Joan Stevenson-Hinde, and Peter Maris, eds., *Attachment Across the Life Cycle* (London: Tavistock/

Routledge, 1991), chapter 4; Carol E. Franz, David C. McClelland, and Joel Weinberger, "Childhood Antecedents of Conventional Social Accomplishment in Midlife Adults: A 36-Year Prospective Study," *Journal of Personality and Social Psychology* 60 (No. 4, 1991), pp. 586–95.

21. Jay Belsky, "Infant Day Care and Socioemotional Development: The United States," *Journal of Child Psychology and Psychiatry* 29 (No. 4, 1988), pp. 397–407; Jay Belsky, "The 'Effects' of Infant Day Care Reconsidered," *Early Childhood Research Quarterly* 3 (1988), pp. 235–72.

22. Deborah Vandell and Mary Corasaniti, "Child Care and the Family: Complex Contributors to Child Development," in K. McCartney, ed., *Child Care and Maternal Employment: A Social Ecological Approach* (San Francisco: Jossey-Bass, 1990); Jay Belsky and David Eggebeen, "Early and Extensive Maternal Employment and Young Children's Socioemotional Development: Children of the National Longitudinal Survey of Youth," *Journal of Marriage and the Family* 53 (No. 4, 1991), pp. 1083–110.

23. Edward F. Zigler and Mary E. Lang, *Child Care Choices* (New York: The Free Press, 1991).

24. Patricia P. Olmstead and David P. Weikart, *How Nations Serve Young Children: Profiles of Child Care and Education in 14 Countries* (Ypsilanti, MI: High/Scope, 1989); Sheila B. Kamerman and Alfred J. Kahn, eds., *Family Policy: Government and Families in Fourteen Countries* (New York Columbia University Press, 1978).

25. Kyle D. Pruett, *The Nurturing Father* (New York: Warner Books, 1987); Michael Lamb, ed., *The Father's Role: Cross-Cultural Perspectives* (Hillsdale, NJ: Lawrence Erlbaum, 1987); Robert A. Lewis and Marvin B. Sussman, eds., *Men's Changing Roles in the Family* (New York: Haworth, 1986).

26. C. Flake-Hobson, B. E. Robinson, and P. Sheen, *Child Development and Relationships* (Reading, MA: Addison Wesley, 1988).

27. Carl N. Degler, *In Search of Human Nature* (New York: Oxford University Press, 1991).

28. *Time*, January 20, 1992, p. 42.

29. Alice Rossi, "Parenthood in Transition: From Lineage to Child to Self-Orientation," in Jane B. Lancaster et al., eds., *Parenting Across the Life Span: Biosocial Dimensions* (New York: Aldine de Gruyter, 1987), pp. 31–81, quote from p. 64.

30. Apparently many Americans agree, causing such books as Deborah Tannen's *You Just Don't Understand—Women and Men in Conversation* (New York: Ballentine Books, 1990) to be on the *New York Times* bestseller list for over two years.

31. Eleanor E. Maccoby and Carol N. Jacklin, *The Psychology of Sex Differences* (Palo Alto, CA: Stanford University Press, 1974); J. Archer and B. Lloyd, *Sex and Gender* (New York: Cambridge University Press, 1985).

32. For an up-to-date review, see Anne Moir and David Jessel, *Brain Sex* (New York: Lyle Stuart, 1991). An interesting discussion of how male-female differences also may stem from a "male wound," the fact that the growing boy but not the girl must differentiate himself psychologically from his mother, is contained in *The Way Men Think: Intellect, Intimacy, and the Erotic Imagination* by Liam Hudson and Bernadine Jacot (New Haven, CT: Yale University Press, 1991).

33. Steven Goldberg, *The Inevitability of Patriarchy* (New York: William Marrow, 1973).

34. Moir and Jessel, *Brain Sex*, p. 17.

35. Martin Daly and Margo Wilson, *Sex, Evolution, and Behavior*, 2d ed. (Belmont, CA: Wadsworth, 1983); D. Symons, *The Evolution of Human Sexuality* (New York: Oxford University Press, 1979).

36. David M. Buss, "Conflict Between the Sexes," *Journal of Personality and Social Psychology* 56 (May 1989), cited in Degler, *In Search of Human Nature*, p. 305.

37. Mary Maxwell Katz and Melvin I. Konner, "The Role of the Father: An Anthropological Perspective," in Michael E. Lamb, cd., *The Role of the Father in Child Development,* 2d ed. (New York: Wiley-Interscience, 1981), pp. 155–85.

38. Patricia Draper and Henry Harpending, "Father Absence and Reproductive Strategy: An Evolutionary Perspective," *Journal of Anthropological Research* 38 (No. 3, 1982), pp. 255–73.

39. D. B. Lynn, *The Father: His Role in Child Development* (Monterey, CA: Brooke/Cole, 1974). This proposition is not unchallenged however, with some scholars even positing a "fathering instinct." Also, males clearly have the "capacity" to become strongly attached to their infants and children.

40. M. M. West and M. L. Konner, "The Role of the Father: An Anthropological Perspective," in Michael E. Lamb, ed., *The Role of the Father in Child Development*, 1st ed. (New York: Wiley-Interscience, 1976), pp. 185–218, cited in Rossi, "Parenthood in Transition," pp. 67–68.

41. The ideas in this section are further explored in David Popenoe, *Life Without Father: Compelling New Evidence That Fatherhood and Marriage are Indispensable for the Good of Children and Society* (New York: Free Press, 1996), chapter 6.

42. Lynn, *The Father*; Irwin Garfinkel and Sara S. McLanahan, *Single Mothers and Their Children: A New American Dilemma* (Washington, DC: Urban Institute, 1986); Michael E. Lamb and David Oppenheim, "Fatherhood and Father-Child Relationships: Five Years of Research," in Stanley H. Cath, Alan Gurwitt, and Linda Gunsberg, eds., *Fathers and Their Families* (Hillsdale, NJ: The Analytic Press, 1989), chapter 1.

43. There is also strong evidence that children are important for the full maturation of men as adults. See Michael E. Lamb, Joseph H. Pleck, and James A. Levine, "The Effects of Paternal Involvement on Fathers and Mothers," in Robert A. Lewis and Marvin B. Sussman, eds., *Men's Changing Roles in the Family* (New York: Haworth, 1986), chapter 6.

44. Alice S. Rossi, "Gender and Parenthood," in Alice S. Rossi, ed., *Gender and the Life Course* (New York: Aldine de Gruyter, 1985), pp. 161–91.

45. Rossi, "Parenthood in Transition," p. 69.

46. Ibid., pp. 57–61.

47. M. W. Yogman, "Development of the Father-Infant Relationship," in H. E. Fitzgerald, B. M. Lester, and M. W. Yogman, eds., *Theory and Research in Behavioral Pediatrics*, vol. 1 (New York: Plenum Press, 1982), pp. 221–80; J. L Roopnarine and N. S. Mounts, "Mother-Child and Father-Child Play," *Early Child Development Care* 20 (1985), pp. 157–69.

48. Diana Baumrind, "Are Androgynous Individuals More Effective Persons and Parents?" *Child Development* 53 (1982), pp. 44–75. In another study of adolescent outcomes, it was found that the most effective parenting was that which was both highly demanding and highly responsive, a difficult task for either a man or a woman to combine. Diana Baumrind, "The Influence of Parenting Style on Adolescent Competence and Substance Use," *Journal of Early Adolescence*, 11 (No. 1, 1991), pp. 56–95. See also Frances K. Grossman, William S. Pollack, and Ellen Golding, "Fathers and Children: Predicting the Quality and Quantity of Fathering," *Developmental Psychology* 24 (No. 1, 1988), pp. 82–92.

49. Willard W. Hartup, "Social Relationship, and Their Developmental Significance," *American Psychologist* (February 1989), pp. 120–26, quote from p. 122.

50. Maggie Gallagher, *Enemies of Eros* (Chicago: Bonus Books, 1989).

51. Graeme Russell, *The Changing Role of Fathers?* (New York: University of Queensland Press, 1983); Philip Blumstein and Pepper Schwartz, *American Couples* (New York: Pocket Books 1983). Despite their hopes, Russell found that shared-caregiving couples had marriages of "significantly lower quality" than traditional couples, and Blumstein and Schwartz concluded, "that when roles are reversed, with men doing housework and women taking over as provider, couples become dreadfully unhappy" (p. 324). An additional problem is that when a divorce comes to a shared-caregiving couple, it is much more likely for a child-custody battle to ensue, since the man wishes to keep the children as much as the woman does.

52. This is an underlying theme in the (brilliant) book of Richard A. Posner, *Sex and Reason* (Cambridge, MA: Harvard University Press, 1992).

53. Ellen Piel Cook, *Psychological Androgyny* (New York: Pergamon, 1985).

54. The late age of marriage is one of the many ways in which this marriage pattern differs significantly from that of the 1950s; in 1957, the average woman who married was still a teenager!

55. Teresa Castro Martin and Larry L. Bumpass, "Recent Trends in Marital Disruption," *Demography* 26 (No. 1, 1989), pp. 37–51.

56. Alice S. Rossi, "Life Span Theories and Women's Lives," *Signs: Journal of Women in Culture and Society* 6 (1980), pp. 4–32; Linda J. Waite, Frances K. Goldscheider, and Christina Witsberger, "Nonfamily Living and the Erosion of Traditional Family Orientations among Young Adults," *American Sociological Review* 51 (No. 4, 1986), pp. 541–54.

57. Arlene Rossen Cardozo, *Sequencing* (New York; Collier Books, 1986); Felice N. Schwartz, *Breaking with Tradition: Women, Management and the New Facts of Life* (New York: Warner, 1992)

58. Phyllis Moen, *Women's Two Roles: A Contemporary Dilemma* (New York: Auburn House, 1992), p. 133.

59. David Gutmann, *Reclaimed Power: Toward a New Psychology of Men and Women in Later Life* (New York: Basic Books, 1987).

60. David Gutmann, "Men, Women, and the Parental Imperative," *Commentary* 56 (No. 5, 1973), pp. 59–64.

10

Challenging the Culture of Fatherlessness

To understand how to renew fatherhood, we must turn to marriage. Marriage is the institution that holds men to their children. Both the economy and the government have no doubt played some part in the marriage decline of the past three decades. But by far the most important factor is the culture, changes in the realm of values, attitudes, and beliefs. "At no time in history, with the possible exception of Imperial Rome," Kingsley Davis, the eminent demographer, says, "has the institution of marriage been more problematic than it is today."[1] As we know, Imperial Rome collapsed, and family difficulties are typically invoked by scholars to help account for its demise.

The Culture of Modernity

The importance of cultural change for marriage decline and fatherlessness, in contrast to effects of the economy and public policy, can clearly be seen through a comparison of modern nations. The modern nation that today leads the pack in fatherlessness and marriage instability, including having the highest divorce rate, is the United States. If family problems are mainly the result of economic deprivation, as is often asserted, it is difficult to reconcile that idea with this nation's status as the world's wealthiest in terms of consumer purchasing power. To be sure, poverty is no friend of marriage. But neither is affluence. In general, affluence breeds personal freedom and opportunity that is corrosive of traditional institutions and social obligations.

Perhaps the American problem, then, rests in the arena of public policy. Government intervention into the economy and the culture is considerably less in the United States than in any other Western nation, and many consider this to be a fundamental cause of our family decline. But consider Sweden, which is widely recognized to have the world's most comprehensive welfare state. Sweden has today what is probably the world's lowest marriage rate, and it also has one of Europe's highest levels of fatherlessness. One reason is the negative effect of welfare provisions on marriage formation, an effect that we have seen clearly in America's "welfare population."[2] The lack of welfare programs should not be considered a contributor to stable family life. But just as important are the unintended consequences of government welfare programs and the welfare culture that grows up around them in discouraging marriages and making them easier to dissolve.

So what can we conclude from the Western world's most laissez-faire nation and its most government-interventionist nation both having serious problems of marital instability and fatherlessness? Let us add one more fact: As the other nations of the West grow wealthier—more modern—their family structures weaken. The common denominator in all of these situations is the ever-expanding culture of modernity, which exists at a mature stage in the United States and Sweden and is rapidly advancing in the other Western nations.

The culture of modernity emphasizes personal freedom and opportunity apart from traditional values and social structures. The reason it is advancing so rapidly is that almost everyone desires it. Who doesn't wish for more freedom and opportunity to do what they want to do, when they want to do it? The problem is that when people's individualistic drives proceed so far that their social responsibilities and obligations are neglected, the social order weakens. And a stable and secure social order is necessary if freedom and opportunity are to be both pervasive and enduring.

The culture of modernity has been gaining momentum in the West for several hundred years. Yet only in the past few decades have we seen signs of an imbalance, in which the individualistic impulses have begun seriously to impinge upon the necessary components of community and order. This recent period, indeed, has been witness to an abrupt and extraordinary transformation of people's values, worldview, and even self-definition, the ground rules by which we live. Large segments of the population have come to regard pure "self-fulfillment" as their dominant life goal, pushing aside such traditional "Victorian" values as self-sacrifice, commitment to others, and institutional obligation. This cultural shift has been widely documented by public opinion surveys. Daniel Yankelovich found, for example, that people today place a much lower value on what they owe others as a matter of moral obligation, and a much higher value on self-realization and personal choice.[3]

One of the most important repercussions of advanced modernity, with its radical individualism, is that the traditional moral legitimacy and authority of almost all social institutions, such as education, religion, and the professions, erode. People lose trust and faith and confidence in them. In this respect, no institution in the past few decades has been harder hit than marriage. Trust and confidence in marriage as a stable, lifelong social endeavor have plummeted. Marriage is the historical basis of family life; as marriage goes, so goes the family. The authors of a recent history of the American family opined: "What Americans have witnessed since 1960 are fundamental challenges to the forms, ideals, and role-expectations that have defined the family for the last century and a half."[4]

Americans still believe in the importance of finding a lifetime mate and in "getting married someday." But marriage has become less a social institution that expresses society's goals and much more a personal, voluntary relationship that individuals can make or break at will in their search for self-fulfillment. "Till death do us part" has been replaced by "so long as I am happy" or "until I change my mind."

The Path to Fatherlessness

Let us briefly review the history of fatherhood in America.[5] In the colonial period, families tended to be heavily fathered. The father was the acknowledged family leader, and he was primarily responsible for his children's education and moral development (which was primarily religious in nature). Both fathers and mothers were in the labor force as farmers or small shopkeepers in or near their own homes, with their children working alongside them.

Then, associated with the rise of industry and towns in the early 1800s, what historians call the "modern nuclear family" arose. The new wage labor in factories and offices required the man to be away from home during the workday, and his income enabled him and his family to leave the farm and live in a town. It also enabled his wife to become a full-time housewife and childrearer. Fathers began to take a backseat in childrearing, leaving the task mainly up to women. But the town-living mothers typically were surrounded by caring relatives and neighbors to help them. Starting in the higher classes and gradually filtering down to the lower classes, this is the family form that predominated in the United States in various guises until the 1960s.

In the twentieth century, however, and especially after 1960, more and more mothers entered the labor force and, like the fathers before them, left the home during the day. Moreover, they now lived not in towns but in suburbs or cities where the supportive "village" was largely absent. Fathers moved in two directions. Some, the so-called "good dads," helped to fill the vacuum left by the working mothers by becoming more involved in day-to-day childcare than their own fathers ever had been.[6] But they were outnumbered by others, the "bad dads," who found great difficulty coming back into domestic life after more than a century of fathers having moved in the opposite direction. Many essentially abandoned their children via divorce and out-of-wedlock births, leaving the care of children solely up to women in single-parent families, which dramatically increased from 9 percent in 1960 to today's 27 percent.

The net effects of these shifts were not only a rapid increase in the number of fatherless children, but a general decline in the amount of time that both parents spend with their children in active childrearing. Children now spend less time than ever before in family interactions, and more time with peers, watching TV, and in school.

Two other cultural shifts in the late nineteenth and twentieth centuries, both fundamental components of the culture of modernity, had a great effect on fathers and fathering. The first was a change in the nature of marriage. Marriage was once a mostly economic and partly arranged relationship. Many husbands and wives undoubtedly loved one another, but love was not the main basis for the marriage, nor was the loss of love a reason to break up. Divorce was mostly out of the question, and out-of-wedlock births were strongly stigmatized. Beginning in the last century, however, romance became the main reason for marriage, and divorce became a possibility. The result is that most marriages today are based entirely on love, and marital partners are expected to be intimate best friends. While this probably has generated many marriages that are more satisfying than those of the past, especially for women, affection alone has proved to be a weak link on which to hang such an important social institution. Should affection in a marital relationship wane, which it does in almost every marriage at least for short periods of time, divorce is now not only a legal possibility in all cases but it is culturally approved as well.

The second recent cultural shift of great consequence is the sexual revolution, in which sexual norms have moved from restrictive to permissive. A central theme of the sexual revolution was to give women many of the same sexual freedoms long granted to men. The rapidly accelerated version of this revolution, beginning in the 1960s, was made possible by the widespread availability for the first time of relatively cheap and reliable contraceptives, plus abortion. The revolution was extended through widespread acceptance of the idea (heavily promulgated by the therapeutic community) that good sex lies at the root of self-fulfillment, through the commercialization of sex, and through the extreme sexualization of popular culture by the media.

Cultural Conditions of Fatherless Today

The end result of the various trends just discussed is a society that is surprisingly unsupportive of fatherhood. Indeed, if one were specifically to design a culture and a social system for the express purpose of undercutting fatherhood and men's contribution to family life, the resulting society would be a close approximation of our own. Consider the following five dimensions of contemporary society.

Marriage

The principal function of marriage is to hold men to the (inherently stronger) mother-child bond. For men everywhere, marriage and parenthood tend to be a package deal. When marriage weakens, as it has today in modern societies, men will inevitably get the message that they no longer are needed or even wanted in family life, and they will remain detached from their children.

The high divorce rate is a major and woefully underdiscussed problem. Because of it, both men and women are increasingly reluctant to enter into marriage, even when children are involved, helping to account for today's extraordinarily high rate of out-of-wedlock births.

But there is an even more potent reason for the dramatic rise of nonmarital births: the decline of "shotgun weddings." Not so long ago it was culturally expected that men would marry the women they impregnated; now it is not. New evidence suggests that the decline of this norm was strongly associated with the introduction of birth regulation technologies, including abortion, in the 1960s. This made the birth or nonbirth of a child a choice for the mother alone, and therefore marriage or nonmarriage a choice for the father alone.[7] At the same time, of course, the stigma against illegitimacy markedly decreased.

Sex

The effect of the sexual revolution on fatherhood has been devastating. Men marry partly, if not mainly, to have a stable sexual life. If men can get as much sex as they like outside of the marital relationship, they will be much less inclined to many. In addition, the glamorization of nonmarital sex by the mass media has inevitably weakened the marital bond through making such sex seem more appealing. A less widely discussed, but no less important, problem is this: Men are less likely to marry the mothers of their children if they do not have confidence that the children are really theirs. There can be no doubt that the sexual revolution has generated a decline in "paternity confidence," a concept now widely invoked by the new field of evolutionary psychology.[8]

Education

Educational trends have had a serious impact on the preparation of young people for fatherhood and family life. At one time in American history, education was mostly a family affair, and parents were the main teachers. Families were large, and the great majority of households included children. With a strong parental interest at stake, children—both boys and girls—were taught about family life and parenting on a regular basis. Today, much of education has been formalized, taken over by schools, and is mainly concerned with preparing the young for jobs that require a high level of skill and knowledge. In general, our educational system, including higher education, disregards childrearing as a major adult responsibility and marriage as important to childrearing. Men, especially, are growing up with little preparation for adult family life, and little realization that their family life will be as important to them—if not more so—as their work life.

The Economy

The market economy, for all its virtues, has never been a great friend of fatherhood or the nuclear family. The rampant material consumerism that is engendered, especially through advertising, overshadows other important dimensions of people's lives. And the single-minded pursuit of profits is often conducted with little thought for its effect on family life.

The mature market economy in modern societies is encumbered with a formidable contradiction.[9] Bombarded by incessant urging to spend money, have a good time, travel, drink beer, and continuously enjoy life, workers find these messages to be in conflict with the older virtues of hard work, frugality, personal responsibility, and moderation. The manipulated desire for instant gratification is a constant threat to the workers' predisposition for social obligation, including obligation to family members and, indeed, to work itself. With the withering away of civil society, which has always served to insulate people from the market, the culture of materialism and instant gratification is making stronger incursions into people's daily lives. Because they are more individualistic to begin with, and also typically more involved in market activities, men are more affected by this than women.

Government

Although a major purpose of government in modern times has been to offset the dysfunctional impacts of the market, in many ways government has also helped to undermine fatherhood and the nuclear family. We can see this in no-fault divorce laws, in the marriage penalty tax codes, and in welfare policies that discriminate against two-parent families.

Cultural Changes Needed

With a modern culture so strongly stacked against it, what are the best levers of social change to renew fatherhood? Let us be clear that the culture can be changed. Just as the Progressives had a major societal impact early in this century, and the race and gender liberationists had a major impact in the second half of the century, so is it possible that pro-nuclear family forces can have a major impact in the early part of the twenty-first century.

The renewal of fatherhood, marriage and the family, and civil society is a tall order. It directly contradicts the dominant cultural ethos of our time: radical individualism that places at center stage the untrammeled self, loaded with a vision of individual rights and in full pursuit of self-development at all costs.

What is needed is a new balance of forces that can maintain the best of the individualistic spirit while reinvigorating those social and cultural structures able to provide the kind of social order without which civilization, including personal freedom and opportunity, cannot survive. Here are three key areas on which to focus change efforts.

First, dampen the sexual revolution. Schools, churches, and parents should urge young people to postpone sexual intercourse through the high school years. Men and women should be encouraged to restrict their sexual activity to marriage, or to relationships that may lead to marriage. Enormous pressure should be placed on the media and the entertainment industry to decrease the sexual content of their products.

Second, teach in every school in the land information about marriage and parenting. This should include the understanding that fathering is as important as mothering and that fathers are expected to play a major role in their children's upbringing. For young adults, educational programs should stress the negative effects of divorce on children and show the value of premarital counseling and marital enrichment programs.

Third, government policies should privilege marriage and the two-parent family. We can no longer afford to be neutral toward all alternative lifestyles.

Renewing Fatherhood

Rethinking and revising the institution of marriage, and especially marital gender-roles, in a way that better combines the three essential traits of friendship, passion, and justice, is central to any renewal of fatherhood. Most women, and many if not most men, do not want to return to the male-dominated marriages of the past. Only when marriage is revitalized—when men and women want to marry again and stay married—will fathers in large numbers stay involved with their children.

Renewing fatherhood is ultimately about infusing into our culture a stronger sense of moral obligation for the well being of others, especially children, and thus counterbalancing the radical strains of individualism. It may be that a fully restored sense of moral obligation can be accomplished entirely through secular means, but I doubt it. Religion has always been the main cultural repository of morality, and it is not likely that we can have permanent moral renewal without a society-wide religious reawakening. What form that reawakening might take, and should take, is an open question.

Notes

1. Kingsley Davis, "The Meaning and Significance of Marriage," in Kingsley Davis, ed., *Contemporary Marriage* (New York: Russell Sage Foundation, 1985), p. 21.
2. See David Popenoe, *Disturbing the Nest: Family Change and Decline in Modern Societies* (New York: Aldine de Gruyter, 1988).
3. Daniel Yankelovich, "How Changes in the Economy are Reshaping American Values," in Henry J. Aaron, Thomas E. Mann, and Timothy Taylor, eds., *Values and Public Policy* (Washington, D.C.: Brookings Institution, 1994), pp. 16–53.
4. Steven Mintz and Susan Kellogg, *Domestic Revolutions: A Social History of American Family Life* (New York: Free Press, 1988), p. 204.
5. For more on this topic, see David Popenoe, *Life Without Father* (New York: Free Press, 1996), Part Two.
6. Frank Furstenberg, Jr., "Good Dads-Bad Dads: Two Faces of Fatherhood," in Andrew Cherlin, ed., *The Changing American Family and Public Policy* (Washington, D.C.: Urban Institute, 1988), pp. 193–218.

7.   George A. Akerlof, Janet L. Yellen, and Michael L. Katz, "An Analysis of Out-of-Wedlock Childbearing in the United States," *Quarterly Journal of Economics* 111 (No. 2, May 1996), pp. 277–317.

8.   For an overview of evolutionary psychology, see Robert Wright, *The Moral Animal* (New York: Pantheon, 1994).

9.   Daniel Bell, *The Cultural Contradictions of Capitalism*, 20th anniversary ed. (New York: Basic Books, 1996).

11

The Marriage Movement

There can be no doubt that popular culture in America and in other modern nations has become increasingly anti-marriage, and has thus helped to generate the continuous weakening of marriage as a central social institution. In television and films, popular music, and leading newspapers and magazines, marriage has been undercut in recent years by such themes as the glories of single life, the joys of nonmarital sex, the self-fulfillment that divorce can bring, and the special strengths of nonmarital families. In contrast, the theme of building and staying in a committed marital relationship for the good of children and society as well as an enriching lifelong partnership has been all but forgotten. Partly as a result, the marriage rate has dropped by more than a third since 1970 and the out-of-wedlock birth ratio remains fixed at about one third of all births. Long-term marriages have become especially decimated, with a divorce rate holding at close to 50 percent compared to about 20 percent in the 1950s.

At the same time, because cultural values are at issue there is some hope for reversing the decline of marriage. Unlike most technological changes, cultural changes are more open to modification by concerted social action. We have seen dramatic changes to the twentieth century in the areas of race, women's roles, gay rights, and even peace and environmental issues. Indeed, the value changes in these areas over a short period of historical time have been quite remarkable. Although many social and economic trends in place made some of these changes inevitable in the long run, surely the changes were encouraged and advanced by strong, well-organized social movements. This essay explores the possibilities for a movement designed to reverse the decline of marriage.

The Marriage Problem

Throughout most of human history, sex, reproduction, and marriage have been culturally interlocked. Yet today—especially since the 1960s—the separation of these three activities has become marked. One no longer needs to marry to have children, much less to have sex. Marriages are now based mainly on love alone, and because love is considered a personal matter the larger institutions and forces that used to help hold marriages together—religion, economics, and the law—have become less involved. Moreover, love is a feeling, and feelings can change over time. As a consequence, the divorce rate has risen steeply and more people realistically question the possibility of committing to one person for a lifetime, thus contributing to the high rate of nonmarital births.

The separation of sex, reproduction, and marriage, in turn, has been strongly shaped by the larger forces of modernity. These forces and trends include the growing affluence and commercialization of life together with the continuing movement toward self-aggrandizing individualism; high personal and social mobility; secularization, cultural relativism, and the withering of moral standards; and the loss of child-centeredness stemming from radically reduced fertility and the mesmerizing attractions of the new workplace. All of these have tended to corrode personal and family relationships and pull people in directions from which neither they nor the larger society ultimately will benefit.

A Marriage Movement?

To counteract some of the antisocial consequences of these forces and trends of modernity, specifically to bring sex and children back into the sanctuary of long-term marriage, would indeed require a social and cultural movement of massive proportions. Such a movement would be possible if there were a strong latent interest in society for the revitalization of marriage. Does such an interest exist at the present time?

There is some evidence that the nation might be ready for a return to marriage. According to public opinion polls, there has been a growing awareness among Americans in the past decade that something has gone wrong with the family. As compared to their parents at the same age, today's generation of young people puts family life slightly higher on its agenda for the future, perhaps because of having had less of it during the growing-up years. Many people have observed that the topic of marriage recently has become somewhat more tolerated in public and professional debate.

Such opinion shifts may already have influenced a change in behavior. For example, the out-of-wedlock birthrate has leveled off and the divorce rate has dropped a little. Teen pregnancies are down. For several years in a row the percentage of children living in single-parent families has not increased.

Building on these few rays of hope, a number of recently organized efforts have been attempting to encourage and advance the cause of marriage. An Internet-based network called the Coalition for Marriage, Family, and Couples Education, founded by a former official of the American Association for Marriage and Family Therapy, focuses on helping people stay in relationships through skills training; it has had highly successful national conferences with mostly pro-marriage themes. The Marriage Savers group, founded by a religion and ethics newspaper columnist and headquartered in Maryland, has had an impact in many communities and a number of states, focusing on getting churches to better educate people for marriage. One branch of the fatherhood movement, the National Fatherhood Initiative, has made the revitalization of marriage a central focus. An academic group called The Religion, Culture, and Family Project, based at the Divinity School of the University of Chicago, is working to make marriage revitalization a concern of the mainline Protestant churches. And groups on the so-called religious right such as Focus on the Family, the Family Research Council, and a loose alliance of family policy organizations in many states, have made marriage central in their activities.

The National Marriage Project was established in 1997 at Rutgers University in New Jersey, and was designed to provide research and education to the American public about what has been happening to marriage, why this is a problem, and the ways in which the institution might be revitalized. Research and public education on marriage are also being conducted at such non-academic, conservative-leaning groups as The Heritage Foundation, based in Washington, D.C., and The Manhattan Institute and The Institute for American Values with its Council on Families, based in New York City.

In several states, notably Oklahoma, Arkansas, Utah, and Florida, governors have embarked on broad-based campaigns to make marriage an issue in an effort to cut the nonmarital birth and divorce rates. Two states, Louisiana and Arizona, have instituted "covenant marriage" laws, designed for couples that want to express an extra level of commitment to their marriage. Many other states are considering various marriage-improvement proposals as well as legal changes.

Do these varied activities add up to a marriage movement? Social and cultural movements typically proceed through several discrete stages. First is a general but unarticulated discontent with a social condition. This is followed by a second stage consisting of efforts to articulate the discontent and bring people together who share a common awareness that something needs to be done. The third stage involves the emergence of formal organizations at the national level with leaders, policies, and programs, all directed to social and cultural change. In the fourth and final stage the movement becomes institutionalized in the culture and, where relevant, in the law. To the degree that one exists, the marriage movement in America today could be said to rest mostly at stage two, articulating the discontent and bringing like-minded professionals together. No national, broad-based, formal organizations focused principally on marriage yet exist (stage three), and obviously the movement is a long way from becoming institutionalized (stage four).

The marriage-movement activities just noted are important and they provide much hope, but unfortunately their effect on our national life so far has been limited. There is surely across the country a general feeling of social discontent about the family, providing the interest necessary for a social movement. But this discontent has not yet been well articulated and the possible remedies remain cloudy. In particular, there has not yet emerged any national agreement that the strengthening of marriage—as distinct, for example, from more daycare centers, better divorces, more help for single-parent families, or pursuing dead-beat dads—is what is needed to solve the problems of the family.

In the political arena, neither major political party and no major political figure at the national level has taken up the issue of marriage in more than episodic fashion. Indeed, most politicians studiously seem to be avoiding it, a reason being perhaps that too many constituents—including the divorced, single parents, gays and lesbians, and radical feminists, not to mention young people who have become wary of what they interpret as "moralizing"—are allied against any serious discussion of marriage. Also, there is a belief that marriage trends are something about which governments can—and perhaps even should—do little. In the cultural sphere, marriage revitalization has not yet been taken up seriously by the academic community, by any of the major national periodicals, or by the mainline religious communities. Most importantly, there is no sign of any grassroots movement for marriage, especially on the part of those who count—the young adults.

Thus, and sadly in the face of a marriage rate that continues to drop rapidly, it is fair to say that the nation as a whole remains mostly uninterested in this issue. The marriage movement today seems not nearly as advanced as, say, the environmental movement, with which it shares some similarities. Even at the basic level of public education—articulating the general social discontent about family trends in a way that makes clear that revitalization of marriage is essential—much remains to be accomplished.

Revitalizing Marriage

In thinking about the future direction of a marriage movement, one's thoughts turn immediately to today's popular culture and its effects on marriage. Can anything be done to generate a more marriage-friendly Hollywood? Unfortunately, the answer is probably not very much.

Through extensive organization and commercialization, popular culture has become highly attuned to meeting the desires of its audience. If there were no market for sex and violence, a popular culture that features these themes would not exist. But of course there is an enormous market for such themes, especially among young adults. In the affluent age of "do everything, try everything," the normal desires and fascination with sex and violence are prime subjects for attention. And, with much of popular culture now driven by advertising, advertisers regard still-impressionable young adults as primary targets.

Moreover, young adulthood today lasts an unusually long time. If measured from puberty to marriage, in fact, the time period is between fifteen and twenty years. By every indicator we have, this period will only lengthen in the coming decades.

In assessing what can be done about popular culture it is also important to consider the place of children in modern life. In previous generations most households contained children, and the adults in such households surely must have had a strong child-consciousness that entered into their behavior and views of life. Today, less than a third of households contain children—down from more than three quarters in the mid-1800s—and one gets the strong impression that adult needs, desires, and fantasies are often molded quite apart from what is best for children. According to every indicator we have, even fewer households in the future will contain children.

In modern times, then, a situation has developed in which unattached and childless young adults, catered to by an ever more powerful and influential popular culture, have come to dominate much of our national life. This is the same group that, if marriage is to be revived, must somehow change its behavior and outlook. The members of this group must take a longer view of life, realize that committed marital relationships would be highly beneficial for themselves, their children, and their society, and begin to think and act in ways that would be more rather than less likely to lead to such relationships. This would mean such things as avoiding promiscuous sex; educating themselves for wiser mate-selection, marriage, and parenthood; and planning and organizing their careers much more around family life.

It is possible that some short-run modifications could be made in popular culture to make it more marriage-friendly. For example, the worst of violence and perverted sex might be withdrawn or at least restricted to later time slots when young children would be less likely to be watching. But popular culture will change only when popular demand changes. To have real success, a movement to reverse the decline of marriage would probably have to bypass popular culture and focus directly on young adults and their parents.

The most likely scenario for a marriage movement is one where popular culture remains about the same but becomes increasingly less influential over the minds of the young because other forces such as family and religion become more influential. At least a strong minority of young people could over time consciously come to reject the popular culture around them, as has already happened to some extent in strongly religious communities and in strong families that seek to protect their children from what they consider to be pernicious cultural elements. From this perspective, a marriage movement would have to start as a countercultural movement among the young, and then spread to ever-larger groups.

How could a countercultural marriage movement among the young be actively supported and encouraged? Such a movement could stem from a religious base, as it already has in the world of evangelicals. But to have society-wide success the movement would need strong secular as well as religious roots. The four main secular possibilities are governments, schools, parents, and voluntary associations.

Our national government has limited influence over family issues because, unlike in most European nations, American family law and most family concerns reside at the state level. But moral and political presidential leadership could be important, along with White House conferences, as could marriage-friendly policies enacted by Congress. In a few Western and Sun Belt states, as noted above, state-level political leadership has recently developed pro-marriage agendas. Indeed, these are currently the most promising developments in the budding marriage movement. Yet it is by no means clear how many other states will follow their lead; possibly not very many.

Our society places a high premium on education as the solution to many of its problems: Many of the state-level efforts, for example, are directed through the educational system, where marriage education courses could prove to be successful in getting students to think more about, and plan for, eventual marriage. Yet the public schools are probably not a reliable source for any kind of countercultural movement. Teachers are typically tied to the dominant liberal culture, and in any event they do not usually find themselves in situations where they can promote controversial topics.

The ultimate success of a marriage movement probably depends on enlisting the support of large numbers of parents. Parents have a very large stake in positive outcomes for such a movement. They want their own children to have stable relationships in adulthood and they desire grandchildren. Even when their own marriages were not successful or lasting, they usually hope their grandchildren will be raised within long-term marriages. Although adolescence and young adulthood are intrinsically times when young people break away from their families of origin and seek to move on, the young during these periods are probably more influenced by their parents than by anyone else. For a return to a marriage-based culture, parents would need to spend more time with their children stressing the benefits of married life and helping them to prepare for marriage, including the wise selection of a mate. In other words, parents would need to do what many of them used to do in times past.

The problem is that parents have been notoriously difficult to combine into a common "interest group." Attempts to organize parents for political and social purposes the way the elderly, for example, have been organized have so far largely been failures. Still, the possibility remains open, and this is where voluntary associations fit in. Voluntary associations that deal with parents as well as youth, ranging from local Scout troops to professional organizations, must be encouraged to make the revitalization of marriage a major part of their activities.

For those parents and organization leaders who are reluctant to support marriage strongly, these key points should be remembered:

- To be healthy and happy we all need warm, intimate relationships with others. People without such relationships are at a distinct disadvantage in life. Throughout most of history this need for intimate relationships has been met through living not only in families but also in larger, close-knit groupings. In modern life, with the growth of both individualism and affluence, such larger groupings are either weak or they no longer exist. The one residual group from the past that still does still exist is the nuclear family based on the long-term union of a man and a woman. Indeed, because the larger groupings have tended to fade away, the marriage-based nuclear family is more important than ever for human well being. People in strong marriages and families gain substantial health and emotional as well as economic benefits.
- The alternative to the modern nuclear family is the voluntary friendship group. But we should not expect friendship groups to have the same lasting power as married nuclear families because the latter are more strongly rooted in human biology. The human species has always been a "pair-bonding" species in which man and woman mated and together raised their children, and our inherited biological predispositions for this presumably have not changed.
- What has changed is the nature of marriage, which at one time was a functional link in the struggle for survival but consists today of an emotional tie in the struggle for happiness. This emotional tie is often fragile and problematic, not only because our standards of happiness have gone up but because marriage now has to carry the emotional load once carried by a wide complex of intimate family and community groupings. This suggests two requirements for the success of modern marriage: adequate premarital preparation, especially training in relationship skills, and a level of personal commitment to the partner, and to the institution, going well beyond that of ordinary friendships.
- By all the evidence at our disposal, the married, two-parent nuclear family is much better for raising children than any alternative. Compared to children from intact families, children from single-parent families and step-families run two to three times the risk of having serious, long-term problems in life. If marriage continues to decline, children will pay a heavy psychological price.

Based on this line of thinking, here is the general message for parents to give to their children: *A good marriage today is more difficult to achieve than ever, but it is also more important because there are no longer many real alternatives either for personal fulfillment or for child well being. This means that you should be preparing for and working at marriage with at least the same amount of focus and attention that you currently give to your career.*

Conclusion

In recent decades modern societies have developed an increasingly laissez-faire attitude toward marriage. Unwed pregnancies have been almost completely destigmatized, divorce has become fully accepted, and nonmarital cohabitation and alternative family forms are viewed with little concern and even approbation. In order to turn these marriage-related trends around and revitalize the institution of marriage we need to find ways to make society more aware of the profound benefits of married living. These benefits—for personal happiness, child development, and the overall success of our society—have been seriously overlooked in recent years.

Compared to other recent and successful social movements, the movement for marriage is still in the early stages. To move forward, it will have to develop a strong countercultural base of operations in the secular society. A massive public education campaign is required to shift public opinion, especially that of young people and their parents, more in favor of actively revitalizing marriage. Whether such a movement can ultimately be successful in changing the culture, of course, remains an open question.

12

Can the Nuclear Family be Revived?

Based on accumulated social research, there now can be little doubt that successful and well-adjusted children in modern societies are most likely to come from two-parent families consisting of the biological father and mother. Alternative family forms that are attempted, such as single-parent families and stepfamilies, have been demonstrated to be inferior in child outcomes. The recent movement away from the two-natural-parent family has led to considerable social malaise among the young, not to mention social decay in general.

It can be argued that child well being would be enhanced if families lived among care-giving relatives and in supportive communities, but this has become an ever-diminishing situation. Historically, a substantial stripping down has occurred of both the extended family and the cohesive neighborhood, and this trend is probably irreversible. The state has tried to fill the vacuum, but without much success. The two-parent nuclear family therefore may be more important today for children, and for society in general, than ever before in history.

Constituting one of the greatest dilemmas faced by modern societies, however, is the fact that nuclear families themselves are breaking apart at dramatically high rates. The chances in some societies are now less than 50-50, thanks mainly to divorce and out-of-wedlock births, that a child will live continuously to adulthood with both natural parents. This is despite the fact that, unlike in times past, parents now almost always live to see their children reach maturity.

One fundamental reason for the high breakup rate is that the nature of marriage has changed. Not so long ago marriage was an economic bond of mutual dependency, a social bond heavily upheld by extended families, and a religious bond of sacramental worth. Today, marriage is none of these. The economic bond has become displaced by affluence, by female economic pursuit, and by state support; extended family pressures on marriages have all but vanished; and modern societies have become increasingly secular. Marriage has become a purely individual pursuit; an implied and not very enforceable contract between two people; a relationship designed to satisfy basic needs for intimacy, dependency, and sex. When these needs change, or when a presumptively better partner is discovered, marriages are easily dissolved. Moreover, more of the everyday needs traditionally met by marriage can be met in other ways, such as through the marketplace.

With its surrounding and supporting social structures collapsing, can there be any hope that the nuclear family can be revived? Yes—the basis for hope lies in the fundamental biological and psychological makeup of humankind. If the evolutionary biologists are correct, human beings are a pair-bonding species. Unlike most other species, we have an innate predisposition to mate with one member of the opposite sex (homosexuals notwithstanding) and form a pair-bond for the purpose of raising children.

Pair-bonds are considered to be an evolutionary development of enormous importance to the human species, a major reason for our extraordinary success in the world of nature. Our predisposition to pair-bond appears to be a legacy of the fact that, in our ancestral environment of evolutionary adaptation, the mother-child bond alone was inadequate for favorable child outcomes. The most successful childrearing occurred when fathers were involved in the endeavor, bonding with the child's mother at least to the extent of providing the resources necessary for survival.

Human nature today still largely functions in these terms, but there is a joker in the deck. The evolved human pair-bond does not seem well matched with the marriage ideal of the modern nuclear family—voluntary, sexually-faithful, lifelong monogamy in which husband and wife share love and companionship. Such monogamy, in fact, has been extremely rare in humankind. Most societies throughout history have had a strong propensity toward polygyny (one husband, several wives), or toward serial monogamy involving a high marital breakup rate, the system that we have in modern societies today. Moreover, adultery is found almost everywhere, certainly among men but to a lesser degree among women as well.

The Modern Nuclear Family

The largest single reason for the historical deficit of faithful, lifelong monogamy, it has been suggested, is the evolved male mind. Whereas women, who necessarily have to make a tremendous personal investment in each offspring, have a strong desire for one mate who will care for them during their time of childbirth dependency, men can sire numerous offspring with little personal investment. Men are therefore pulled in two directions, one toward pair-bonding and the other toward sexual promiscuity. In most societies, a whole variety of cultural factors has helped to prevent widespread promiscuity, including the desires and influence of women and the self-protective attitudes and actions of men toward one another. Where these cultural factors fail, however, the male promiscuity option wins by default. One could argue that the default option is especially evident today in certain sections of America's inner cities.

It is important to stress the historical uniqueness of the modern nuclear family. Before its rise in the West several centuries ago, such monogamy as existed was typically maintained by extended family pressures, by strong economic dependencies between husband and wife, by the lack of legal alternatives, and by religious sanctions. The marriages in these families were quite unlike those of today. As the distinguished family historian Lawrence Stone has noted, "until fairly recent times the purpose of marriage had nothing to do with romantic love, sexual passion, or even necessarily friendship." Pre-modern marriages seem to have been mostly-arranged partnerships for the purposes of economic production and extended family connection.

The modern nuclear family was a truly remarkable development in the history of human social organization, and probably the only example in history in which voluntary lifelong monogamy was widely practiced. This family form consists of a monogamous married couple living with their children, apart from other relatives, with the husband working outside the home and the wife being a mother and full-time housewife. The marriage partnership is freely chosen and based on love and companionship. First arising among the bourgeoisie in northwestern Europe, this family form endured as a dominant ideal in the West through the Victorian era and up until the 1960s. The linchpin of its success was the still strongly internalized norm of marital permanence. Especially in the Victorian era, in addition, the family form was maintained by other strict moral codes that involved substantial sexual repression and to some extent the subjugation of women.

Due to this remarkable family organization, and thanks to rapidly decreasing parental death rates, by the 1950s more children in the industrialized nations were growing up with both of their natural parents than at any other time in world history. But after that, the modern nuclear family was diminished as a widespread cultural ideal by accelerating cultural, social, and economic trends together with new technological developments. In the realm of technology, new contraceptive techniques plus abortion permitted women for the first time in history to have active sexual lives without the near certainty of pregnancy and childbirth, and television and other mass communications media revolutionized the organized entertainment industry and, thereby, popular culture. Of seminal importance, also, was the unparalleled economic growth and affluence of the post-World War II years, which brought the possibility of unprecedented personal choice, for example in lifestyles, as well as rampant materialism heavily promoted by the advertising industry. Also important was the new mixing of men and women in the workplace, the decline of parental and adult authority, and the breakup of intact and culturally integrated neighborhoods and communities.

These trends were part of a larger ideological shift away from collective identities and toward an isolating and eventually destructive individualism. Even though the modern nuclear family had been built largely around individualism, the trend of individualism continued developing into the extreme form of a highly expressive or self-focused individualism. This differed from the individualism of the earlier era in which the purpose of self-development was more oriented to benefit the group and larger causes beyond the self. Several new cultural ideologies were involved in this shift, especially the therapeutic ideology with its goal of self-fulfillment, a playboy-style sexual opportunism and rejection of responsibilities by males, and a radical feminism that looked at the modern nuclear family as an oppressive institution. Also implicated were the cultural relativism of the social sciences and the humanities, and extreme rights-oriented political movements.

In view of this barrage of forces, what can be done to nourish the cultural ideal that must be restored if we are to revive the nuclear family: voluntary lifelong monogamy? First, let us realize that many things probably can't be changed. Among the things we can't rid ourselves of, or change to any significant degree, are the following: the biological makeup of males and females; modern technologies; the isolated nuclear family (few people wish to return to the earlier system of living in extended families); women in the workplace (except for certain periods of their lives, such as childrearing, women are in the workplace to stay); the nature of the marital relationship (no one wants to go back to arranged marriages, patriarchy, and gross economic dependence); and material affluence (despite the possibility of temporary economic recessions and depressions).

Our efforts must obviously be concentrated on those factors that can be changed, and they fall into two areas: cultural, moral, and religious beliefs and norms; and government policies, programs, and legislation. Of the two, the cultural realm is by far the most important. Some would argue that the culture cannot be changed, but they are wrong. Think of the dramatic changes in recent decades in our attitudes and beliefs about women, blacks, sex, the environment, the role of government, and perhaps even the option of war.

To repeat: If the nuclear family is to be revived, *we must restore the cultural importance of voluntary, lifelong monogamy.* Here are the three most important focal points for such efforts:

1. Counter the Sexual Revolution.

- Promote sexual abstinence at least through the high school years. Most parents certainly favor this and probably most high schools students do as well.
- Encourage women and men to lead their premarital sex lives with eventual marriage more strongly in mind. For example, what our grandmothers supposedly knew might well be true: if a woman wants a man

to marry her, wisdom dictates a measure of playing hard to get.
- Rein in the organized entertainment industry. At one time the entertainment industry did have a moral conscience, so we know it is possible. The main levers today are mass protests and boycotts.

2. *Promote Marriage.*

- Spread the word about the emotional, economic, and health benefits of lifelong monogamy, and about how it is superior to other family forms. This can be done by high schools and universities, churches, voluntary associations, and even by federal and state governments.
- Educate people about the nature of modern marriage—that it is not merely finding the perfect mate and living a life of passion and romance. It is a long-term friendship between a man and a woman that requires constant effort and care plus a strong moral commitment to the institution, in addition to special communications skills.
- Widely promulgate the findings about how marriage failure damages children.
- Continue to privilege marriage through public policy and at the same time discourage the formation of alternative lifestyles.

3. *Renew a Cultural Focus on Children.*

- Parents want to do what is best for their children. So do most adults. We should not let the age-old cultural priority on childrearing—the sentiment that children are our future—slip from our grasp, as now seems to be happening. A serious problem is that less than one-third of households today contain children, down from more than three-quarters in prior centuries. The task will not be easy.

13

A Marriage Research Agenda for the Twenty-First Century: Ten Critical Questions

Introduction

The institution of marriage has undergone such rapid and far-reaching changes in recent times that reliable information about modern marriage is sparse. Much new research and thinking are needed if we are to better understand what has been happening to marriage, the social, economic, and cultural conditions now shaping the institution, and how marriage can best be strengthened. The following ten questions have been developed to try to pinpoint some key issues about which a deeper understanding is needed. I address the questions roughly in order of importance and priority to strengthening marriage in the twenty-first century.

The Ten Questions

Young Adulthood

1. The age of marriage has been moving upward while the age of puberty has been moving downward, thus lengthening the period of life in which people are sexually mature yet unmarried. The patterns of living during this new and relatively long period of adolescence and young adulthood are often associated with values and behaviors that are antithetical to marriage.

How can we best insure that the life experiences during adolescence and young adulthood will contribute to, rather than detract from, eventual marriage?

Discussion: It used to be the case that young people, especially women, lived at home in a family-friendly environment until they married. Today, the average American woman reaches puberty at perhaps age eleven, and marries at age twenty-five, resulting in a period of about fourteen years in which she could be sexually active yet unmarried. The data for men are similar. If current trends continue, this time period will lengthen; puberty could start slightly earlier, and marriage will probably begin later. In several Scandinavian nations today the average age of marriage for women has nearly reached thirty.

At least half of this post-puberty, pre-marriage period typically is lived apart from parents and other family members in a sexually active singles culture that is mainly focused on work, career, and recreation rather than family and children. In America, especially, the nonfamily character of the subculture of young adulthood is accentuated by the entertainment industry in which the serious concerns of marriage and parenthood are seldom addressed. Indeed, a growing number of young people put marriage and children out of their minds during these years and when married family life finally comes it is one of the most stressful times of life, representing as it does a radical shift from the independent and freedom-loving lifestyle that preceded it. The rapidly declining birthrates in all modern societies undoubtedly reflect the difficulty in shifting from young-adult singlehood to responsible marriage and parenthood.

A recent conservative answer to this dilemma calls for earlier marriage. The way to solve the problem, it is argued, is to marry young and thus avoid the singles culture and the temptation for premarital sex. Aside from the fact that this proposal runs directly counter to current trends and would thus be difficult to put into effect, it has some other important failings. Most notably, early marriage—especially in the teen years—has been found by social research to be the strongest risk factor for divorce ever identified.[1] There can be little doubt that modern marriage, which is based on lifelong intimate friendship rather more than the functional relationship of earlier historical periods, depends on the wise and mature selection of a mate. This presumably is more effectively achieved at older ages when personalities have been more clearly formed and work and careers better established.

But if not early marriage, then what? Based on the assumption that the overwhelming majority of young people eventually want to marry,[2] we need as a first step to bring marriage concerns and plans back into the subculture of young adulthood. This might be done through incorporating marriage and parenthood education in the high school and college curricula, reinvolving parents in the mating lives of their children, making the workplace more flexible for family concerns, and encouraging the media to portray marriage positively more often. Some messages that could be stressed are the importance of not waiting too long to marry if children are desired, and taking a longer view of life—focusing on the many lifelong benefits of marriage and children for health, happiness, and prosperity. It might also be useful to permit tax-deferred accounts in young, single adulthood that could be used later for childrearing expenses. A careful program of research is needed to evaluate these various policies and programs.

Sexual Restriction

2. Strong marriage systems of the past have been accompanied by a high degree of sexual restriction, especially of women's sexuality. The sexual revo-

lution has generated unparalleled sexual freedom for both men and women but also probably has lowered the chances for long-lasting marriages and thus harmed children. It is hard to imagine rebuilding a strong marriage system in today's sexual climate.

Is it possible to move toward a more culturally restrictive sexual system for both men and women and if so, how, and how restrictive should it be?

Discussion: Over the course of history, societies have fluctuated between restrictive and permissive sexual regimes, and we are now pretty far out in the permissive direction. The time may be ripe for a shift back. Despite the sexual libertinism promulgated by the urban elite and the entertainment industry, as well as the widespread proliferation of pornography on the Internet, I believe that most young people realize the explosive downside of unrestricted sex and want to find some way to generate a more humane and responsible sexual culture. Because of the commercialization of sex and the power of new technologies, the achievement of a more restrictive marriage- and child-friendly sexual regime will surely be difficult to achieve, but does not seem impossible.

First, families probably will have to become countercultural in order to protect their children from the oversexualized culture. If enough families engage in cultural protest and boycotts against the media, insisting that we find better ways to protect children from premature sexualization, it could have an effect. Second, it seems wise to promote sexual abstinence at least through the high school years. This would seem to be an achievable goal, one that is favored by most parents and probably most high school students as well.

A goal that does not seem achievable is the prohibition of all sexual activity until marriage. The weight of evidence from the social sciences suggests that the premarital period now is simply too long and the sexualization of culture too extreme to hold this as a realistic goal, as much as it may be desired by many and held as a moral and religious value. In its place we should be developing norms in which young adults seek to lead their premarital sex lives with eventual marriage more strongly in mind. The leadership for this probably will have to be taken by women; they are traditionally assumed to be the gatekeepers of sexuality. One such norm is the one our grandmothers thought might be true: if a woman wants a man to marry her, wisdom dictates a measure of playing hard to get. This could mean, for example, that a woman would refuse to cohabit except when marriage is clearly planned, that is, when she becomes engaged. And in such cases the cohabitation should be only on her terms, and usually in her domicile. Another moderate sexual norm that now seems all but forgotten is abstinence from sex until a strong, intimate relationship has been established. The reestablishment of this norm does not seem out of the question, but it would likely have to be reestablished by a large majority of women.

Father Absence and Paternal Investment

3. The historical record indicates that if women are economically able to raise children without men they will often do so; and that, without marriage, men will stray from their children. In the modern era, more and more women are economically independent and are parenting alone, marriage is weakening, and more men are straying. Thus children lose the benefit of fathers, and society loses the benefit of the civilizing force of marriage and children on men.

How can we reverse the tide of father absence and ensure that men remain actively involved in childrearing?

Discussion: It is no secret that modern societies face growing fatherlessness. In the United States, for example, the percentage of children not living with their biological fathers jumped from 17 percent in 1960 to more than 35 percent by the century's end.[3] The factors that have led to high paternal involvement in societies throughout history have been fairly well established and they go well beyond economics.[4] Most of these factors are now weakening and, in combination, they represent a most important focus for future research.

First, high paternal involvement occurs when a father has a high degree of confidence that a child is really his. Men are much more willing to make parental investments in their biological children than in children who are genetically unrelated. Given today's sexual climate, paternity confidence must surely be diminishing.

Second, high paternal involvement takes place when alternative mating opportunities for males are restricted, forcing men into a strategy of making higher investments in a few children rather than lower investments in many— the reproductive option they possess far more than females. Today, especially with cohabitation and the ease of divorce and despite our socially imposed monogamy, the alternative mating opportunities available to men are high.

Third, men make strong investments in children if they think that such investments are truly important for child outcomes. Today, with the help of the government, low-income women are at least able to get by, and high-income women are financially self-sufficient—thus diminishing the man's economic importance. Moreover, the cultural perception has arisen that men may even be superfluous to childrearing.

Fourth, high paternal investments traditionally have been accentuated through pressure from extended family members who also have a biological stake in child outcomes, and such pressure has often been contributed as well by peers and through the larger culture. These pressures are notoriously weak today.

Fifth, fathers contribute more if they sense that successful offspring will lead to their own economic enrichment, as, for example, on a family farm or through expected care in old age. Today, children are seen more as an economic drain than an asset (see question 8 below).

Sixth, paternal investments are mediated through the marriage relationship. If the relationship is strong, men will go the extra mile to please their wives through childcare activities. If the marital relationship breaks down, men have tended to leave both the woman and the child. Given the state of marriage today, this phenomenon obviously has serious social implications.

In the face of these six factors, reversing the tide of fatherlessness is surely a daunting challenge. Among the possible solutions, in addition to shoring up the institution of marriage and partially reversing the sexual revolution, are more widely publicizing both the importance of fathers for child outcomes and the benefit to male psychological well being of close ties to children, and engaging fathers in early childcare so that they will be more likely to bond with their children and stay with them even if their marriage breaks down.

Marital Bonds

4. Marriages of the past typically were held together by strong bonds of economic dependency between husbands and wives, religious meaning, extended family solidarity, and societal approval, all based around the importance of reproduction and childrearing. Today, in many marriages, the only major bond is adult psychological need, which has proven to be quite fragile in holding marriages together over the long run.

If modern marriages are to be made stronger and longer lasting, aren't some additional marriage bonds needed? If so, which ones?

Discussion: The primary purpose of marriage throughout history has been the raising of children. The need of every society for successful childrearing is why marriage has been a public institution and a focus of religious concern. In times past, children not reared by a mother and a father who stayed together faced significantly higher risks of negative life outcomes, including early death.

Today, marriage is thought to be more a couples relationship—a friendship between two adults—in which children are an option. Children have been pushed ever more to the sidelines of modern life and are even perceived by a growing number of adults as impediments to the good life. It can reasonably be argued that married people are happier, healthier, and wealthier than single people and that therefore marriage is a social good.[5] But without children, it is much more difficult to envision the institution of marriage as something that requires public attention and regulation. After all, it is a social good for people to have lots of friends, but we don't consider that to be a public issue subject to government regulation.

Frankly, in the absence of children, I do not know what other bonds can be added to the modern marital relationship. And, as marriage becomes increasingly a private relationship between two (or more!) adults, I believe that it will become much more difficult to think of it as a social institution that should be subject to government and religious concern. But this is surely a critical area for further thought and discussion.

Division of Labor

5. In every society throughout history, except under abnormal circumstances, husbands have been the primary breadwinners and wives have been the primary childrearers. Today, the changing nature of the economy increasingly has blended these marital role assignments.

To what extent can the traditional marital division of labor be discarded without damaging the success of marriages or the sense of well being of either men or women?

Discussion: One of the axioms of contemporary evolutionary psychology is that, in mate selection, women prefer men who can provide economic resources whereas men prefer women who are young, attractive, and fertile. This pattern is so common that it likely has a genetic base. That is, it was selected for through adaptation in our ancestral environment. Moreover, throughout history men have been the family leaders—presumably not only because they were the main economic providers but also because they possessed greater size and strength. Yet women today seemingly are in the workforce to stay, more and more families involve joint wage earners, and we see a growing number of couples that break from the common pattern, such as wealthier women with struggling male artists and career women who have househusbands. What do these trends mean for the future of marriage?

It is worth remembering that the extreme marital division of labor—with women serving as full-time mothers and homemakers and not in the labor force, and men serving as the exclusive breadwinners, working outside the home, and remaining somewhat distant from day-to-day family life—dates from the nineteenth century and even then only in the urban middle classes. Throughout most of history, to the degree that childcare permitted, women have shared breadwinning and been in the labor force, mostly in agricultural pursuits. Much of our marital gender-role tension today, then, seems to concern the shift from the "modern nuclear family" of the past century, with its defined roles, to today's nuclear family. This limited time span provides some hope for a successful resolution. Indeed, we apparently have returned to a family situation, not unlike that found in our ancestral environment, in which the predominant family form is nuclear, both husbands and wives are in the labor force and have a relatively egalitarian relationship with one another, and men have a reasonably active and hands-on fathering role.

Still, it is highly unlikely, given human nature, that we will ever see a general role reversal, with women becoming the primary breadwinners and men the primary childrearers. In fact, there is some evidence to suggest that marriages in which this has taken place are unhappy and have a high breakup rate.[6] Unless human nature somehow radically shifts, therefore, we will probably continue to see some differentiation based on women's stronger ties to children with the attendant traits of nurturing and caring, and men's stronger ties to hierarchy with the attendant traits of competitiveness and aggressiveness. But this is obviously an area in which far more knowledge is needed.

Friendship Outside of Marriage

6. Up until the modern era, no marriage system expected husbands and wives to be each other's nearly exclusive best friend and confidant. In prior periods the close friendships of husbands and wives were much more likely to have been with others of the same sex or close relatives or both.

To what degree does exclusive marital friendship place a burden on modern marriages, and if a serious burden, how can it best be surmounted?

Discussion: For many people in modern life, especially men, marriage (along with nonmarital cohabitation) has become the only social structure that concerns intimate relationships. This is unfortunate, because it puts enormous pressure on a fragile institution. Just as married women need same-sex friends apart from their husbands, so do men. Because it is more difficult for men to make and keep friends than it is for women, the "isolated nuclear family" is not an especially healthy environment for men. With the reasonable goal of gaining further access to public life, feminism has sought to break down male-only bastions where, in fact, male friendships were once formed. In the future it might be wise to reconstruct some male-only places outside of bastions of public power where married men can seek same-sex companionship and intimacy.

Sexual Fidelity and the Modem Workplace

7. Historically, in most societies, men and women have been gender segregated in their work lives, and the kin group and local communities have closely controlled their sexual behavior. Married men and women seldom were in situations where intimate contact with others of the opposite sex could occur. Today, men and women are thrown together in the workplace, and their behavior takes place largely apart from the observation and control of relatives and neighbors; married men and women operate in conditions identical to those of the unmarried. Under such conditions, the normal, biological male and female sexual and mate-selection proclivities can be expected to come into play, helping to generate marital breakdown.

Can explicit norms and workplace policies be developed that inhibit intimate contact among coworkers, especially those who are married?

Discussion: This is a serious problem. The workplace has not only become the venue in which much mate selection takes place but probably also the environment in which many marriages are dissolved. In the absence of gender-segregated settings, a new normative structure will have to be developed if we want to regain some control over the situation. Sexual harassment legislation is one response already in place; the worry is that it will dampen the prospects for successful mate selection. More important, in my view, is the development of a normative code that places married people off limits to sexual approaches. It is hard to see how law could impose this; it would have to arise informally. Shouldn't people at least feel some remorse from going after someone else's wife or husband? The moral obliviousness about this in today's popular culture is as remarkable as it is unfortunate.

Economics of Children

8. Marriages of the past were heavily based on the fact that both the husband and the wife had a mutual interest in their children's well being because the children would become part of the family workforce and the parents would become economically dependent on those children in their older years. In other words, children were enormous economic assets to the married couple. Today, children have become more of an economic liability to parents than an asset, and the economic support of dependent elderly has largely been taken over by the state.

Is there any way to make children an economic asset to their parents again, and thus strengthen the marriage bond?

Discussion: There is only one way I know of to do this in modern societies, and that is to reformulate social security and old-age pension systems so that a parent's income in old age is based partly on the child's earnings. Economist Shirley P. Burggraf has recently put one proposal forward.[7] Under the current system of collectivized social security, young people pay into a system that provides generous retirement benefits for all older persons, irrespective of whether they have been good parents. As she notes, "People who never have children, parents who abuse or neglect or abandon their children, deadbeat dads who don't pay child support—all have as much claim (in many cases more) on the earnings of the next generation as the most dutiful parents." Under Burggraf's proposal, the parental retirement pension would come from taxes on their children's earnings that had been invested in a trust fund. Parents who invest more in their children might thereby reap the most economic benefits in the long run. The system would not discriminate against the childless; adults without children would be expected to set up their own retirement trust funds; they could, in effect, invest in the stock market instead of in children.

The problem is that turning children again into potential economic assets might be morally unacceptable in today's society. A national discussion of these issues would be useful, but in the end we will probably have to rely on children being psychic rather than economic assets.

Support During the Transition to Parenthood

9. The arrival of the first child has proven to be a critical time of stress in many modern marriages.[8] There are many reasons for this, but a prominent one is that so many children today are born into households that are isolated from other family members, relatives, neighbors, friends, and supportive services. In the past, childrearing was largely a group experience; mothers had much assistance from others and children were often raised as much by the local community as by the parents.

How can we bring today's childrearing households into closer contact with others for the provision of mutual assistance and support, or provide such support through other means?

Discussion: It is surely the case that a "village" is an important adjunct to childrearing, and that today's isolated nuclear family is distinctly disadvantageous for children. One answer to this question rests in building communities that are better focused on the needs of childrearing families. In many respects, American communities today are woefully inadequate for children, ranging from the absence of public transportation to the lack of pedestrian access. Another answer is a better network of childcare centers, at least for preschool children.

One outstanding issue is the seeming need for both parents to work when the children are young, thus making childrearing that much more difficult. This problem might be helped through enabling pre-married single people, during the years when they have good incomes and no dependents, to setup tax-deferred accounts to be used for childrearing expenses after marriage. We should also consider expanding parental leave to a longer time period with partial pay, and providing more relief for families with young children from the current high level of taxation. In addition, we need to do much more education for parenthood in high schools and colleges, as well as for couples who are expecting their first child.

Attachment Experiences

10. There is substantial evolutionary and psychological evidence that the early attachment experiences of infants are related to the intimate relationships and procreational behavior of those infants when they become adults.[9] In other words, weak and insecure early attachment can generate poor adult relationships, including unstable marriages and unhealthy sexuality.

To what degree are today's high divorce rates and nonmarital birthrates related to inadequate attachment in childhood and, if the connection is strong, what should we be doing to improve the attachment experiences of today's children?

Discussion: Perhaps the greatest tragedy of recent family decline is the weakening of attachment experiences in children. Because weak attachments in childhood seem to lead to weak attachments in adulthood, and since good intimate relationships are one of life's most meaningful and important attributes, we may be on a course in modern societies in which people become increasingly rich but decreasingly happy. What a sad commentary that would be on human progress. We should be conducting major longitudinal studies to pin down the precise relationship between childhood attachment and adult outcomes, to determine the kind of family units in which attachment is fostered, and to assess the impact of the childrearing process called "attachment parenting."

Conclusion

These questions obviously are framed from broad academic and interdisciplinary perspectives, including historical, cross-cultural, and evolutionary. Especially for an institution as central and important as marriage, such broad perspectives are essential if we are to have a full understanding of the issues involved. It is clear that marriage issues cannot adequately be addressed by the approach of a single discipline, or even by the social sciences as they currently are established. Marriage is much more than a social institution; it is based in the biological realities of the human species.

Notes

1.   See, for example, T. C. Martin and L. Bumpass, "Recent Trends in Marital Disruption," *Demography* 26 (1989), pp. 37-51. One recent study has concluded that the increase in median age at first marriage since the 1960s is the most important factor accounting for the recent leveling off of divorce rates. Tim B. Heaton, "Factors Contributing to Increasing Marital Stability in the United States," *Journal of Family Issues* (in press).

2.   In the 1996-98 period, 81 percent of high school senior girls and 72 percent of high school senior boys stated that having a good marriage and family life was "extremely important" to them. From Monitoring the Future surveys reported in *The State of Our Unions: 2000*, National Marriage Project, Rutgers University, New Brunswick, NJ.

3.   Calculations from government sources for David Popenoe, *Life Without Father* (New York: Free Press, 1996).

4.   See David C. Geary, "Evolution and Proximate Expression of Human Paternal Investment," *Psychological Bulletin* 126 (2000), pp. 55-77 and Patricia Draper, "Why Should Fathers Father?" in Alan Booth and Ann C. Crouter, eds., *Men in Families* (Mahwah, NJ: Lawrence Erlbaum, 1998), pp. 111-121.

5.   Linda Waite and Maggie Gallagher, *The Case for Marriage* (New York: Doubleday, 2000).

6.   Graeme Russell, *The Changing Role of Fathers?* (New York: University of Queensland Press, 1983); Philip Blumstein and Pepper Schwartz, *American Couples* (New York: Pocket Books, 1983).

7.   Shirley P. Burggraf, *The Feminine Economy and Economic Man* (Reading, MA: Addison-Wesley, 1997).

8. Carolyn P. Cowan and Philip A. Cowan, *When Partners Become Parents: The Big Life Change for Couples* (New York: Basic Books, 1992).

9. See Robert Karen, *Becoming Attached* (New York: Warner Books, 1994).

Part 4

Looking Back

14

Remembering My Father: An Intellectual Portrait of "The Man Who Saved Marriages"

A few months ago I drove down Sunset Boulevard in Los Angeles, past the building not too far from Hollywood and Vine that once housed my father's American Institute of Family Relations. This used to be one of the spiffy areas of Hollywood, and I remember how proud he and my mother were when the building was purchased and renovated after World War II: he was able to move his Institute—the oldest and for nearly half a century the largest family counseling organization in the nation—out from an office in the center of downtown Los Angeles where he had founded it in 1930. My father spent the rest of his working life in this building; he thought of it as his international headquarters. In the late 1940s, before I went east to college, I spent many a Saturday there helping him, usually stuffing envelopes and licking stamps with the clerical staff.

In returning to Hollywood I wasn't sure what to expect. My father died in 1979 at the age of ninety. He had relinquished the reins of the Institute a few years before that, after reluctantly acknowledging his failing memory, and spent his last year in a nursing home near one of my older brothers in Florida. After his death, realizing that the area was turning seedy, the new managers had moved the Institute in the early 1980s out to the North Hollywood-San Fernando Valley area. Later, struggling to survive, it was merged with another counseling organization. Last I heard it had vanished from the American scene.

The building was still there—itself a surprise in southern California, the obsolescence capital of the world. It now houses something called the Annex of the American Radio Network. But most of the old neighborhood was gone, having become an area of fast food joints, rundown and boarded-up stores, homeless, and streetwalkers. The only tie to the past could be found on the side of the building where, although the actual letters had long since been taken down, I could see embossed on the stucco the faint image, "The American Institute of Family Relations." I was reminded of how, in my father's day, the next-door neighbor had put up a billboard on his property that completely covered up the Institute sign. He claimed that it was his "constitutional property right" (another southern California affectation), and apparently it was—at least my father was never able to get rid of the billboard. Now, of course, with nothing to obstruct, the billboard was gone.

It is not surprising that the Institute, except by a few years, failed to outlive its founder. In a 1960 article in *Your Life* entitled "Paul Popenoe—Marriage Mender," the author wrote: "a wise man once said, 'An institution is the lengthened shadow of one man…and Dr. Paul Popenoe…is indeed a man with a lengthened shadow.'" The converse of this is, when the man goes, so goes the shadow, no matter how lengthened it is. This certainly happened in the Institute's case. But what has puzzled me is how fast my father's name passed into oblivion. Today, for example, the person once generally regarded as having founded and popularized marriage counseling in America is all but forgotten in the professional field of marriage and family relations.

Although I fully recognize that a man's stature may be greatest in his son's eyes, I always thought of my father as a great man. At the peak of his career, in the 1950s and early 1960s, Paul Popenoe was probably the best known "family relations" expert in the nation. In addition to running the Institute he had a nationally syndicated daily newspaper column, "Your Family and You," was host of a popular "unrehearsed and unscripted" television program titled *Divorce Hearing* in which he counseled real-life clients, and was a regular guest on the Art Linkletter *House Party* and other radio and TV shows. He had lectured at over 200 colleges and universities and was the author of some seventeen books and hundreds of articles, both scientific and popular. He is perhaps best remembered for the *Ladies Home Journal* advice column "Can This Marriage be Saved?" which he developed in 1953 with the writer Dorothy Cameron Disney and which, for its first few decades, carried his introduction and picture and was based on actual files from the Institute. Still running, the column is currently billed as "the most popular, most enduring women's magazine feature in the world." In 1960, the *Ladies Home Journal* carried a feature article on my father entitled "The Man Who Saves Marriages." At least in southern California, which is all I knew about, he had become a celebrity through frequent TV appearances. One could seldom go into a restaurant, for example, without people recognizing and coming up to him.

Paul Popenoe's television and radio popularity was no doubt generated by his strong and unique personality. A highly learned, even brilliant man, who was well versed in the classics and knew eight languages, he possessed a fabulous memory, a sharp, ever-present wit, and a down-to-earth manner that gave him a compelling presence in public. The author of "The Man Who Saves Marriages" described him as "a fascinating conversationalist, he peppers his words with the spice of funny anecdotes, endless statistics and pertinent quotations from the Bible and Shakespeare…he has a dry, crisp, staccato way of talking and a wide smile both bashful and kind." A friend of fifty years once said of him, "the most successful man I know with the least self-conceit," and "infinitely wise."

He was a direct, no-nonsense, roll-up-your-sleeves kind of man. "Call him about some matter and it's done—bang!—practically by the time you hang up the receiver," one writer stated. This quality of directness may account for some of the immense, long-lasting appeal of the "Can This Marriage Be Saved?" column, in which one reads the wife's story, then the husband's, and then bang—the necessary steps to be taken to save the marriage. No beating around the bush.

Yet, while Paul Popenoe is still remembered by those senior citizens who looked at his materials or watched him on TV, his impact in the professions and in the worlds of elite and academic discourse seems to be nil. There could be many reasons for this turn of events. He was largely a professional loner who remained aloof from professional associations and was unable even to find a suitable protégé to take his place at the Institute. And, although he was an accomplished scholar, he desperately wanted to improve the world and therefore became a popularizer, putting out his message directly to the people in speeches and popular articles, rather than in academic journals. Academics and professionals have never taken kindly to such behavior (and, over the years, he did not always take very kindly to them, either).

But surely one important reason for the swift fading of his reputation is that his was a message people no longer wanted to hear. He was a man of the old school, one who believed in strong family men who sacrificed for their children, in premarital virginity for both men and women, in breadwinner/housewife marital roles, in strict marital fidelity, and in two-parent families. In short, he was a fervent proponent of what we now call the traditional nuclear family. Needless to say, this message came under heavy attack in the cultural revolution that began in the middle of the 1960s. And, from his side, he was thoroughly repelled by the personal liberation ideology, new age consciousness, playboy mentality, and alternative life styles that then came into vogue. He found these cultural shifts to be in opposition to everything he stood for. Thus it may be that Paul Popenoe and his views were swept away in a cultural tide.

Today in the 1990s, however, with the huge cohort of baby boomers having finally reached the middle of the family stage of the lifecycle, the cultural revolution that began in the 1960s is looking ever more frail. There is a new spirit of familism afoot, a realization that many children have been damaged by "me generation" upbringings in the past thirty years, a sense that men culturally have been cast adrift, and a growing feeling that we must try harder to foster social bonds and family values. One even hears with increasing frequency the thought expressed that perhaps we should try to undo the sexual and gender revolutions and restore the traditional nuclear family. Paul Popenoe would have loved this aspect of the nineties; he would have thought that society might be shifting back to his basic view that "successful marriage and sound family life are the basis of any enduring civilization."

In light of this possible cultural shift toward a "new familism," it has been especially intriguing for me to have the opportunity to reconsider Paul Popenoe and his views. I wanted to come to terms with just how much of what he believed about families, and especially the role of fathers, I consider still to be valid today. And I thought it might be of interest to others to know what kind of father, husband, and family man Paul Popenoe was. That is a subject on which little has ever been written, least of all by one of his sons, and it speaks directly to the issue of the validity of his views. In this regard, I'm sure that I am not alone in holding the opinion that one of the best tests of a person's views is how well they work out in practice.

His Life Story

My father often called himself a Victorian man and turn-of-the-century Republican. He was born the eldest of three sons in 1888 in Topeka, Kansas, into a family whose forebears on his mother's side (Bowman) came over on the Mayflower and on his father's side (of French Huguenot extraction) immigrated around 1690. He was very proud of his blueblood and American pioneer background (one relative was reputed to have fought alongside Daniel Boone at Boonesboro), and like many strong familists he maintained a life-long interest in family genealogy. (My mother's family background, however—maiden name Stankovitch and of Croatian descent—interested him considerably less.)

My grandfather grew up on a farm outside of Topeka (the family having moved out from Illinois, and before that from Ohio and Kentucky). He married a banker's daughter originally from Boston, and later became a man of modest wealth as owner of the Topeka Daily Capital. For part of his childhood, my father lived in a Topeka "mansion" on the edge of town; although he liked to refer to his "dirt farm" background, this was plainly more a cultural than an economic legacy. Kansas may best be known as the backwater state featured in *The Wizard of Oz*, but Topeka at that time was something of a cultural mecca by Midwestern standards and was the spawning ground for a number of prominent Americans, such as the Menninger brothers.

As pioneer families are wont to do, my father's family eventually moved on to California around the turn of the twentieth century, being among the early settlers in the Pasadena area. The "official" reason given for the move was my grandfather's health, but it also appears that he had somehow lost a good deal of his Kansas-earned money. Southern California at that time (and especially Pasadena) was made up mainly of Midwesterners who worked diligently to uphold their imported bourgeois values. What an era it must have been—an upright and hardworking people with a sense of unlimited progress in one of the most beautiful places on earth. As a true product of this Midwestern Victorian culture, my father's most strongly held moral virtues were honesty, hard work, a powerful drive for personal achievement, and overall moral rectitude. His father constantly stressed to him that the goal of a man's life was to leave his mark, and the virtue that Paul Popenoe most often emphasized with his own four sons was, "Popenoe's aren't 'can't' people." As a young man he wore stiff white collars, inhabited a world mainly of men, and absolutely adored his mother (when he was very old, any mention of her would bring tears to his eyes).

In good Victorian fashion, he also exhibited what many today would call a profound sexual prudishness. He claimed to have been a virgin at the time of his marriage at age thirty-two and even to have successfully eschewed masturbation; he viewed prostitution and pornography as among the world's great evils. Around women, he was awkward and shy.

But in other respects he could be marked as a California man, a free thinker. He gave up religion when he was still young (after teaching Sunday school for many years in the Congregational church) and became a secular humanist, often jokingly replying when you asked his religion that he was a member of "the First Evangelical Church of the Living Truth." He was one of the early California vegetarians, refraining from eating meat around 1905 after a fainting spell following a steak dinner at a restaurant; he kept to a meatless diet for the rest of his life. (In the Freudian spirit of the time, we—his four sons— typically interpreted this as a misguided attempt by him to curtail his overly aggressive impulses.) And it could be argued that he never would have taken up the profession of marriage counseling had he remained in the Midwest, away from "the Hollywood scene" where the need for such counseling was constantly staring one in the face.

Paul Popenoe was a mostly self-educated and self-made man. After completing two years at Occidental College and his junior year at Stanford, majoring in English but taking many courses in biology, he had to quit college to care for his ailing father (he would have graduated with the Stanford class of 1909). His "doctors degree" was an honorary one, granted to him by Occidental in 1929. Following college he worked for several years as a newspaper editor in Pasadena and then, after taking the proverbial Grand Tour of Europe for six months (with a difference—he later referred to it as a "tramp trip" on a reported $2 a day), he became an agricultural explorer on behalf of his father, who in retirement had become a nurseryman. For this assignment he learned Arabic, and his travels in the Middle East to collect date palms resulted in his first book, *Date Growing in the New and Old Worlds* (1913), a complete manual for the horticulturist. But his career really began when he went to Washington in 1913 to become editor of the recently established *Journal of Heredity*. This was thanks mainly to a Kansas contact, David Fairchild, who was a prominent agricultural explorer and U.S. Department of Agriculture official, married to the daughter of Alexander Graham Bell.

Intellectually, the young Paul Popenoe was a true child of the Progressive era, a combination of Darwinian scientist, William James pragmatist, and Teddy Roosevelt progressive. Charles Darwin was his idol, and he was also greatly influenced by the eminent biologist David Starr Jordan, president and then chancellor of Stanford from 1891 to 1916, under whom he had studied. More than anything else, he was a devout advocate of science and the scientific approach, and believed that the path to human betterment lay in the application of science to society. In later years he was often quoted as saying that his mission was "to bring to bear all the resources of modern science in promoting successful marriage and family life." Although he sometimes called his approach sociological, which it surely was in an applied sense, he typically referred to himself as a "social biologist." He had never formally studied sociology and in fact became somewhat alienated from that profession over time, claiming that it had become marked by excessive cultural determinism and value neutrality.

My father's major interests in the years around World War I were heredity, and its chief social application of the time, eugenics. It has never been clear to me just how and where he picked up his vast knowledge of heredity, but his interest in both heredity and eugenics was surely in keeping with one of the major intellectual fashions of that era. Although eugenics is thoroughly repudiated today as deeply reactionary and misguided, mainly due to the racism with which it often was associated, it was then considered liberal and progressive. Living in the wake of the Darwinian revolution, as Carl Degler has recently pointed out in *In Search of Human Nature: The Decline and Revival of Darwinism in American Social Thought*, most of the intellectual Progressives of that day—in America as well as in Europe—were eugenists. This included Teddy Roosevelt, Harvard's president Charles W. Eliot, many of the leading sociologists, the socialists Beatrice and Sydney Webb, and many, many others. They fully accepted the hereditarian precepts that many personal traits are passed along genetically and therefore heredity is the key to understanding human behavior, and they further believed in the social regulation of heredity, or eugenics—controlling human reproduction in various ways for the good of society.

Amidst a group of young intellectuals centered around, and financially supported by, Alexander Graham Bell, who had become interested in heredity and eugenics through the hereditary deafness of his wife and sheep breeding experiments at his summer home in Nova Scotia, Paul Popenoe developed rapidly as a self-taught scientist and something of a now-urban raconteur. The group, which included the prominent American geneticist Sewell Wright who shared an apartment with my father, often met for discussions at Bell's home either in Washington or in Nova Scotia. These must have been golden years for a young man still in his twenties to have been in Washington; at least that is how he often remembered them. During this period my father wrote (with

Roswell Johnson, another of the group's intellectuals) the first major textbook on eugenics entitled *Applied Eugenics* (1918). The book became a standard reference in the field, coming out in a revised edition in 1933 and a sixth printing in 1949.

But then the War intervened and my father was inducted into the officer corps, ending up as captain in charge of the section on vice and liquor control of the War Department Commission on Training Camp Activities. This meant essentially, according to him, directing "the clearing out of liquor and prostitutes from around the army training camps." (It was said at the time that venereal disease was eliminating as many soldiers from combat as were battle wounds.) What a perfect job for a Kansas republican and Victorian moralist (he was a lifetime teetotaler)! He seemed to have accepted the assignment with relish. As he later told the story, when he found "vice" close to an army base he went to the local mayor and chief of police and told them to act; if they did not, he ordered them put into jail. These experiences never left him, and he was fond of telling about them in later years. (As an aside, my father was always averse to his sons referring to him as "dad" or "daddy;" according to my mother, this was because the prostitutes of that day used to bait him by calling out to him "sugar daddy.")

After the War, Paul Popenoe spent a year in New York City as executive secretary of the American Social Hygiene Association, a group trying to achieve for America—through public education—something similar, one might say, to what my father had tried to accomplish around the army camps. Social hygiene was a euphemism for sexual hygiene, with a heavy focus on premarital virginity, but the group was generally progressive in its outlook and was an early promoter, for example, of birth control and sex education.

It was in New York that my father met my mother. After he had finally made up his mind that it was time to get married, and let that be known, a mutual friend told my father that he had found "just the right girl for you." My mother, Betty, came from an economically poor and rather disturbed family situation, and had only completed nine grades of schooling (albeit some at New York's excellent Friends Academy), but her mother was very ambitious for her. A beautiful and graceful girl, Betty had embarked on a promising career as a rhythmic dancer in the pattern of Ruth St. Dennis and Dick Shawn. She had already had several New York performances and been taken under the wing of Frank Crowninshield of the Algonquin set and an editor of *Vanity Fair* magazine, which had done a pictorial write-up on her. For my father, it was love (or lust) at first sight. And even though he came from a totally foreign cultural environment, how could Betty turn down this handsome and debonair man of the world? The goal of almost every woman of the day was marriage, not career. After knowing one another for only six months, they were married privately in New York City in 1920 by a justice of the peace; my mother had just turned nineteen.

This marriage was in itself another major turning point in the life of Paul Popenoe. Still a Kansas boy at heart, and brought up with the Jeffersonian view that cities were a principal source of evil, he found New York City (and post-War society in general) to be an increasingly alienating environment and with his new marriage sought to make a clean break. Immediately after the marriage Paul and Betty left for California, stopping in Topeka so that my mother could meet his relatives. They were headed for the Coachella Valley desert in the Palm Springs-Indio area, at that time very sparsely populated and one of the last of the frontier territories of the American West. It was also the center, not incidentally, of the American date palm industry. My father's idea was to go back to the land and grow dates, cotton, and whatever else would sell, and they bought a farm (called in California a "ranch") near the village of Coachella. Until the agricultural market collapsed and my parents gravitated back to the Los Angeles area, they lived there for six years and bore two children.

For my mother, who had known little but city life, the move to the desert was a wrenching experience. Pursuing the clearly etched female gender roles of her time, she desperately sought to be the good wife and mother, but the social isolation, the intense heat, the inadequate housing, the sandstorms, the scorpions, and the need to carry a pistol to kill rattlesnakes were terribly trying for her, to say the least. Making matters worse, my father was seemingly a virtual illiterate in the culture and character of females, a real psychological primitive. For example, when they first arrived in the desert they shared a cabin with one of my father's associates, and their domestic area was separated from his by only a sheet. My mother's consequent deep embarrassment at performing marital activities virtually "in public" was something that was hard for my father to fathom.

But he was a fast learner, and devoted himself not only to adjusting to marriage but to intellectually mastering what he thought of as the strange and entirely separate world of women. It was this marital adjustment process, in fact, that led to his first family book, *Modern Marriage* (1925). The subtitle of this book was "A Handbook for Men," and in the preface was the statement: "the book is addressed to men, primarily because I happen to belong to that sex myself, and do not feel qualified to write for women." On the front cover was the quote, "Popenoe has stated many things which a thoughtful father would like his son to know before marrying, but finds it difficult to tell." One might add, "things that he learned the hard way through trial and error." In fact, the book was very much a summary statement of everything he had recently learned about what a man had to do to adjust to an intimate life with a woman. And, although there must have been many times early in his marriage when he worried that the opposite might be true, a central theme of the book was, "monogamy is not inharmonious with man's nature."

With further marital experience, the caveat about "not feeling qualified to write for women" was soon dropped and most of his later work became unisex;

indeed, his main lifetime audience was women. *Modern Marriage* was extensively rewritten, based on his later Institute experiences, for a 1940 second edition and, by 1958, the book was in its fifteenth printing.

For Paul Popenoe the desert years had gradually shifted from farming back to intellectual pursuits. As is well known, there is nothing like having a wife and children for a man to discover the importance of "family," and the family began to loom ever larger in his interests. His marital advice book was shortly followed by a more sociological and philosophical one, *The Conservation of the Family* (1926). Intended as a companion volume to *Modern Marriage*, which had focused on "the things that an individual can do to make his marriage more successful," the new book considered "mainly the things that an individual cannot do for himself, and which society must do for him."

My father never considered his move from biologist and hereditarian to marriage and family relations specialist to be anything unusual. His biological interests remained very much alive in the 1920s and early 1930s, and he regarded his new family interests as an outgrowth of them. *Modern Marriage* was data-based and expressly "written from a biological point of view;" *Conservation of the Family* was billed on the cover as "the first book to consider family life from a biological point of view" (although much of the data in both books was more sociological than biological). During this period, he also wrote numerous articles and three books on heredity, including a major textbook entitled *The Child's Heredity* (1929), plus several more books on eugenics.

In keeping with the decline of hereditarianism in American intellectual life, Paul Popenoe gradually shifted his professional efforts from genetic improvement to family improvement. With the help of some influential financial donors, he started the American Institute of Family Relations (then called the Institute of Family Relations) in 1930. At first a one-man operation, it grew over the decades into an organization with as many as seventy counselors and by 1977 claimed to have counseled over 300,000 men, women, and children. Here is what he later said was the connection of this new enterprise with his earlier biological interests: "I had the idea that to improve the race, we should first start with the family. And since the family often suffers problems which threaten its stability, we must treat those problems. In other words, we should establish a marriage counseling center where maladjustments might be brought, studied, classified—and helped if possible."

He is said to have coined the term "marriage counselor," although he admittedly borrowed it and the idea behind it from Germany, where marriage counseling had been first developed in the 1920s. Through his work at the Institute he became best known as a popularizer of marriage and family counseling, yet he also developed a particular approach to counseling that is now coming back into fashion. In keeping with his no-nonsense personality, the marriage counseling he conducted and promoted was highly directive. He gave his clients information and encouragement and eschewed the use of the term "therapy," preferring to think of marriage counseling as more an educational than a psychological or medical process. He was especially critical of Freudian analysis, often saying that "people should be encouraged to go into action, not lie down on a couch."

While he maintained most of his Victorian values to the end, in other respects he was a progressive in his field. Among the many instances that come to mind, he was an early and vociferous advocate of both birth control and sex education in the schools, at a time when these were considered by many to be the height of moral decadence. He was a strong believer in the importance of fathers, urging them to take a more active role in their children's upbringing. And, according to a *Time Magazine* article in 1956, he devised with Art Linkletter the first computer dating service for Univac.

Late in my father's career his growing isolation from a changing American culture became ever more apparent. Throughout most of his life, for example, his closest associates were leading scientists and professionals. Considered a mainstream figure, he shared with them both a strong scientific approach toward life and a philosophy of familism. Yet by the late 1960s and 1970s his younger colleagues were mostly religious conservatives. Many of his assistants at the Institute were ordained ministers or other devoutly religious people from such denominations as the Baptists and the Mormons (one was Dr. James C. Dobson, now president of Focus on the Family), and a large portion of the hundreds of marriage counselors trained at the Institute in those years were clergymen. My father was no more religious than ever, but these were his new professional and ideological allies and protégées. The elite of the rapidly growing helping professions, meanwhile, had headed in an entirely secular and individualistic direction, one that dismissed "bourgeois moral values," stressed cultural relativism, promoted self-oriented therapeutic ideologies, and seemed to favor self-fulfillment over family obligation. In a final irony, after years of battling the Roman Catholic Church over such issues as birth control and sex education he came to think of it, too, as an ideological ally. The Church, in his mind, was at least on the pro-family side.

His Marriage

What kind of marriage did Paul Popenoe himself have? Dark hints often emanated from Hollywood scandal sheets that the man who saves marriages must have a troubled marriage himself, and there were constant rumors that he had been divorced. (The latter were particularly troubling to him, because until about 1970 he required all of his marriage counselors to be currently married and never divorced; he believed that to be an effective marriage counselor it was important to have been successful with your own marriage.) I once read in a tabloid that he was "one of three men" in Lana Turner's troubled life, another being Johnny Stompanato (who was eventually killed by her daughter). It is true that my father gave Ms. Turner marriage counseling; in fact, to maintain privacy she came to our house. I can still clearly recall my brothers and I peeking out from the backyard, to which we had been sent, and seeing this glamorous blonde walking up our driveway wearing dark glasses. So much for privacy. But my father would have been the last person in the world to be unfaithful, with Lana Turner or anyone else. And in 1970, at a big family gathering, my parents happily celebrated their golden wedding anniversary.

This is not to say that their marriage was untroubled. No two people could have been much more different than my father and mother, the one rational, scientific, aggressive, and restless, the other intuitive, artistic, submissive, and nurturing. Indeed, they personified the stereotypical traits of the ideal man and woman of the time. (In my father's writings he made much of what he felt were the enormous differences between men and women and the absolute necessity, in happy marriages, for each partner to take those differences into account. This message, of course, was the subject of a withering attack by the feminist movement, but it is now returning to the center of the cultural dialogue with such enormously popular books as Deborah Tannen's *You Just Don't Understand*.)

By today's standards you would wonder just what my parents had in common. Certainly not much in any intellectual sense. But their marriage was conceived, as were most traditional marriages of that era, as a symbiotic partnership of opposites. My father, a workaholic, was totally involved in his work and did almost nothing within the home; to my knowledge he never cleaned, cooked, washed a dish, or changed a diaper while his children were growing up. Yet he did bring home the bacon (or at least a vegetarian's version of this) and had a very active interest in his garden, thus taking care of all the "outside" tasks. My mother was a full-time mother and homemaker for almost thirty years (four boys, spaced three and a half years apart). Her mothering time would have been even longer except that we boys, from a very early age, were taught independence; this meant leaving home as soon as possible, which we all did by about age seventeen, and seldom returning. Although mother never was able to return to her dancing, as we grew older and left home she did resume seriously other of her artistic talents—painting and sculpture.

Opposites may attract, but that certainly doesn't mean they will have no problems of adjustment. My parents had numerous memorable marriage squabbles, and I often felt that many of my mother's allergies and minor illnesses were somehow the result of being suppressed and unfulfilled in a male-dominated marriage and a masculine world (it didn't help in this regard that she had only sons!). In the late 1960s I was talking with one of my brothers about people we knew who were "self-actualized," and I suggested that our father fit that bill to a tee. My brother quickly agreed. Part of the reason was surely that he had a loving, kind, dutiful wife who literally took care of his every need at home. But one would never have said that my mother was self-actualized. She was not an open complainer, and she relished her life as a wife and mother (yet often felt inadequate and uncomfortable as the wife of a famous person), but we all sensed that her life of total sacrifice for others left something to be desired. (On the other hand, a male counselor and top administrator at the Institute wrote in an obituary of my father that while my father was "not easy to work for," my mother was "one of the finest human beings I've ever known.")

It came as a tragic surprise when our mother, who was thirteen years younger than my father, was the first to die—of a stroke at age seventy-seven. In hindsight it appears that she may have sacrificed herself to an early death. She had often said that she did not want to live on past her husband's death, that he was her entire life, and that she wouldn't know what to do without him. At the time of her death our parents were still living in our boyhood home and father, in his late eighties, had serious memory loss and was even more cantankerous and demanding than usual. He was not an easy person to handle. Desiring to relinquish the terrible burdens of being both nurse and home maintainer, mother had long expressed a wish to move into a retirement home. We all thought, however, that father would live longer if he could stay in his home environment, so this idea was resisted. For mother's sake, we probably resisted too long. It is true, however, that father, once put into a nursing home, completely lost his memory and lasted only a year. In any event, this is how one traditional nuclear family came to an end.

Paul Popenoe as a Father

What kind of father was Paul Popenoe? Within the parameters of the Victorian or bourgeois family ideal of his time, he was the very personification of "the good family man." He worked hard and long, but always seemed to make time for his boys—whom he adored. Some of my fondest memories are going to work with him to downtown Los Angeles, usually with a friend, on the old southern California red trolley cars. My friend and I would hang out around his office for a while, then look around town (invariably spending some time riding on the new escalators at Bullock's Department Store), and meet him again for lunch. We would always go to a special cafeteria, Clifton's, and he was fond of telling the story that he would follow behind us in line and just order a glass of water and a toothpick; he claimed that there was more than ample food for him left on our trays at the end of the meal! Another fond memory was the entire family sitting on his bed and listening to him read stories to us.

He traveled around the United States a lot, but would frequently send us a brief postcard. I still have many of them: "Valentine's Day—and I'm certainly enjoying the butter scotch." "Glad to hear from mother about what a fine birthday party you had;" and (at camp) "are you getting in some nature study along with your crafts? and are you doing any fishing?" When he wasn't traveling, he had the work situation that most fathers (and their children) can only dream about—a home office in the rear of our property; we would frequently go back there and visit with him. And he placed special importance on the regular family meal; those were times of discussion, reflection, and much good humor.

At the same time, in true Victorian style, he was a relatively authoritarian person and a strict disciplinarian, which I'm sure was harder on my older brothers than it was on me, the youngest of the four boys. (Like most fathers, he mellowed over time.) There were a great many family rules to be followed, and punishments meted out accordingly. One punishment, if we called our mother a dirty name, was to hold us over the bathtub and wash out our mouths with soap (a frequent, highly symbolic practice in the first half of this century); another, for unruly behavior, was to lock us up in a small closet (with a window) for a while until we calmed down. He was never actually with us that much—that was my mother's role—but he was ever the distant threat "who would spank us when he got home." And occasionally we were spanked. He also believed strongly in children having household chores, and we all had various daily assignments, both outdoors and indoors (having no sisters, we had to do their work too!). We spent every Saturday morning carrying out special chores, mostly in the garden, from a long list that he had prepared for each of us.

In private, he was what today we would call emotionally repressed, or at the very least highly reserved. He was rather stiff and formal in demeanor (and always stood about a yard away from whomever he was speaking to); when we were growing up he never hugged or kissed us, and we never saw him cry. But these are characteristic traits of males from an Anglo-Saxon background and they, too, diminished as he got older.

Looking back, it is hard for me to fault him as a father. I had an idyllic childhood. One testimony to my parents' childrearing approach was that even though my brothers and I did all of the things that young boys did in those days, including "wars" with neighborhood "gangs," none of us ever broke a limb or had a major accident. Of course it helped that we grew up in a benign, upper-middle-class suburb, during a time of great social order in America. He did set very high standards, and pushed us hard to excel. This was a constant source of anxiety, especially when we were teenagers, but we nevertheless all turned out to be reasonably happy and successful adults. If any fault is to be found it is on a psychological level. Despite his fame as a counselor he was no "sympathetic listener;" he told you what was to be done, and that was it—no back talk.

Evaluating Our Family

Yet in later life, as young adults, we seldom returned home (much to my mother's sadness), and when we did, we didn't feel like staying for very long.

Partly this was because we were males, taught to leave home and make our own way in life. But there was something else, something about the subculture of the family, that drove us to distraction. For one thing we all had become liberals, the products of a relatively freethinking family. (When my father was once asked, "Why are you a Republican, but all of your children became Democrats?" he replied, "if I had been a Democrat, all of them would have become Republicans!") I looked down on my parents' stuffy, Victorian sex code, on the fact that just about the only thing my mother ever read was the *Readers Digest* (she kept it by the toilet), and on their antipathy toward Roosevelt, Truman, and John F. Kennedy and their love for fellow Kansan Dwight D. Eisenhower (actually I think my mother, like many women, may have been a closet Democrat, unwilling to speak up). More than anything else, anticipating the baby boom generation that was to come, I objected to all of their "moralizing." "Come on, lighten up, get with it, times are changing."

Something in the family seemed amiss on a psychological level. My brothers and I were never intimately close either with each other or with our parents. I never felt, for example, as if I could talk over my problems with any of them. Much of our family interaction involved good-natured but rather strained bantering, expressed through an ever-present psychological front that was dominated by concerns about personal achievement.

Also, my parents were too different from each other; the relationship was too one-sided. My father, the all-powerful rational autocrat, my mother, the passionate submissive; how were you supposed to put the two pieces together? It was partly this extreme one-sidedness that caused me to believe that my mother had not gotten all that she could have out of life. What happened to her dancing? Why was she never educated? Was it right for her to have devoted her entire adult career to waiting on my father and to raising us? Her life was clearly not as fulfilled as my father's.

Lessons for Today

In this brief description of Paul Popenoe's marriage, his father-role, and his family, you have, in some respects, a social cost-benefit analysis of the traditional nuclear family—only one family, to be sure, but prototypic of its time. In summary, it was very good for men, quite good for children, and not so good for women. Can we do any better today? "Moralizing" is now coming back into style, biological explanations of human behavior are being revived, the gender and sex revolutions are easing, and new talk of "familism" fills the media. It is an opportune time to look closely at just what the continuing relevance is, if any, of the father-role that Paul Popenoe embodied, and of the family type that he personally fostered and professionally espoused.

The answer depends on where one locates the optimum balance point among the varying needs of women, of men, of children, and of society as a whole. In the past thirty years the needs of women for autonomy and self-fulfillment have been significantly advanced, and the sexual desires of men have been catered to as never before. But the needs of children have been neglected, mainly the result of family changes, and the social order has therefore weakened. There have been sharp increases in the rates of many juvenile pathologies, such as delinquency, depression, substance abuse, and suicide.

With the deteriorating conditions of childhood in mind, and assuming that it could be accomplished, a return to the traditional nuclear family has much to recommend it. That family type was both more child-centered and more enduring than ours today; the values were clear and discipline was strong. Such family qualities seem absolutely essential to the good society. Indeed, without enduring, child-centered families that teach strong values, it is likely that society over the long term cannot survive.

The traditional nuclear family, however, had two major disadvantages: male dominance, an ancient historical legacy, and the very restricted role for women, in part a product of the industrial revolution. I have two daughters whose attitudes are fairly typical of the female achievers of their generation; they are still in graduate school, one studying to become an anthropologist and the other in training to become a physician. Both are very family oriented and dearly want to have children; in this, but in few other ways, they are like my mother. They have postponed marriage and have been living with men out of wedlock; they plan to take time off from their careers to raise children, but then return. Most of all, they would find it very difficult to be married to a man like my father. They would recoil at the stay-at-home servant role he expected, and they would certainly not relish his male authoritarianism. They anticipate from their husband more of a fifty-fifty relationship (my father always advocated professionally a fifty-fifty marriage, but he didn't mean what my daughters mean by it).

These young women will probably never find a man who will agree to split fifty-fifty with them both breadwinning and childcare, the goal of some feminists. And I don't think they even want that; they value a man who can be a premier wage earner and they believe that, at least in the years of infancy, mothers should have the commanding role in childcare. Still, they will almost certainly marry a more fifty-fifty partner than my father was, and partly for that reason their lives will probably be much more fulfilled than my mother's was.

The big question is, to paraphrase Freud, what do men want today? My daughters will doubtless have a difficult time in the struggle to have both a family and a career, but they know clearly that they want them both. The breakdown of the traditional nuclear family has in some respects had more important consequences for men than for women, although we don't usually think of it in that way. Just as my father predicted, the sexual and gender revolutions have plainly weakened men's devotion to marriage and children. Compared to my father's era a lot more men today help out at home, but the statistics on nonmarital births, divorce, and male desertion suggest that a lot more men also have largely abandoned children and family life. The old tradeoff placed by women (and society) before men to generate the traditional nuclear family was this: if you want sex, marry me; and after you marry me, you can also have the masculine satisfaction of protecting and economically taking care of me and our children. This tradeoff is now history. A man can get sex outside of marriage anytime and anywhere he wants it; and a growing number of men today are looking for women they don't have to provide for economically, partly so that they can have more money for themselves.

The revolution that brought self-fulfillment to women has promoted self-indulgence in men. From a family perspective, we live in an age of the vanishing male. Both men and women are less involved in family life and childcare today than at any other time in our history, but the differential between men and women in this respect is growing. Both men and women are postponing marriage and increasingly not marrying at all, even when children are involved. Yet it is men who typically balk at marriage, and we now have a historically high rate of nonmarital births. And the new ease of divorce, together with the active labor market participation of wives, make it easy for men to break out of their marriages to pursue other women, at relatively little cost to themselves. The result: more than fifty percent of children growing up in America today will spend some time before adulthood living in a household without a father.

A major task of our time is to get men to act in more socially responsible ways. We need to find new mechanisms to replace the tradeoff that lay behind the traditional nuclear family. Over the past few decades, we have tried culturally to bolster the single-parent family, asserting myopically that, after all, the traditional nuclear family was a male-tyranny and the single-parent family may be just as good, perhaps even an improvement. Many single-parent families are no doubt doing a fine job, and they should be supported, but accumulating evidence of the negative effects of single parenting on children suggests that this view is far off base. The best family is the one instinctively favored by every child—the family with a caring mother and a functioning father present. With the gender revolution now a partial success as far as women are concerned, the needed revolution in the nineties and beyond is to readjust men to the new social conditions.

Despite the disadvantages of the traditional nuclear family for women, male responsibility in the era of the traditional family form was greater than it is today. Men worked harder to maintain their families and curtail their sexual exploits, they felt a stronger sense of family and community obligation. Yet we cannot go back; there is no undoing the revolutions that have brought economic security, public participation, and sexual freedom for women.

What must be salvaged is the nuclear family—not the traditional nuclear family. That is a difficult, but not unachievable, goal. We must strive for a nuclear family in which there is an enduring sense of family obligation on the part of both sexes, along with a strong desire to put children first. But it should be a nuclear family in modern form, in which there is a fifty-fifty division of power and decision-making between wife and husband, and a firm understanding that both women and men will share a common (though not necessarily identical) commitment to the workforce over the course of their lives.

What could possibly hold men to such a family? A good answer is close companionship and understanding between the sexes at a level never before achieved on a mass scale. The new family meets one of the most basic of human needs: intimate attachment to at least one other person. That, at least, is the carrot. There also needs to be a bigger stick. Margaret Mead once observed that no society exists anywhere in the world in which people have stayed married without enormous community pressure to do so. Such pressure has weakened considerably in recent years, and we should be seeking ways to increase the social insistence that men fulfill their social and family obligations.

Conclusion

Paul Popenoe was largely a man of the nineteenth century. We are about to enter the twenty-first century. It would be surprising, indeed, if everything he said were still relevant today, and it is not. His strong support for the traditional nuclear family is no longer justifiable. Yet he was right on target in his rock-bottom belief in the fundamental importance of the strong family for the good society. And he sensed, and welcomed, many needed family changes. In the conclusion to his *Conservation of the Family*, published in 1926, he predicted what the future family would look like. Although perhaps based as much on hope as on reality, his first five predictions at that time still provide an invaluable set of social goals. He said, "the family of the future will, I think, be marked by (1) much better mate selection, (2) much greater understanding, making for permanence of love, (3) more intelligent consideration of children, (4) greater concern for individual development, particularly of women, (5) more democracy."

These words were written well before he began his fifty-year career as a marriage and family counselor, but I do not think that he ever encountered anything in that career to cause him to revise them. Nor do I think there is any cause for us to revise them today. Indeed, at a time when our culture appears to be swinging in a more familistic direction, they are more relevant than ever.

15

The War Over the Family: America's Debate Over the Decline of the Two-Parent Family

Few social issues in the United States have been more controversial in recent decades than concerns about what is happening to the American family. In the past forty years the divorce rate has more than doubled, the out-of-wedlock birth ratio has increased over 600 percent, and the marriage rate has fallen by 37 percent. In view of these facts, has the family really weakened or "declined?" If so, does it need to be strengthened? Remarkably, these are issues that have polarized the nation. Many scholars and intellectuals, along with much of the media, have believed that family weakening should not be a concern, except to the extent that some families are poor and need economic assistance. They have generally downplayed the importance of high divorce and out-of-wedlock birthrates. Others, mostly on the cultural right, hold that the married, two-parent family has been badly damaged in recent decades and believe this is a serious problem for children and our nation. They have called for "moral renewal" and a social movement to regenerate stronger families.

Yet in the past ten years or so, after decades of controversy and dissention, there are signs of a marked change in elite opinion. The decline of the two-parent family and of marriage itself has begun to be taken seriously, and a new consensus has emerged about the need to strengthen families. For many, the issue now is what to do about the problem. This is the story of how and why a pro-family shift in the United States is taking place, together with some speculations about the future. Interestingly, it is an account in which empirical research in the social sciences has played a major role.

Historical Backdrop

Concerns about what is happening to the American family are nothing new; indeed, they go back almost to the nation's founding. But they first became pronounced around the turn of the twentieth century, when some startling trends were revealed to the nation by a newly established government census unit. A phenomenal decrease in fertility rates over the course of the nineteenth century was documented, from seven children per native-born white family in 1800 to just 3.56 in 1900. This was accompanied in that century's second half by rapidly rising divorce rates, leading many in the Progressive Era prior to World War I to believe that the family was under great stress if not, in fact, in a crisis. In that time period new social programs of all kinds were suggested by, among others, the new field of sociology, which devoted its third annual conference in 1908 to the "family crisis." Many of the conference papers investigated the effects on the family of rapid industrialization and urbanization, and a particular concern was the high divorce rate. An early sociology text in 1898, written by a former U.S. commissioner of labor, referred to "the menace to which the family is exposed through the complications of modern society."

After World War I a new emphasis on individualism and self-fulfillment, often referred to as "cultural modernity," took hold strongly in the United States, and the rise of sexually liberated urban lifestyles in the "roaring"1920s is sometimes regarded as the beginning of the family-shattering trends that emerged full blown in the 1960s. In the decade of the 1920s a more affluent economy of mass production focused on personal and household consumption, together with a rapidly expanding organized entertainment industry, were radically changing the values by which Americans lived. The new culture featured personal freedom, youthful innovation and constant technological and social change; the Victorian values of self-reliance, self-sacrifice, frugality, and sexual self-control were slowly giving way to a new morality of self-expression and self-gratification. As James Q. Wilson has pointed out, if it were not for the Great Depression and World War II, with its highly familistic aftermath, we would probably be talking about the twenties rather than the sixties as the beginning of the modern era of family decline.

Certainly some concerns about the fate of the family were expressed publicly in the 1920s and 1930s, especially about the negative consequences for the family of the Great Depression and the rising influence of Hollywood. Yet family issues both in the public debate and in government policies were heavily superceded by economic concerns. President Roosevelt's New Deal policies, for example, were focused not on family strengthening but on individual and societal economic relief.

The family changes of the 1950s era, roughly from the end of World War II in 1945 to the early 1960s, were as momentous as they were virtually unexpected. At this time a remarkable return to higher fertility generated the famous baby boom, and high marriage and low divorce rates spawned a suburban-based era of family togetherness in a period of rapidly increasing wealth. Concerns about the American family became almost completely muted during the 1950s; very few people were discussing family decline in any form. Indeed, rather than being concerned about families breaking apart, the social criticism of the time focused on over-organization, over-conformity, and the loss of personal autonomy—too much family!

The dramatic social changes that followed the fifties were again almost entirely unpredicted. In one sense they represented a social correction from what some thought of as the "smug and conformist" fifties. This correction could be considered one of many historical examples in which societies adjust to seek a better balance point between the need for tradition and social order and the desire for personal freedom and social change. In another sense the social changes represented a rapid extension of cultural modernity themes first seen in the 1920s. Beginning in the early 1960s, personal liberation became the dominant motif first of the cultural left and then much of America. As a part of the move toward personal liberation and "alternative lifestyles," a concerted attack on "bourgeois family values" was launched. The ideological attack combined a new radical feminist movement with its view that the family is an archaic and authoritarian institution that oppresses women, a gay liberation movement that wanted its lifestyle to be accorded symbolic and practical equality with the traditional heterosexual family, and a "new age" sensitivity and self-realization movement that found the nuclear family too confining for personal growth. Also involved were a New Left political movement that was highly critical of America in general, including the family, and a less organized but culturally powerful new "singles subculture" that became the darling of advertisers. Each of these efforts co-opted the language of the civil rights movement that had become so successful in combating the segregation of blacks.

By the end of the 1970s the movement toward personal liberation and against the traditional family had achieved remarkable success, helped immeasurably by the birth control pill and the availability of legal abortion. The age-old cultural stigmas against premarital sex, illegitimacy, divorce, and single parenthood all but vanished. Amidst much talk of sexual liberation, "open" marriages, and good divorces, the traditional, two-married-parent nuclear family took a huge hit. Between 1960 and 1980 the divorce rate more than doubled, the percentage of births to unmarried women climbed from 5 percent to 18 percent and, after 1970, the marriage rate started to drop dramatically. As a result, the percentage of children living with a single parent jumped from 9 percent in 1960 (the same percentage as in 1900), to 20 percent in 1980. And child poverty, which thanks to economic good times had dropped to only 15 percent of all children in 1970, climbed again to 22 percent by 1985, the same percentage it had been in the mid-1960s.

The War Over the Family Begins

In the mid-1960s, black families became the harbinger, the canaries in the mine if you will, for what was to happen later to families across America: 25

percent of black births were out of wedlock and close to 30 percent of black children lived with a single parent. These statistics were featured in a famous report by Daniel Patrick Moynihan, then a minor cabinet official in the administration of President Lyndon Johnson, that proclaimed the Negro family to be "in the deepest trouble" and referred to its weaknesses as a "tangle of pathology." President Johnson relied on the report in a major speech in 1965 in which he spoke strongly about the need to strengthen families as a part of the "war on poverty." But the reaction from the cultural left was so vituperative—claiming that Moynihan's charges asserted a collective abnormality among blacks that was implicitly racist and in any event unwarranted—that a planned White House conference on the topic was cancelled, Moynihan was sent into intellectual exile, and any further official national discussion of family strengthening policies was banished for years.

President Nixon in the early 1970s again raised the issue of family weakening among the poor, this time through his efforts to achieve welfare reform through the establishment of income supports or "guaranteed incomes," government monetary support if one's income falls below a certain level. His proposals never were approved by Congress, however, one reason being an important research finding that income supports for the poor actually increased family instability by raising divorce rates. In a controlled experiment, it was found that when offered a guaranteed income a disproportionate number of poor families took the money and ran—from their marriages! In the 1970s it also was becoming clear that family problems were not limited to the poor. Divorce, for example, was skyrocketing in all segments of society.

The first president to focus on the general problem of family decline was Jimmy Carter. He ran for office in 1976 deploring what he called "the steady erosion and weakening of our families" and called for an administration that would reverse these trends. Unfortunately, he got no further in this effort than his predecessors. In national discussions leading up to his ill-fated White House Conference on Families, he ran into two major hurdles. The first was the firm belief of many Americans, throughout the nation's history, that government has no business in people's private lives. The second concerned the definition of family, and it was a portent of a conflict that would take many years to resolve. If the government were to play some role, should the target of family policy be "the family," in other words the two-parent nuclear family, or "the diversity of families"? In a pluralistic society, the cultural left strongly argued, who was to say that one family form was better than another? In part over such matters of definition, Carter's family conference split apart before anything could be achieved and virtually no family legislation ever was passed. The left's inability to distinguish among "good" and "bad" family forms went on to become a central issue in the family debates that followed. And any idea of a national family policy was essentially dropped, as was masterfully chronicled in Gilbert Y. Steiner's 1981 book, *The Futility of Family Policy*, which concluded that, "organizing on behalf of family policy is not feasible."

During the Reagan-Bush years in the 1980s and early 1990s, little was said or done in the area of family strengthening policies. This was a time when both the presidents and the nation leaned in the direction of government nonintervention, fiscal restraint, and reliance on market forces, Another factor, probably, was the fact that Reagan was the first divorced president the nation had ever had. It was during the Reagan-Bush years, however, that the nationwide "culture war" over the family began to pick up steam.

The main group that arose to question the direction of family trends in America was loosely referred to as the religious right. Consisting mostly of conservative Christian denominations, the religious right interpreted what was taking place as a serious form of moral decline. Their viewpoint was based strongly on biblical scripture as well as what they called "traditional family values." They often linked their concerns about family decline to their condemnation of abortion and homosexuality, which had become perhaps the most controversial domestic issues of the day. Thus a broader ideological or cultural war emerged in America between mostly secular elite groups on one side, led by the various movements for personal liberation, and on the other side by people with more bourgeois values and conservative religious leanings. To this day, many constituents of the main political parties in America—Democratic and Republican—reflect this dichotomy. Interestingly, both the far left and the far right agreed on one thing—that the family was changing in a dramatic fashion. The far left often seemed to be cheering on these changes, however, while the far right was aghast.

What did academics, the great majority of whom considered themselves part of the cultural left, have to say about the weakening family? The brief answer is, up until the late 1980s, very little. The memory in the academic community of what happened to Daniel Patrick Moynihan remained strong. In order to support alternative family forms and not stigmatize minorities, combat patriarchal attitudes, and not provide any ammunition for the cultural right, a strong ethos emerged within the social science community—almost a conspiracy of silence—to say nothing negative about recent changes in family structure. There were a few exceptions. As early as the mid-1970s Cornell psychologist Urie Bronfenbrenner, for example, wrote an op-ed for the *Washington Post* entitled "The Calamitous Decline of the American Family." But it is not clear what impact this op-ed had, if any.

Indeed, despite the massive changes in family structure, many supposedly dispassionate and objective academics who wrote on the topic, most of them social scientists, commonly referred to family decline as a myth. Political scientist Mary Jo Bane, for example, the author of a best-selling book in the mid-1970s entitled *Here to Stay: American Families in the Twentieth Century*, asserted that "the myth of the decaying American family is often publicly used to bolster arguments for legislative action." Another popular book in 1981, *What's Happening to the American Family?* by two economists, Sar A. Levitan and Richard S. Belous, noted about the family that "currently fashionable gloom scenarios miss the essential process of adjustment and change." A prominent sociologist, Theodore Caplow, even put forth suggestions about why those who believed the myth did so. These people can "discover with pleasure that their own families are better than other peoples," and they provide a "consoling explanation" that "offers some comfort for certain frustrations."

In keeping with this academic perspective, much of the research of the era found many benefits and few problems with the changing family structure. The research on divorce was a case in point. Divorce was seen as something that ended oppressive, patriarchal marriages and liberated women. As for children, little evidence was found that children were seriously hurt by divorce. And if they were hurt, it was either due to the problems in the marriage before the divorce took place, or because the divorce was not a "good" one—that is, it didn't go smoothly, which it could have if there were not so much social stigma against divorce, if the divorce laws were changed, and so forth. The media, which itself was heavily allied with the cultural left, tended to follow the mainstream of academia on these issues.

By the end of the 1980s, however, the massive family changes underway since 1960 were becoming inescapably obvious and urgent. And new social science research was becoming available showing that the consequences of family change were far from benign. In a 1988 second edition of the work noted above, *What's Happening to the American Family?*, the authors recanted their earlier view, now saying that "American families are besieged from all sides." Also in 1988, I published the first book to tackle the issue of modern family decline from a cross-national perspective. Entitled *Disturbing the Nest: Family Change and Decline in Modern Societies*, it was an historical and comparative look at family change focused on Sweden but looking at the situation in several other countries, including the United States. I concluded that the forces of modernization were weakening family structures everywhere, but perhaps most of all in Sweden.

The reviews of *Disturbing the Nest* were mixed. Those who shared my views thought it was an important contribution to comparative sociology. But Sweden had become (and largely still is) the great utopia for many in the social science community, and even though much of my book was favorable toward Swedish society and family policies, any criticisms of that country were not welcome. A common theme among critics was that I was unfairly characterizing Sweden and, even worse, nostalgically trying to set the clock back— calling for the return of the traditional, patriarchal family.

Probably the first academic conference to consider the issue of family decline took place at Stanford University in November 1989. It was sponsored by The Institute for American Values, an organization formed by David Blankenhorn in the late 1980s primarily to open "a national conversation about the status and future of the family as a social institution," together with the Stanford Center for the Study of Families, Children and Youth, and the William Petschek National Jewish Family Center. The papers given at the conference by leading American family scholars, including Urie Bronfenbrenner, were collected into a book entitled *Rebuilding the Nest: A New Commitment to the American Family*. The opening section of the book was headed "Conditions: Is the Family in Decline?" in answer to which the authors provided a firm, scholarly-based "yes." But a sharp schism between the right and the left on family issues emerged at the conference, with the left more strongly concerned with such things as the stigmatization of single parents and the return of patriarchal families. The book published by Family Service America didn't make much of a splash, certainly in the academic world.

Several government commissions also became involved at this time in the family debate. The bipartisan National Commission on Children, headed by Senator John D. Rockefeller IV, reported in 1991 that "dramatic social, demographic and economic changes during the past 30 years have transformed the American family." There were bitter battles on the commission between conservatives and liberals, but it was finally agreed that "these changes have had largely deleterious effects on family life and have caused a dramatic decline in the quality of life for many American children." Later, in the final days of the first Bush administration in January 1993, a more politically partisan Report of the National Commission on America's Urban Families was released. Headed by now Attorney General John Ashcroft, the report found that "the family unit in America is weakening" and "child well-being is declining." Neither of these reports made much of an impact, although they clearly signaled that a shift of attitudes about family decline was in the making.

By the early 1990s most people on the cultural left, including so-called family scholars as well as prominent members of the media, still saw the family changes in a favorable light and dismissed many of the negative effects on children as well as on adults and society as a whole. An article in a leading sociology journal—summarizing what it thought was the current state of knowledge—referred to "the misleading belief that children will receive better parenting in intact families." And a 1992 front page article in the *Washington Post* announced that according to "a searching reevaluation by social scientists" the "conventional two-parent household may be far less critical to the healthy development of children than previously believed." Divorce was still seen to be a liberating experience for adults and the belief was that it did not seriously hurt children in any long-term way. Out-of-wedlock births were viewed as the unintended and not particularly negative result of a new freedom for women that gave them the choice of not having to remain tied to an inappropriate man.

In order not to offend anyone, even the term "broken home" was shunned. There are many different kinds of families, each good in its own way, it was said, and it is pejorative to label one family form as broken. Shunning new data showing that children are statistically much more likely to succeed in life when raised by their two natural parents, it was endlessly argued that any family form could be good at raising children—it is what the parents (or care-takers) do that counts. It was often claimed, for example, that homes without fathers can function just as effectively as homes with fathers. And any serious concern about the high dissolution rate of black families was derided, just as it had been in response to the Moynihan report, as "blaming the victim" of racism and inequality. The general idea was that adults should be left alone to organize their intimate relationships as they see fit; moreover, society shouldn't be so judgmental about it all.

This perspective on the family was clearly seen when Vice President Dan Quayle, running for reelection with President George H. W. Bush, gave his now-famous speech in 1992 criticizing the television program "Murphy Brown" for glorifying unwed motherhood. Although that theme was a minor part of his speech, it touched a raw nerve. Many intellectuals across the nation and of course the Hollywood entertainment community expressed outrage at Quayle's "stigmatization of single motherhood." Yet this speech and its aftermath also marked an important event—for the first time the nation as a whole began to discuss seriously such issues as the dramatic rise of unwed births and single parenthood.

The Intellectual Shift

At the peak of the divorce revolution, in the 1970s and early 1980s, a number of major social science studies were begun that followed the children of divorce over time. By the early 1990s the results of this research were coming in, and they showed negative consequences for children occurring two to three times more often in divorced families than in two-parent families. The negative consequences examined included such things as dropping out of high school, becoming a delinquent, and having a teenage pregnancy. (The most influential book on this topic is *Growing Up With a Single Parent* [1994], by sociologists Sara McLanahan and Gary Sandefur.) Getting this new information into the public debate became the goal of a small group of scholars and intellectuals centered around the New York-based Institute for American Values, which had co-sponsored the Stanford Conference of the late 1980s.

One of the first media shifts in favor of the two-parent family occurred when the *New York Times* accepted an op-ed I had written entitled "The Controversial Truth: Two-Parent Families are Better," which was partly in response to the front page article in the *Washington Post* noted above minimizing the harmful effects of divorce on children. The piece highlighted the compelling social science evidence for the importance of two-parent families and raised the question of why, in view of this evidence, the decline of two-parent families was being taken so lightly. The letters to the editors published subsequently, from well-known family scholars, indicated that the war over the family was far from over. Themes developed in these letters were to prevail in the media for years to come: Pointing out the benefits of two-parent families, the letters claimed, is "misguided nostalgia for 'Ozzie and Harriet' land," and "needlessly stigmatize[s] children reared in families that don't meet the 'Ozzie and Harriet' model." (*The Adventures of Ozzie and Harriet* was a hit television show running from 1952 to 1966 that featured a traditional, two-parent family.)

The next major media shift came in April 1993, when the *Atlantic* published a long article by social historian and critic Barbara Dafoe Whitehead carefully reviewing all of the latest research on the negative consequences of divorce and unwed births. She had previously written an op-ed in the *Washington Post* that triggered the Dan Quayle speech. The article began on the front cover of the magazine: "After decades of public dispute about so-called family diversity, the evidence from social science research is coming in: The dissolution of two-parent families, though it may benefit the adults involved, is harmful to many children and dramatically undermines our society." Much to Whitehead's surprise, the *Atlantic* chose the provocative title: "Dan Quayle was Right." It proved to be one of the mostly widely read articles that the *Atlantic* had ever published.

The article generated a flood of letters to the editor, most of which were negative. One came from a group of eleven leading "divorce scholars" who took Whitehead to task for writing a one-sided article that grossly overplayed the social science findings of harm to kids, stating that "the evidence...suggests that divorce does not cause serious long-term problems for the large majority of children who experience it." This probably represented the prevailing view of most marriage and family researchers at the time. In other words, despite the enormous impact of this article, the nation's professionals in this field remained for the most part unconvinced.

Within the academic community the family debate continued the following August in the leading academic forum for family scholars, the *Journal of Marriage and the Family*. This journal agreed to accept an article I had written entitled "American Family Decline: 1960-1990: A Review and Appraisal." Loosely based on my book *Disturbing the Nest*, the article succinctly but comprehensively laid out for the family scholar community, for the first time, the major facts about changing family structure and what they meant for children, for adults, and for the nation as a whole. It set off an academic firestorm. Although the article was given top billing in the journal, the editors would not run it without critical responses, and it was at this time that one of the critics came up with the notion that we were engaged in "national family wars."

Speaking of me and my ideological colleagues, this critic said: "the nostalgia for the family that they peddle is singularly unhelpful to children."

Despite the compelling social science evidence, lone voices like mine and Barbara Dafoe Whitehead's would obviously never be sufficient to convince the nation's media that two parents really were best. What was needed was a body of eminent leaders who could examine the research, deliberate together, and lend their weight to the issue. A huge step in this direction was made with the formation of the Council on Families in America in 1992, under the aegis of Institute for American Values, consisting of a group of like-minded scholars and leading intellectuals who could speak with one voice and receive media attention. The capstone contribution of the Council, of which I served as co-chair with political scientist Jean Bethke Elshtain, was the release in March 1995 of "Marriage in America: A Report to the Nation." Many of the Council members were solidly in the liberal camp politically, so it was no easy task to meld right and left opinions into a coherent statement. But the final document was emphatic in its point of view. The executive summary read:

> The divorce revolution...has failed. It has created terrible hardships for children, in-curred unsupportable social costs, and failed to deliver on its promise of greater adult happiness. The time has come to shift the focus of national attention from divorce to marriage and to rebuild a family culture based on enduring marital relationships.... We must reclaim the ideal of marital permanence and recognize that out-of-wedlock child-bearing does harm.

This strong language, together with the Council's prestigious group of members, succeeded in garnering impressive nationwide media attention. Family decline and marriage seemed finally to be gaining a foothold in the national discussion.

After 1995, efforts on behalf of marriage and the two-parent family spread across America and began to take on the characteristics of a social movement. Many new pro-family groups were formed, the rhetoric was beginning tangibly to affect behavior, and the public debate about family issues moved in a positive direction much faster than any of us would have predicted. There was an important progression of ideas in the public debate: 1) children are hurt; 2) fathers are important; and 3) marriage is essential. As the media and the public finally understood the fact that children are seriously hurt by family breakup, the next stage was to convince them that family breakup means absent fathers, and fathers are important. Once that intellectual hurdle was overcome, the next (and current) stage of the debate is that the way to keep fathers at home and families intact is to strengthen the institution of marriage.

1996 proved to be a big year for family issues. President Clinton devoted nearly a third of his State of the Union speech to family topics (without once, however, using the "M word": marriage). A major contributor to the text was Clinton advisor and Council on Families in America member William Galston.

Most importantly, a bipartisan welfare reform bill was passed which for the first time gave importance to changing family structure. Three out of the four legal goals of the welfare reform law were marriage related: promote "marriage, encourage...two parent families and reduce...out-of-wedlock births." As subsequent years would show, welfare reform proved to be a remarkable success story in the annals of public policy.

Since 1996 a "marriage movement" in America has blossomed. Seemingly almost overnight, the National Fatherhood Initiative founded in 1993 became a national organization with a wide following and measurable impact. An Internet-based network called the Coalition for Marriage, Family, and Couples Education, led by Diane Sollee, has had highly successful national conferences with pro-marriage themes. It focuses on helping people stay in relationships through skills training. In 1997, Barbara Dafoe Whitehead and I established at Rutgers University the nation's first academic center focused on marriage, the National Marriage Project. The Project publishes each year, with widespread media publicity, an annual report on the social health of marriage in America called *The State of Our Unions*. Also in 1997 the Washington, DC-based Family Impact Seminar drew together marriage researchers and movers for an important conference entitled "Strategies to Strengthen Marriage," later publishing a report, *Toward More Perfect Unions: Putting Marriage on the Public Agenda.*

As other signs of a widespread marriage movement, conservative institutions such as the Heritage Foundation, the Manhattan Institute, Focus on the Family, the Family Research Council, and the Rockford Institute have developed or strengthened a focus on marriage and family issues, and several conservative luminaries have written important books on marriage. A group called Marriage Savers has had an impact in many communities around the nation, focusing on getting churches to better educate people for marriage. In several states, notably Oklahoma, Arkansas, Utah, and Florida, governors have embarked on broad-based campaigns to strengthen marriage in an effort to cut the nonmarital birth and divorce rates. In the year 2000, led by David Blankenhorn and the Institute for American Values, a marriage movement "statement of principles" was released that now has over 2500 signatories. It received support from both Gore and Bush in the presidential election of that year.

In the academic world, dramatic changes have also been seen. Many of the same scholars who had signed the letter of protest about Whitehead's *Atlantic* article got together with other family researchers in 1994 in Middleburg, Virginia, to try to develop what amounted to a counterstatement about the effects of divorce. Three years would pass before the statement was finalized and the results published. During that time the findings of important new research about the effects of divorce became available, and much of the steam behind the protest dissipated. Indeed, in the final version of the statement, it is difficult to detect much disagreement with Whitehead:

Overall, most children of divorce experience dramatic declines in their economic circumstances, abandonment (or fear of abandonment) by one or both of their parents, the diminished capacity of both parents to attend meaningfully and constructively to their children's needs…and diminished contact with many familiar or potential sources of psychosocial support…as well as familiar living settings. As a consequence, the experience of divorce is a psychosocial stressor and a significant life transition for most children, with long-term repercussions for many.

Today's new and revised academic position on the effects of family structure was clearly stated recently by the highly-respected Washington, DC, research group Child Trends, in their fact sheet summarizing the current state of knowledge titled *Marriage and Children's Well-Being: What the Research Tells Us*. The report confirms that children develop best in families formed by both biological parents in a low conflict marriage (it took a long time to gain social science acceptance for inserting the word *biological*, but that is another story), and that children born to unmarried mothers are disadvantaged relative to children born to married mothers.

What has happened in the media? Over the years I have noticed that the many reporters with whom I speak have become much less antagonistic about the two-parent family issue. Indeed, they now mostly seem to be on the same wavelength that I am. They are aware of the social science data, and they assume that two parents are best. As one sign of the times, in a stunning admission to the media in the late 1990s the actress Candice Bergen, who played Murphy Brown in the TV series, said that Dan Quayle had picked "the right theme to hammer home." The body of his speech was "completely sound," she told the *Los Angeles Times*, and indicated of Murphy's childrearing experience that "I didn't think it was a good message to be sending out." And recently, in July, 2002, she said to the Television Critics Association that "…his speech was a perfectly intelligent speech about fathers not being dispensable and nobody agreed with that more than I did." Referring to the present time, she noted, "I think all of us feel that family values have to sort of come back front and center."

Perhaps the most vivid culmination of the intellectual shift in favor of marriage and the family appeared in August 2001, in a page-one article in the *New York Times* entitled "2-Parent Families Rise After Change in Welfare Laws." It is interesting to compare this with the statement noted above that was made in the *Washington Post* nine years earlier. The reporter wrote,

a powerful consensus has emerged in recent years among social scientists, as well as state and federal policy makers. It sees single-parent families as the dismal foundries that produced decades of child poverty, delinquency and crime. And it views the rise of such families, which began in the early 1960s and continued until about five years ago, as a singularly important indicator of child pathology…. From a child's point of view, according to a growing body of social research, the most supportive household is one with two biological parents in a low-conflict marriage.

The Federal Government Takes Up the Issue of Marriage

With the social science community and the media finally coming around to the importance of married two-parent families, and the national family wars thus essentially ended, the federal government has also come on board. Important initial overtures were taken in the welfare reform bill of 1996 under the regime of President Clinton, but as noted above he said virtually nothing at the time about the key ingredient of family decline, the weakening of marriage. National political figures have long had an extreme reluctance to talk about marriage, believing it to be too sensitive an issue for political discussion. This is despite the fact that over the years numerous federal programs have impacted and in many ways privileged married couples: the federal government has never been neutral, much less opposed, to marriage. At last, however, in an address given during the presidential election campaign of 2000, candidate George W. Bush became the first major presidential candidate in modern times to state publicly that the federal government should do more to support marriage: "My administration will give unprecedented support to strengthening marriages." After he was elected president he followed through on this pledge. He proposed that a substantial portion of welfare monies be devoted to the goal of strengthening marriage and appointed Wade Horn, the very successful head of the National Fatherhood Initiative and a prominent leader of the marriage movement, to oversee the program as Assistant Secretary of Health and Human Services.

Federal marriage strengthening programs, however, have yet to be put into effect. The provisions of the welfare reform bill of 1996, featuring a new emphasis on work and family structure, were scheduled to end in 2002, and as of this writing efforts to renew it have not passed Congress. In recent debates over welfare renewal it has become clear that most Democrats do not want any specific marriage strengthening measures. But in keeping with the new social science consensus their concern seems to be more strategic than substantive. Most do not oppose or diminish the importance of marriage; rather, they believe that government programs will be ineffective and also take money away from the real economic needs of the poor. A few marriage promotion measures will probably soon be put into effect by the Bush administration, yet due to this political infighting they will probably not come close to the scale of programs desired by the marriage movement.

Can the Married Two-Parent Family Actually be Revived?

The new national agreement that a weakening family structure has important negative effects and that two parents are best is surely, in my mind, a victory for common sense, if nothing else. But the stance of Democrats in Congress does raise an important question: Can anything really be done to halt modern family decline and revive the married two-parent family? We should never underestimate the power of research and new information and media persuasion to change our minds and hearts. Indeed, some experts are already talking about a "family turnaround." By the second half of the 1990s the percentage of single-parent families and teen pregnancies were dropping, especially in those populations at greatest risk. Crime rates were diminishing, including youth crimes. And child poverty steadily decreased to below 16 percent, the lowest level since 1979.

Still, there are good reasons for skepticism. The demise of the two-parent family is a product of many forces that are ingrained in modern times, including the technologies of birth control, the organized entertainment industry, the breakup of intact neighborhoods and communities, unprecedented material affluence, and the rise of an expressive, self-centered individualism—in other words, modern culture. Short of some kind of counter-cultural revolution or religious reformation, most aspects of modern culture surely cannot be changed. Nor do most people want them to be changed; they bring many advantages as well as disadvantages. Moreover, the main reason for the married, two-parent family has always been the need to have a stable social structure for childrearing. As children lessen as a personal and societal focus, which clearly seems to be happening, further family weakening seems bound to continue.

Just because a social trend has moved in one direction for a period of time, however, doesn't mean that it will necessarily continue in the same direction. History is filled with many surprises in that regard. It may well be that adults in modern societies can rediscover the fact that a solid marriage offers the best hope for a satisfying life. And that those who still have children will, wanting to do right by their offspring, realize that a sound marriage offers those children their best shot for a successful future. At this time in history there is surely everything to be gained, and nothing lost, by serious society-wide efforts to try to restore the married, two-parent family to a central place in modern life. Certainly, as the basis for childrearing, personal happiness, and the civil order, no better alternative has yet turned up in the annals of science, religion, or philosophy.

Index